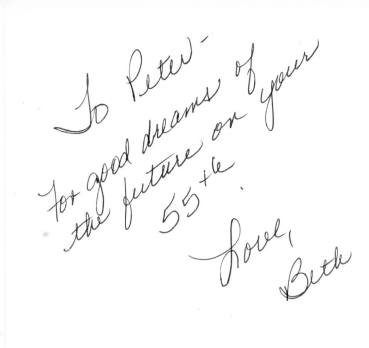

To Peter—

For good dreams of the future on your 55th.

Love,
Beth

PINEHURST STORIES

A Celebration of Great Golf and Good Times

by Lee Pace

with a Foreword by Ron Green and original essays by
Charles Price, Dick Taylor and Herbert Warren Wind

PINEHURST

A Celebration Of Great Golf

STORIES
And Good Times

"The man who doesn't feel emotionally stirred when he golfs at Pinehurst beneath those clear blue skies and with the pine fragrance in his nostrils is one who should be ruled out of golf for life."

Tommy Armour

Photography on these and preceding six pages:
Pinehurst Country Club with the first and 18th holes of the No. 2 course in the background; the Pinehurst
Hotel with its copper roof glistening in the morning sun; the natural beauty of Donald Ross's work on the 14th
and 16th holes of No. 2; the innovative 16th hole designed by Rees Jones on the No. 7 course. © Paul Barton

PINEHURST STORIES

A Celebration of Great Golf and Good Times

Published by Resorts Of Pinehurst Inc.
P.O. Box 4000   Pinehurst, NC 28374

Library of Congress Catalog Card Number: 91-66283
ISBN: 0-9630688-0-6

Dust jacket design by Leslie Adverstising Inc., Greenville, S.C.
Front cover photograph from the files of Pinehurst Resort & Country Club
Back cover photograph © Paul Barton
Front end sheet photograph from the Tufts Archives; color-tinting by Frank Pierce
Back end sheet map from the Pinehurst Outlook

Printed by The Hickory Printing Group Inc.
at its commercial sheet-fed division in High Point, N.C.

*Many hundreds of people have
contributed to Pinehurst becoming
"The St. Andrews of American Golf."
This book is dedicated to the memory
of the two men who helped the most,
Richard S. Tufts and Donald J. Ross.*

Golfers have been searching for the magic keys to better golf for nearly a century now on "Maniac Hill."
© Tom Casalini

CONTENTS

*"Pinehurst reminds me of a quote I read not long ago.
'Golf is not a matter of life and death to these people.
It's more important than that.'"*

Tom Watson

*"I've always felt it's not what championships you
won, it's where you won them. I have won in various
cities, but winning in Pinehurst meant more to me. It
was something totally different."*

Billy Joe Patton

FOREWORD

Among all the addresses to which work or the pursuit of pleasure have taken me over the years, not a handful can rival this lovely village called Pinehurst. I'm not certain of this, of course, but I believe that when good golfers die (those who let faster players through and don't lie excessively about their scores), they come to Pinehurst and are given mulligans and preferred starting times through all eternity.

Pinehurst. Thirty-five or so years after I first set foot on this fair and storied ground, the place still has magic for me. Despite my familiarity with this town that residents still prefer to call a village, I never come to Pinehurst that I don't feel the spell cast over me.

Pinehurst grows and suffers the clutter of condominiums here and there. The annual spring and fall influx of golfing tourists, lured by an ever-increasing number of courses, escalates into the large thousands. But somehow Pinehurst manages to retain its charm.

You drive out of the throbbing cities and through the nondescript little towns and trail pickup trucks down highways past sprawling farms, and then suddenly you're in Pinehurst, a thousand miles away from where you were minutes earlier.

Author John P. Marquand, one of its many famous residents over the years, wrote: "Pinehurst's greatest attribute is its friendliness and calm. Even on the most crowded days of the spring season, when individuals are struggling feverishly for starting times on the golf courses and when hotels have run out of reservations, peace never wholly leaves Pinehurst. It never loses the spiritual lack of haste or the impression of leisure and repose and hospitality that its founder designed for it."

If there were a hall of fame for golfing resorts, Pinehurst would be one of the original inductees, and if there were a hall of fame for golf courses, Pinehurst's No. 2 would be one of the first to be honored.

I've tried to figure out what it is about this place that is so endearing. It's beautiful, of course, a Mona Lisa of fair land, and placid, and it embraces the game with a motherly hug. But there's more to it than that.

There's a special feeling here, something spiritual. Ghosts walk here, some ghosts of the living, some ghosts of the dead. Some came to play golf, some to live, some simply to enjoy the air and the peace that lies over the place.

You walk the fairways of No. 2 and are aware that this is where Ben Hogan won his first professional championship. Jack Nicklaus won the North and South Amateur. Legendary figures like Walter Hagen, Jim Barnes, Tommy Armour, Francis Ouimet, Harry Vardon, Bobby Jones, Babe Zaharias, Patty Berg, Gene Sarazen, Byron Nelson, Sam Snead and Gary Player have walked these fairways.

It's a place that has been home or a vacation retreat for people like John D. Rockefeller, John Philip Sousa, Annie Oakley, J.P. Morgan, Will Rogers, Warren Harding, Al Smith, Gloria Swanson, Eddie Rickenbacker, Bette Davis and Gen. George C. Marshall.

And it is a place rich with stories. In this book, Lee Pace and his all-star collection of contributors tell many of the best and in the telling, give us a valuable history of Pinehurst.

This was not a task to be trusted simply to a typist. It called for a person with an understanding of golf and of Pinehurst, someone who could feel and capture the grace of the village, the fascination of the golf courses and the glory of what has happened there. Lee Pace has done that faithfully.

Ron Green
Charlotte, July 1991

VIVIEN WELLER

"Pinehurst is more than good golf courses. It is a state of mind and a feeling for the game, its aesthetics, courtesies and emotions."

William C. Campbell

"I almost can't tell you how good the golf course is. It might not be the hardest golf course in the world, but for pleasure, for going out and having a pleasurable time with a smile on your face, it can't be beat. It's hard to get mad when you play Pinehurst."

Johnny Miller

INTRODUCTION

T his story might be a little macabre for some tastes. But of all the tales I've encountered the last year compiling this book on Pinehurst, this one has a little more oomph to it.

A trio of visiting golfers showed up in the Pinehurst Country Club golf shop one morning in the late 1970s for their tee time on the No. 2 course. The shop attendant informed them that one of them would have to pay a full cart fee since the final member of their group wasn't with them. The golfers weren't particularly happy with that news, then bickered among themselves over who would get stuck riding solo.

And the absent member of the group? He lay covered by a sheet in Moore Regional Hospital after suffering a heart attack early that morning in the Pinehurst Hotel.

"We're expecting a call from the family telling us where to send the body," one of the golfers told the stunned girl at the counter. "Will you take the information and let us know when we finish?"

Noting the girl's amazement that they would play golf under such circumstances, one of them said, "He'd be doing the same thing if it were one of us."

And then there was the time a golfer hit his tee shot on the 11th hole of No. 2, suffered a coronary and expired on the spot. "I can't think of a better way to go," said his playing partner.

Golf is like that in Pinehurst. It transcends all else. It's a town where you see customized license plates: DIVOTTEE. PAR4US. SANDIRON. TEEITUP. Where a man can walk down the street, pronating his wrist and not look the fool. Where your shoulder turn and swing plane are more important than the prime rate and the cost of prime rib.

This book is not an attempt to tell the history of Pinehurst. The facts and dates contained herein are superfluous. There is much that there's not enough time or room to deal with: the village, the churches and all the other pursuits that require horses and rackets and mallets.

It is a book of *stories,* of golf stories, of anecdotes and musings and memories of the people who've made a mark here. If somehow you could collect the Ben Hogans and Sam Sneads and Billy Joe Pattons of the golf world around a cold beer and a crock of cheese after 18 holes, this book is what you'd hear.

It's been a memorable year planning and collecting this book. And collecting is the right word. That's all I've done. The stories were there; it was merely a matter of asking for them. What's been amazing is the reception I've gotten. People *love* to talk about Pinehurst.

Herbert Warren Wind has had 5,000 words on Richard S. Tufts in him for decades. It's just that no one ever asked him to put them on paper. Curtis Strange was reluctant to schedule a formal interview in advance through his agent. But I approached him walking from green to tee during a practice round at Doral Country Club last February and said, "Fletcher Gaines says hello." Strange brightened and invited me inside the ropes to walk with him and talk about winning two North and South Amateurs with the legendary caddie carrying his bag. I'll remember Pete Dye talking long into the night about golf-course architecture and Donald Ross. I'll remember the emotion in Billy Joe Patton's voice as he talked about the springtime of his golfing life he spent in Pinehurst.

My goal is that the people who've known and loved Pinehurst from days long ago will enjoy this book and acknowledge that maybe, just maybe, it captures a little something of what's made Pinehurst so special.

Lee Pace
Chapel Hill, July 1991

A NEW GOLF LINKS

A large gallery surrounds a square, sand green in 1910 postcard; the original Pinehurst clubhouse in 1898 (inset).

A nine-hole golf course has been laid out after the famous St. Andrews, near Edinburgh, Scotland. Mr. Tufts is giving his personal attention to the construction and we may expect as fine links as there are in the country. The spot selected is an ideal one, situated upon the hill south of the Village Commons. The grounds cover sixty acres of thoroughly cleared land, well fenced in, and covered with a thick growth of rye, which will be kept short by a flock of more than a hundred sheep. A large force of men have been at work on the links, which are now in good condition. Many good golfers are with us and anxiously awaiting the opening day.

As quite a few of our townspeople have not participated in the fascinating game, the question has been asked: "Is golf really a great game? Shorn of all the glamour and glitter of a new sport, will it wear well?" The answer comes from all parts of the country: "It will." It is a game that requires only moderate exertion; it does not tire one, but it creates a love for walking, develops the muscles of the arms and back, and cultivates a true eye and steady nerve. Like cycling, golf brings out of doors many who are not trained athletes. It is possible to the young, the middle aged, and even the old, and women can join in it no less than in lawn tennis or cycling. It gives to its

followers the best kind of tonic known to science—plenty of fresh air. But the greatest characteristic of the game is that it can be played all the year around. He whom the mighty Caledonian game has won, is perennially present, going over the course with increasing zest and pleasure.

Turning the page in the history of Pinehurst, we note that the historian dwelt lovingly over the glory of tennis, croquet and other

sports with more care than was ever given to the stories of the early saints by cloistered scribes picturing their triumphs with masters' brushes and pens. The popular out-door sport of the day is unquestionably golf, and the good old historian is compelled to admit to the new page the fact that the games that have been so popular in the past have settled into a state

Sweaters, ties and plus-fours were standard garb for early Pinehurst guests on the golf course (L); another view of the early 1900s clubhouse (inset); Bobby Cruickshank putts out on the fourth hole of No. 2 in the 1935 North and South Open (above); that hole became the current sixth hole with the opening later that year of new fourth and fifth holes.

¶ Without entering into any detailed description, the distances of the various holes are given below:

1—385 yards		10—311 yards	
2—375 "		11—153 "	
3—116 "		12—317 "	
4—310 "		13—285 "	
5—213 "		14—500 "	
6—386 "		15—257 "	
7—437 "		16—505 "	
8—213 "		17—152 "	
9—355 "		18—385 "	
Out 2,790 "		In 2,865 "	

Total, 5,655 yards.

(Length of nine-hole course, 2,750 yards.)

¶ The amateur record for the course, 36 holes, is 71-69—140, and 18 holes, 69 strokes, both held by Mr. Walter J. Travis. The professional record is 70, made by Alex. Ross.

¶ The bogey is 79.

An early course layout with Donald Ross's photograph in Pinehurst brochure (top); Chick Evans drives from sand tee while winning 1911 North and South Open (above); Pinehurst founder James Walker Tufts (R).

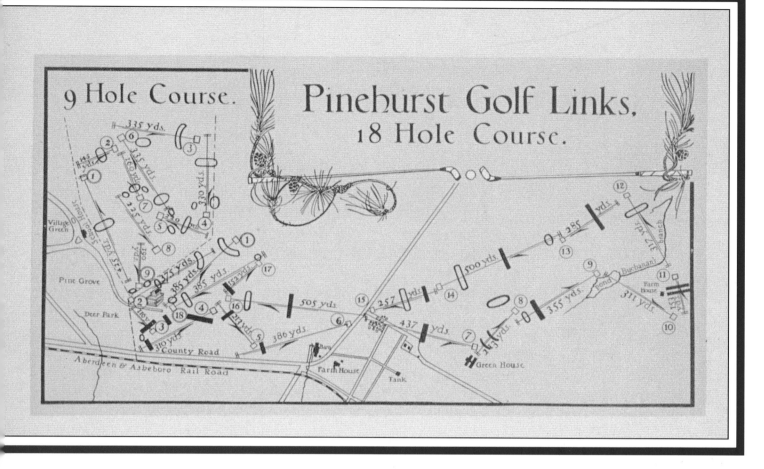

9 Hole Course.

Pinehurst Golf Links,
18 Hole Course.

of "innocuous desuetude," and is now ready to illuminate with red letters the birth of the Scotch national game at Pinehurst.

The word "links" in Scotland is applied to the sandy stretches of country near the sea; so the Pinehurst links have been laid out upon the white sand of Southern soil. Resorts of the North can boast of grass covered meadows, dotted here and there with trees. To be sure groves of trees beautify the landscape, but mar the joy of the game for him whose ill-directed drive has landed his ball in the midst of the foliage. This lack of appreciation of the beautiful in Nature is a feature of golf. No matter how artistic or picturesque with woods and ravines may be the course, the golfer only sees in them so many more or less insurmountable "hazards" and "bunkers." We are happy to say that there are no obstructions other than those placed there in connection with the few hills met with on our course, and those lend interest to the game.

There are no links in the South to be compared with those at Pinehurst, and they will prove the great magnet of attraction to lovers of the game. ∎

From "The Pinehurst Outlook," February 18, 1898

BOOK ONE

PINEHURST MEMORIES

From Hogan to Snead to Nicklaus to Campbell:
Eighteen stories of how some of the greatest names in golf
carved their niche in the annals of Pinehurst history.

Long-time Pinehurst regular Dick Chapman tees off as (L-R) Jimmy Demaret, Ben Hogan and Frank Stranahan look on.

BEN HOGAN

Ben Hogan spent seven grueling and frustrating years on the pro golf tour without winning—and was about to kiss his dream good-bye for the security of a club pro job. Then he won in Pinehurst in 1940. The rest, as they say, is history.

he Ben Hogan Company sits on a five-acre tract in the southwest corner of Fort Worth, Texas, less than a mile from the campus of Texas Christian University and alongside plants that manufacture and process such goods as steel, lumber and wooden cabinets.

On a blue awning that stretches from the front entrance, a red silhouette of Hogan watching the flight of his one-iron to the 72nd hole of the 1950 U.S. Open makes an elegant statement about the activity inside. It's the company Hogan started in 1953, his best year in golf (he won the U.S. and British Opens and the Masters). "I wanted to make golf clubs that were jewel-like in quality," Hogan once said, remembering $150,000 worth of clunkers in his first batch of irons. "I just ate them and started over."

Fifty years and nine months after he won a watershed golf tournament in Pinehurst, the proprietor is neatly dressed in gray slacks, a tweed jacket, white shirt and tie. On one wall is a large photograph of the four golfers who have won golf's four majors: Hogan, Gene Sarazen, Jack Nicklaus and Gary Player. Hogan is pleasant and warm.

There are so many things to talk about where Ben Hogan and Pinehurst are concerned:

The 1940 North and South championship, Hogan's first on the pro tour after seven years of frustration. The subsequent victories in Greensboro and in Asheville. The North and South titles in 1942 and '46. The grand times Ben and Valerie Hogan enjoyed with Byron and Louise Nelson, dressing in black tie and tails for dinner in the Carolina Hotel dining room. The 11th hole on Pinehurst No. 2, which Hogan once described as his favorite par-four. The 1951 Ryder Cup lambasting of the Brits.

"I always loved to play Pinehurst," Hogan is saying, interrupting his usual morning of office work before retiring to Shady Oaks Country Club for lunch. "I thought it was a great place. I thoroughly enjoyed every minute I stayed there. I must have played No. 2 I don't know how many times. But my record shows I won it three times.

"The whole golf course was a most pleasant

and testing golf course. It's a real test of golf. The North and South Open was a major then. At least I thought it was. It seems to me it was played in the fall of the year, after all the eastern courses had closed and the fellows were migrating south. It was a golf mecca. They had a very nice hotel, accommodations for everybody. It was great. It had a super reputation. Everybody wanted to go to Pinehurst."

* * *

William Benjamin Hogan was not a happy camper when the tour migrated to Pinehurst in March, 1940. One report said he had $30 in his pockets and bald tires on his second-hand automobile. Since first trying the tour in 1932, he'd yet to win a tournament, and for five years would occasionally need money so badly that he'd drop off the tour, spend the summer as pro at the Country Club in White Plains, N.Y., and the fall with his folks in Fort Worth. He often stretched his limited funds by making meals of the free oranges available to golfers when the tour swung through California and Florida.

"In 1937 I decided it might as well be sink or swim," he said. "If I played the tournament round and did well, so much the better. If it turned out I wasn't good enough to keep up with the rest of the boys, I could go home to Fort Worth and be broke again."

Hogan's teen-aged contemporaries, fellow Texans Byron Nelson and Ralph Guldahl, had four Western Opens, three U.S. Opens and two Masters between them. Hogan, on the other hand, could only score better than two men in the 1939 U.S. Open at the Spring Mill course at Philadelphia Country Club, shooting 78-80 in the final two rounds.

Hogan was viewed as an oddity on the tour because of his relentless work ethic and long practice hours. Other golfers avoided rooming next to him, for fear that the "thump-thump-thump" of Hogan putting long into the night on the hotel-room floor would rob them of sleep.

"The rules and the equipment are fine," Hogan once said. "The only thing that golfers need is more daylight. There isn't enough time during the day to practice and play to keep one's game to where it needs to be."

And on another occasion: "The best part of

golf is practicing and improving. You get your fun out of golf from practice."

While some thought his obsession with practice curious, others wondered if he had the mechanics to be a champion. "Hogan will never make it," Gene Sarazen once said. "That swing of his ... he should have won by now if he's ever going to do it with that swing."

The 1940 season was showing some promise, but several near misses added salt to his long-festering wounds. Hogan was the second-leading money winner, with $3,038 to his credit, when the tour arrived in Pinehurst and had finished second six times—to six different players—in the last 14 months. Hogan was in

the clubhouse in Phoenix with what appeared to be a safe lead, but Porky Oliver shot a 29 on the final nine to edge him by one stroke. Jimmy Demaret beat him in another tournament by a stroke. So did Nelson.

Hogan saw a sliver of hope in the narrow misses, however, reasoning to Valerie that if six different players were one shot better than him, there wasn't one player head and shoulders above him. "One day I'll get so far ahead no one can catch me," he said.

"Ben Hogan was starving for a tournament triumph as the 1940 tour began," Gene Gregston wrote in *Hogan: The Man Who Played for Glory*. "The achievements of Guldahl and

Hogan returned for North and South Open wins in 1942 and 1946 and was on the American Ryder Cup team that beat the British in 1951 on Pinehurst No. 2.

Nelson did not dishearten him, just the contrary. They added fuel to the fires smoldering within him until he was walking around the golf course like a volcano on the verge of eruption."

Despite his compact size—Hogan stood only five feet, eight inches and weighed 140 pounds—he still was one of the longest hitters on tour. He struck his woods and irons with vigor, furiously pouring every ounce of determination into his golf swing and grimacing if he even hit so much as a tail-end draw on his tee shots. In a long-drive contest earlier in the year in Los Angeles, Hogan's blast of 253 yards took second to Jimmy Thomson's 265. Thomson weighed 70 pounds more than Hogan.

Pinehurst and the North and South Open of 1940 had the aura reserved today for the major championships, and the Carolina Hotel and surrounding inns overflowed with the pros and the other guests who could watch golf—or better yet, *play* golf—or partake of the resort's other pleasures. "Back then, the pros wanted to win the North and South more than any other tournament, except the U.S. Open," Henry Picard said. Gymkahnas—outdoor festivals of contests such as pig races and musical chairs on horseback—were popular on the side lawn (where the pool stands today). Minstrels provided musical entertainment on a washboard, harmonica and guitar, and W.C. Fields' "My Little Chickadee" played in the Pinehurst Theatre. The only thing to dampen the mood was the specter of war; the day before the North and South opened, Adolf Hitler visited Italian Premier Benito Mussolini in Rome to plot battle plans.

Admission to the event cost only $1.25 the first two days and $1.50 the final day (36 holes), and the purse was minuscule, too, by today's standards: $4,000, with $1,000 to the winner. Pinehurst was the first leg of a four-tournament northern swing that closed the winter tour (later it would be played, as Hogan remembers, in November). The Greater Greensboro Open, the

EDGAR A. GUEST: PINEHURST'S "POET LAUREATE"

Poet Edgar A. Guest was an avid golfer and frequent visitor to Pinehurst. His verse appeared regularly in *The Pinehurst Outlook*, and quite frequently he composed poetry saluting the colossal Pinehurst experience. One of those poems appears below, and several others are scattered throughout *Pinehurst Stories*.

Guest was also an accomplished practical joker. Once he and friends of Fred Wardell of the Detroit Golf Club conspired for a laugh at Wardell's expense by having Guest made up to look like a caddie.

High wagers were made on the match, and Wardell was constantly distracted from his golf by the incompetence and insubordination of his caddie. Guest dropped the bag of clubs just as Wardell was putting and stepped on his ball in a bunker. Wardell fired the caddie on the 11th hole, but the caddie refused to leave until he'd been paid for a full 18 holes. As a fond farewell, Guest then kissed Wardell and removed his wig.

PINEHURST

There are other spots on this gracious earth,
  Where the sky is just as blue;
There are scenes like these, with the gentle breeze,
  And the kindly sunshine too;
There are haunts made fine by the stalwart pine,
  Where the charms of June are known,
But I've learned today in a curious way
  Why Pinehurst stands alone.

There are gardens fair in the sunny south
  Where rich magnolias bloom,
There are fairy scenes with the wealth of greens,
  And the scent of a sweet perfume.
But more than a sky where the sun shines high,
  And more than ridge of pine,
Or a sea or a lake, God needs to make
  An earthly golfers' shrine.

The Lord has lavished his treasures rich
  All over the orb of earth,

Yet some are base with the common place,
  And some are lost to mirth.
But Pinehurst holds in its friendly folds
  The lure of an honest grip,
And a manhood fine adds to gifts divine
  The wealth of its fellowship.

It isn't the pines with its flowering fronds
  Upraised to the God on high,
Or the fragrant air that men come to share,
  And it isn't along the sky.
It's the hand clasp true, that they seek anew,
  The smile on the cheery lip,
Here honor counts more than the victory,
  And a man is more than his gold;
Here love of the game means more than the fame,
  Or the joy that the prize may hold.
Oh, Pinehurst gleams with the finest dreams,
  And best we mortals know,
It is rich in the things that a true life brings,
  God grant you may keep it so.
© 1922 by Edgar A Guest

Land of the Sky Open in Asheville and the Masters Tournament in Augusta would follow, each paying $5,000.

The field lacked the tour's top money-winner. Jimmy Demaret—who had won $6,125 but was still obscure enough that many fans were pronouncing his name "Dem-a-RAY" instead of "De-MER-it"—had returned to Houston to handle club business, but the rest of the tour's top 10 money-winners and Vardon point holders were there. Among them were Byron Nelson, coming off his 1939 North and South and U.S. Open victories, as well as Craig Wood, Lawson Little, Jug McSpaden, Paul Runyan, Dick Metz, Horton Smith, Sam Snead and Clayton Heafner. Even Bobby Jones was there as a spectator.

The crowds marveled at the sun-tanned faces, just up from Florida, and most gathered around Charlotte native Heafner, then a pro out of Linville, who was joined in the first round by Horton Smith and Dick Metz. In the gallery was legendary Duke University football coach Wallace Wade.

So the stage was set on March 19, 1940 for Benny Hogan, as he was then called. Wearing gray slacks, a dark green sweater, a white shirt and dark tie and the trademark white linen cap, Hogan got off on the right foot—he birdied the first hole with a drive, seven-iron and 12-foot putt, as well as the second with a drive, six-iron and four-footer. He went to three-under with a birdie on four. The new 14-ounce MacGregor driver he'd been loaned by Nelson felt good; his tee shots were long and true. Hogan froze a tabby-cat scowl on his face, walked fast and left a trail of cigarettes in his wake. His precision was painstaking: on one putt of an inch, he went through all the footwork and positioning of a 10-footer. He holed a bunker shot on 11 for a three and didn't miss one fairway. Hogan shot a six-under 66, tying the competitive course record set the year before by Harry Cooper. Runyan was next at 69.

"There's something about this new driver that fits me like a glove," Hogan said. "I tell you, I've never driven the ball better."

Hogan widened his margin to seven after 36 holes with a 67. His 133 total led Snead and Revolta, at 140. Never had Hogan felt more confident. Perhaps he'd finally acquired that insurmountable lead he'd spoken to his wife

"Gymkahnas" were held on weekend afternoons on the side lawn of the Carolina Hotel and drew interest from young and old alike as guests played a variety of games on horseback.

BOBBY JONES VISITS PINEHURST

While Bobby Jones was taking his golf game to legendary heights in the 1920s, he was noticeably absent from the Pinehurst golf scene. Jones played in Pinehurst as a 15-year-old in 1917, but, according to the March 26, 1932 *Pinehurst Outlook*, didn't return for 15 more years. But Jones, who had retired from competitive golf only two years before, snuffed any impressions that he was not partial to Pinehurst.

"I always have regarded Pinehurst as one of the garden spots of the South," he said. "I thought always, and still think, it has golf courses that are very fine tests of golf and very beautiful. I have not been able to come here oftener simply because I had to be home sometimes, and my spare time for big golf has had to be devoted to national or international play. I think the public realizes that just to keep in form and play in the national tournaments entails considerable sacrifice of time.

"Moreover, Donald Ross is an old and very highly esteemed friend of mine, and had I been able to come here oftener I would have done so if only to keep in closer touch with this fine golfer and genuine fellow.

"Well, now that I'm more foot loose as regarding golfing, and have renewed my contact with Pinehurst, I hope to see more of it in the future."

about. Sarazen was still skeptical: "He's never won before, he won't win this time. He's been out front before. Someone will catch him."

The last day, a Thursday, was unseasonably chilly. Hogan was paired in the last group, with Revolta and Heafner, and his early aggressive, confident approach had turned tentative. He under-clubbed several times in the morning round and shot a 74, but his lead at lunchtime was still six strokes. Among his closest challengers up ahead, Sarazen was shooting a final-round 75 and Snead a 67. The latter holed a 20-footer for a birdie on 18, closing with an eight-under 280 total. But Hogan, back on 16, made a birdie to go 11-under. Two closing pars would beat Snead by three shots and clip two strokes off the tournament record set in 1938 by Vic Ghezzi.

"Don't pinch me," Valerie Hogan said as her husband did indeed par 17 and 18 for a 70-277 finish. "I'm afraid I'll wake up. Ben always said the only way he would win his first title would be to get so far out in front of the field that nobody could catch him on the final day. That seems to have happened now. But I don't believe it. Ben has been so close so many times, only to see one fatal shot crumble all his hopes. He's never given up trying, though, even in his darkest hours. That's why I'm so proud of him now."

At the presentation ceremony, Hogan was offered the trophy and $1,000 in fresh, green bills by Edward J. Cheyney of Cleveland, a USGA official and friend of Pinehurst's Richard Tufts. Worried about carrying so much cash with him, Hogan instead asked that a check be

drawn and sent to him that weekend in Greensboro.

Then he drank a glass of milk and told newsmen:

"I won one just in time. I had finished second and third so many times I was beginning to think I was an also-ran. I needed that win. They've kidded me about practicing so much. I'd go out there before a round and practice, and when I was through I'd practice some more. Well, they can kid me all they want because it finally paid off. I know it's what finally got me in the groove to win."

And what a groove it turned out to be. The volcano had erupted. (It would take time, though, for "Hogan" to become a household name. That night at the *Greensboro Daily News*, a typesetter looked at an editor's hand-scrawled headline and thought the name "Hogan" must surely be "Hagen." So the paper's early edition read, "Hagen's 277 Leaves Snead 3 Strokes Behind." John Derr, on the staff at the time, caught the mistake after the early edition went to press and corrected the error.)

The tour moved on to Greensboro for the first two rounds at Starmount Forest Country Club, then a 36-hole finale on Monday at Sedgefield CC. Hogan and Heafner each shot 69s to open the tournament and tie for the lead, and then on Easter Sunday, March 24, something very strange happened:

It snowed.

Fourteen threesomes had teed off amid cold and flurries when play was halted. "Okay, fellows, let's ski off," Sarazen cracked. Eventually three to four inches fell, postponing the second round until Wednesday. Rounds three and four would be played Thursday, and the Land of the Sky Open in Asheville had been set back and wouldn't begin until Friday.

Hogan was quiet during the delay, spending his days playing bridge, but his presence was felt now that he'd won a tournament. His biggest concern was that his $1,000 check hadn't arrived from Pinehurst. "He's a fine golfer, he's been long overdue," Heafner said. "He's one of the best. He'll be hard to beat in this tournament."

Hogan shot a 68 in the second round, with three birdies and no bogeys. Heafner faded to a 76, and Hogan led Sarazen and Guldahl by three at the halfway mark. It was no contest. Hogan lapped the field with a 66 and 67 on the final day, for a tournament-record 270 and nine-shot win over Craig Wood. He collected the

$1,200 and was apprised by wire from Donald Ross at Pinehurst that his North and South winnings would be in Asheville upon his arrival.

"The game becomes monotonous the way the slender man plays it," newspaperman Jake Wade commented afterward. "He has all the shots and he tears into the ball with amazing power for one of such slight build. It is a straight, true and unwavering game."

Said Johnny Revolta: "It was easy to see we couldn't catch that fellow, the way he is playing. You can't beat perfection."

The players drove through heavy fog on the way up to Asheville that Thursday night for 18 holes at Asheville Country Club, 18 at Beaver Lake and 36 at Biltmore Forest. Hogan continued his stellar play with a 67, but was three behind Metz, Guldahl and Lloyd Mangrum. Hogan and Mangrum were tied for second at 135 behind Guldahl's 134 after two rounds. A pair of 69s on the final day gave Hogan a 273 total and three-shot win over Guldahl. Hogan pocketed another $1,200 and, yes, his $1,000 from Pinehurst was there.

In three tournaments, Hogan played 216 holes 34-under-par, breaking par 11 of 12 rounds. He broke 70 on all but two rounds. He three-putted just two greens, both in Asheville. Ten of 12 rounds were on Donald Ross golf courses (the exception being Starmount Forest). Hogan had now won $6,438 in three months, and he eventually won the 1940 top-money prize with $10,655 and collected the Vardon Trophy as well.

Given that nudge of confidence from two weeks in North Carolina, Hogan went on to become one of the top three or four golfers of all time. He claimed the money-winning and Vardon titles again the following two years, won North and Souths again in 1942 and '46 and became one of four players to win a career grand slam: four U.S. Opens, two Masters, two PGA Championships and one British Open. He was a member of the 1951 Ryder Cup team that whipped the British 9 1/2 to 2 1/2. That was the scene of one of his career shots. In a singles

match against Charles Ward, Hogan was 2-up when he hooked his tee shot on the par-five 10th into the woods. He punched out into the fairway, then launched a two-wood nearly 300 yards to the green's fringe. Hogan drained a 75-foot putt for a birdie.

"Yes, it was as good as any I've ever hit in my life," Hogan said. "When the adrenaline is running, you can hit a ball further, and I guess my adrenaline was going full speed. It surprised me that I hit the brassie so far."

* * *

Many of the specifics are fuzzy, but the overall feeling is still there for Ben Hogan this

December, 1990, morning.

"The people from the North who'd go South for the winter, and they'd do it for years and years and years, they'd always stop at Pinehurst," the 79-year-old says. "They'd play golf for a few days and stay overnight and move on. They had three or four golf courses right there at the Carolina Hotel."

Hogan is told there are now seven courses at Pinehurst Country Club.

"Seven golf courses. Goodness gracious," he says. "Are any the equal to No. 2?"

"It would be hard to equal No. 2, don't you think?" comes the response.

"You're right, of course," he says, then soon after bids adieu to his visitor.

"Tell everyone in Pinehurst hello for me," Ben Hogan says cheerfully. ∎

Congratulations: Donald Ross (L) and Hogan share a handshake following Hogan's landmark triumph in 1940.

GOLF WORLD MAGAZINE

SAM SNEAD

Sam Snead won three North and South Opens, signed one incorrect scorecard, found a legendary caddie and generally had a blast in Pinehurst. Whether or not he won playing a slot machine is open for debate.

I t was the perfect Sam Snead-at-Pinehurst story. There've been plenty of good tales, of course, about the man from Virginia spreading his molasses golf swing across the Sandhills. He'd won three North and South Opens. He'd won the 1971 PGA Club Professional title on No. 2. He'd told everyone from Riviera to Turnberry for half a century that among his top five golf courses—maybe even his favorite—was Pinehurst No. 2. Didn't he find his favorite caddie of all time, Jimmy Steed, at Pinehurst Country Club? And wasn't he second to Ben Hogan during that 1940 North and South when that tiny stick of Texas dynamite exploded onto the world of golf?

But there it was one day on the microfilm reader, in a story by-lined Arch Murray that dealt with the 1938 Greater Greensboro Open:

"I don't think there was ever a more discouraged youngster than Sam Snead when he took to the dusty trail from Pinehurst to Greensboro ....."

It was like discovering gold in that March 24, 1940 *Greensboro Daily News*. It seems a disconsolate Sam Snead wasn't having that great a spring as the 1938 pro tour season moved into

Pinehurst. He'd won the Bing Crosby Pro-Am, but aside from that, the article said, he was suffering the "sophomore jinx." And what happened when he got to Pinehurst? He shot a fat DQ after accidentally signing an incorrect scorecard.

Snead wandered into a drugstore in the village late that night, dropped a nickel into a slot machine and—*whoosh*—out poured a stream of coins.

"As the silver rushed out, this boy with the mark of the mountains hard upon him sensed that this was the big turn," Murray wrote.

And the big turn was in Pinehurst, N.C., of all places. The next week he won his first of eight career Greensboro Opens, clicked off six more wins for the year and spent the next 30 years collecting 81 official PGA Tour wins and every honor in the game. It was like a Hollywood script writer had cranked it out.

So, Mr. Snead, what drugstore was it? What time of night was it? How much money did you win? What did you do after winning the money? Did you go to the hotel bar and buy drinks for the house? What did you shoot in Greensboro the next day?

Samuel Jackson Snead, 79 and spry as a fox,

Waiting on the tee in 1949 (L-R): Johnny Bulla, Snead, Gene Sarazen and Paul Runyan.

draws a blank when he hears the story.

"Never happened," he says.

What?

"Never happened," he repeats. "I never messed with those things. We played in Las Vegas one year and I didn't play those slot machines then."

Well, maybe the old boy's lost a little over the years. Surely someone else has heard the story.

"Sounds like something Fred Corcoran made up," Al Barkow, editor of *Golf Illustrated* and noted historian, says of the former tour administrator and Snead manager who was known to dole little stories out in the pressroom like they dispense lollipops in nursery school.

"If Sam said it didn't happen, I'd tend to believe him," says Irwin Smallwood, a retired newspaperman in Greensboro. "You might try Carson Bain. He and Sam were good buddies. They went fishing a lot."

"I never heard that one," says Bain, who led the effort to get the entrance road to Starmount Forest CC in Greensboro renamed Sam Snead Drive. "Stories seemed to magnify around Sam. Sam never drank on the tour, but people would come up to him and say, 'Sam, remember me? We got drunk one night in L.A.,' and you knew it never happened because Sam didn't drink."

Rats.

All right, no great Sam Snead-at-Pinehurst story. But a bunch of good ones.

"I did get disqualified in 1938, that much is true," Snead says one morning at his winter home in Ft. Pierce, Fla. Under foot is Meister, a seven-year-old retriever who does just that: Snead's slippers, golf balls, whatever. "Somebody hits one in the woods, he finds it. Went into the woods the other day and found 11 golf balls," Snead says proudly, rubbing the dog's head.

Snead hasn't all day to talk. He lives only a driver from the clubhouse at Meadowbrook, a club/residential community he lives in December through March. Billboards on I-95 and surrounding roads hawk his photograph and beckon sales inquiries. "I got a couple pigeons coming in. I've got to be at the golf club by 11 or so," he says.

Snead was playing with Gene Sarazen and Paul Runyan in the second round of the '38

North and South Open. For some reason that Snead doesn't remember, he was keeping all the scores on one card. He made a bogey-five on 18 but mistakenly gave himself a four and penciled one of his partners, who made a four, with a five.

"Five thousand people saw me make a five," Snead says. "I wasn't going to put a four down on purpose. They were supposed to check my score as I checked theirs. I had a five the last hole. I would have won that tournament, too. I had 73, not 72.

"All the pros got together and said, 'That's not right.' They said I shouldn't have had to keep three scores on one card. Only two people didn't back me: Horton Smith and Sam Parks. I'm practicing, here comes Dick Tufts. He said, 'Sam ... well ... geez.' And I said, 'I know, you want me to leave, don't you?'

"He says, 'Well, there are two guys who won't support you. They're kicking up a storm.' That old Smith. I called him an old woman. Poor devil, I shouldn't talk about him. It was an honest mistake.

"Tufts said, 'I'm awful sorry. Two guys won't go to bat for you.'"

It is true, also, that Snead left Pinehurst that

If ever there was a "company town," Pinehurst was it under the Tufts, who owned the village, the fire department, the power company—and the money. When times got tough during the Depression, the company resorted to paying its employees in script that was redeemable for merchandise in the Village General Store.

Pinehurst, N.C.
December 13, 1926

Mr. Martin
Mr. Hemmer
Mr. Werden
Mr. Severance:

For the rest of my life I shall be writing you letters probably—every so often—absolutely contradicting themselves on the subject of conventions. We get a good convention down here and it may add from ten to fifteen thousand dollars to our profits—if I don't happen to run across any of our regular guests at that time, especially if business has been a little dull. I am all for conventions and you may hear from me to push conventions. If, on the other hand, we have a convention of people who get gloriously (or ingloriously) drunk or who are complained of to me by many of our old guests and if these guests tell me that this business is stopping many people from coming to Pinehurst you will get a letter from me condemning conventions.

For the next little while, until you hear from me to the contrary, I would go easy on convention publicity. Business is good and there has been a good deal of criticism of conventions.

Yours very truly,
Leonard Tufts

week, traveled to Greensboro and won there for the first of his many GGO titles. It's also fact that at Pinehurst Snead found the caddie who would help him to three North and South Open titles in 10 years, all his GGO success and sometimes work for Snead outside the state. Jimmy Steed carried Snead's bag, chomped on a cigar and always had the right club.

"Some of the fellows on tour think one reason Sam won Greensboro so often was because of Jimmy Steed," says Bill Campbell, a fellow native of the Blue Ridge that runs through West Virginia and Virginia and a four-time North and South Amateur winner. "Sam has a great many talents, but one of them is not confidence in selecting clubs. He accepts the advice of caddies, and looks for it. Jimmy Steed had the knack of giving Sam clubs, whether right or wrong, and Sam had confidence in Jimmy."

Snead even arranged for Steed to be his caddie in the 1956 U.S. Open at Oak Hill Country Club in Rochester, N.Y. Since the USGA required at the time that local caddies be used instead of traveling caddies, Snead arranged for Steed to move temporarily to Rochester and join the Oak Hill caddie staff. But USGA official Joe Dey stepped in.

"Joe Dey took him away from me," Snead

says, still ruffled today at the memory of the one major championship he never won. "Jimmy caddied all year up there so he could caddie for me. They had assigned me another caddie, so Jimmy and he just switched bags. Joe Dey saw Jimmy carrying my bag and said, 'Oh no, you can't do that.' And I said, 'What do you mean? He's a caddie here. He's been here all year.'

"He said, 'You still can't do that.' Well, I think that cost me the tournament, because I was really playing well.'

"Jimmy was great. At the end, though, I went to playing by yardages and he couldn't handle that very well. He went by sight. He'd always say something like, 'Hook your seven-iron,' or 'Let's hit a high five.' Or 'Let's cut a six.' He'd get a big kick out of it. Then I said, 'Jimmy, don't go by sight any more, I need to know the yardage.' He'd pull out three or four clubs. He had no idea. He just couldn't caddie like that."

Snead won the North and South Open in 1941, 1949 and 1950, and in that 10-year span finished second three other times. The '41 Nortl and South was particularly memorable because of an eagle on the monstrous par-five 10th hole—Snead was on in two and rolled in a 50-footer for a three—and because it featured Snead, Ben Hogan and Clayton Heafner (a Charlotte native and Linville pro) in the final group for the third day's 36-hole finale. Snead won with a final-round 69 and a 277 total, three shots ahead of Heafner. He clipped two other North Carolina natives for his other titles, beating Burlington's Johnny Bulla in '49 with a 274 and Badin's Johnny Palmer in '50 with a 275. The latter two wins earned him jackpots of $1,500.

Snead also was a member of the 1951 Ryder Cup team that whipped Great Britain, 9 1/2 to 2 1/2, and Snead was six-under through 33 holes in beating Max Faulkner, 4-and-3. Bad weather on Friday kept the U.S. team from sporting its red, white and blue golf shoes, and Saturday was an off-day because officials feared poor attendance on a day when the University of Tennessee's top-ranked football team was to play 70 miles up the road in Chapel Hill.

The North and South Open was scheduled to follow immediately, but according to one newspaper report, only Snead, Heafner, Skip Alexander, Porky Oliver and Henry Ransom remained to enter. Lloyd Mangrum, Jackie Burke, Jimmy Demaret and Hogan were among those who left. But Ransom was the only one to finish four rounds. Snead, *The Charlotte Observer* reported, got disgusted over slow play, withdrew after two rounds and hopped a train to Miami. "Scrammin' Sammy," they called him in Pinehurst. The others withdrew for assorted reasons. Pinehurst's Tufts took offense at the pros' actions and promptly discontinued the North and South Open; it would be 22 years before the pro tour would return to Pinehurst.

When Snead returned in 1973 for the World Open, he was incensed at some of the changes made since the Tufts family sold the property to Diamondhead Corp. Snead gets riled up talking about one of his favorite holes, the third.

"I've always thought the third hole was one of the nicest little holes," he says. "It had chocolate drops down the left side. On the right side was sandy waste area. The fairway got narrower as you went. Then you had that bunch grass. If you get up against that you'd have to pitch it sideways. There were more fives than threes made there.

"Then this new group came in there and took all those mounds out, took that sand and covered it up and put two little pot bunkers down there. You could hit anything (off the tee). There were more threes than fives. It ruined the hole. The other, if you wanted to hit a big club, you go ahead, but brother you miss it to the left of one of those mounds and you're done for. It's a pitch out, you see. And the same way in that waste bunker on the other side. Actually it was bare sand with that bunch grass. Had to play a two or three or four-iron off the tee, and they had four good pin placements. If the pin was on the left and you fooled around going for that flag, brother, you were going to get into trouble.

"I always said I'd like to have that one hole in every 18. I was going to do a course in Palm Springs, but the fellow died. I was going to do that hole on that course. It would have been absolutely perfect, 340, 330 yards."

Which leads to two more Sam Snead stories—one from Campbell, the former USGA president who administers his golf, business and life with such precision that if he tells a story, you put it in the bank. And the other, again, from the *Greensboro Daily News*, whose credibility is teetering a little.

"There's a wonderful story on the 16th hole of the North and South Open," Campbell says. "Sam hit a long drive and had 230, 240 yards to the hole. Jimmy gave him a one-iron and said, 'I'd take a one-iron, Sam, and I'd drill it.' Sam

hit it absolutely on the button by all appearance, but it came up about 20 yards short on the upslope to the green. Sam whirled around in his quick anger. Jimmy looked at him and he had that cigar, and he said, 'Sam, I said, *Drill it.*' Jimmy's the only man who could get by with not choosing the right club and saying that to Sam."

Okay, Mr. Snead. How about that one?

"No, it was a five-iron," he says. "I really jumped on it. I turned around, I said, 'Jimmy, you know you had me hitting that five-iron 200 yards.' He went, 'Heh, heh, heh.' He had that funny giggle."

Final story. North and South Open, 1941, fourth round. Snead is two shots up on Heafner through 16 holes. Snead hits his tee shot on the par-three 17th to 10 feet.

"All right, Heafner, beat that," Snead says. And it's in black and white. Right on Page 21 of the March 21 *Greensboro Daily News*, in a story by Bill Boni of the Associated Press. The caddies supposedly giggled when he said it (Steed had

America's first miniature golf course: James Barber couldn't get enough golf, so in 1916 he built an 18-hole "Lilliputian" golf course on the grounds of his home behind the Carolina Hotel. He looked at the work of architect Edward Wisell and declared, "This'll do!" and from then on the course was called "Thistle Dhu." Here Donald Ross tries his hand at the course that players negotiated with putters and niblicks.

Off for Pinehurst: The "Golf Boy" was the forerunner to the Pinehurst "Putter Boy" and appeared in all the resort's early advertising.

wagered his gabardine trousers against the overalls of Heafner's caddie).

Heafner almost hits the flagstick. The ball stops 10 inches from the cup.

"No, I never said that in my life," Sam Snead says. "I never said that. I learned young you don't give anyone the needle.

"It was the 1935 Cascades Open, the first tournament I ever played in. Guy I worked for, Fay Ingalls, cost me that one. I was leading by three shots. My boss, he's shooting 80, he's playing with me and (Bobby) Cruickshank. I birdied the first hole. The second hole, he said, 'How do you expect to ever play golf with that elbow coming up?' The Ingalls family owned the Homestead. Fay Ingalls said he didn't want to see me win. 'Assistant pro wins tournament, we won't get any publicity out of that. We need one of the tour players to win.' So they gave me that needle. I had a strong grip with the right hand. On the next shot, I said, 'I'll keep the elbow down,' and I put it halfway up that mountain and made eight. I shot 40 or something that side.

"My brother came up to me and said, 'What the hell happened to you?' I said, 'Ingalls just gave me a needle back on the second tee.' He said, 'I'll go knock him down.' I said, 'No, I've learned a lesson. I'll know the next time.'"

No slot machine. No one-iron to 16 from 230 yards. No needle to Clayton Heafner.

Your commitment to truth and accuracy is admirable, Sam Snead, but you sure can ruin a good story.

EPILOGUE: A box full of notes obtained near press time that was compiled by former "Charlotte News" writer Bob Saunders has references to Snead being disqualified in 1937, not 1938. And there's also on a faded sheet of paper a paragraph about Snead hitting that phantom jackpot—but in 1939, not 1938.

Back to the microfilm.

In the lower right-hand corner of the lead sports page of the March 23, 1939 "Greensboro Daily News," is a small box headlined "Sam Hits Jackpot!—An Omen?"

A one-paragraph story signed by Wilton Garrison began as follows: "Sam Snead, the West Virginia hill-billy, dropped into a drug store here tonight for a soda. He casually flipped a nickel into a slot machine and promptly hit the jackpot. 'It's back,' he whooped as he raked in his money, 'my golden touch is back. Now watch me hit that thousand-dollar jackpot tomorrow. Whoopee!'"

Byron Nelson actually hit that jackpot the following day, winning the 1939 North and South Open. But maybe there's something to that story, after all.

Your witness, Mr. Snead. ∎

Legend has it that Walter Hagen arrived on the first tee at Pinehurst for a North and South Open round straight from an all-night soiree. He topped his tee shot only a short distance, but soon settled down and shot a 66. Hagen won the event in 1918, 1923 and 1924.

HARVIE WARD

Harvie Ward could chip. He could putt. And boy could he play to the crowd. Pair him against one of golf's very best amateurs, Frank Stranahan, and the result was two North and South finals matches unrivaled for their intensity and flair.

ord first circulated through the Zeta Psi fraternity house in Chapel Hill late that Friday afternoon in April, 1948. It filtered over to the SAE house, through Big Fraternity Court and then spread like a fire through an autumn hayfield down Franklin Street, where students at the University of North Carolina were beginning their weekend rounds of the Goody Shop, Harry's, the Curve Inn and the Ranch House.

Harvie Ward had just beaten Arnold Palmer and would play Saturday in the final of the North and South Amateur.

Road trip.

They piled into cars the next morning and the Zeta brothers and Tar Heel golf team led a caravan down Hwy. 15-501 to Pinehurst and its No. 2 golf course, where Ward and Frank Stranahan of Toledo, Ohio, would square off in the 36-hole match that day.

A crowd estimated near 2,000 lined the fairways. *Golf World* magazine described the scene like this: "A number of attractive coeds from Chapel Hill, some in bare feet with painted toes, were included in an exuberant gallery of collegians, wealthy tourists, town folks and Negro caddies on the championship course at Pinehurst Saturday, April 24."

The contrasts in the competitors were striking.

Stranahan, 25, the heir to the Champion spark-plug fortune, was a fine golfer. But his deportment was gray and cool, his game methodical and disciplined. He played power golf as his arms bulged with the muscles honed through religious weight-lifting. He'd been hooked on weights since his teens, when he took the Charles Atlas course to beef up for prep school football. He carried his weights on the road, and the Pinehurst bellboys knew they were in for a workout unloading Stranahan's barbells each spring. (Stranahan once posed wearing a loin-cloth with muscles flexed for Pinehurst photographer John Hemmer, and the photo ran in a New York newspaper). He was polite but distant. His handsome face was tanned after a spring of full-time competition on the professional golf tour.

Ward, 22, the son of a Tarboro pharmacist, had never met a stranger. He epitomized a golden era in post-war Chapel Hill where students had little money and few cars, so they jitterbugged to Les Brown and his Band of Renown, cheered "Choo Choo" Justice on fall Saturdays, and campus became like one big, happy family. The frisky 21-year-old was more of a finesse player. One of his favorite shots was a little punch wedge that could make the golf ball dance on the bermuda-grass greens. Another was *anything* struck with his ancient, hickory-shafted putter he found some eight years before in the locker room of Hilma Golf Club in Tarboro.

"You had the austere Stranahan, the Greek god, who played a subdued game and rarely said anything," says Bob Cox, a Carolina golfer at the time who now lives in Charlotte. "Harvie was one of the most popular students ever at Carolina. He had a certain rhythm and motion and romance about his game. Harvie would be walking down the fairway talking to people."

Or, as fellow Zeta Collier Cobb III of Chapel Hill remembers: "Harvie was the happy-go-lucky type. He'd be walking down the fairway with his arm around a girl."

So they set out early that Saturday morning, and, over 36 holes that day and another 35 one year later, Ward and Stranahan would make North and South history with the most hotly contested rivalry in the half-century of the event. In 71 consecutive holes of match play, Stranahan would hold a one-hole edge. Each would win a championship. But there was no doubt about the crowd favorite.

"It was kind of embarrassing," says Ward. "Most of the kids from Chapel Hill knew nothing about golf. The game was kind of in its infancy. Every time Frank would miss a shot or miss a chip, they'd cheer. The only people Frank had pulling for him were his mother and father and sister. Anytime I'd get the ball airborne they'd go nuts. You'd have thought they were in Kenan Stadium at a football game."

Stranahan adds two names to his rooting section: "Art Wall and Mike Souchak, who played for Duke, were cheering for me." (Today

JOHN HEMMER

Ward and caddie Barney Google stretch out for best view of a stymie during 1948 North and South. Two-time British Open champ Henry Cotton (C) was on hand to present the winner's and runner-up awards to Ward (L) and Stranahan.

Stranahan lives in Palm Beach, Fla.; he doesn't play golf anymore but still lifts weights and runs in frequent marathons.)

"But it was something," Ward continues. "It was the first big golf tournament I was ever in, and it was certainly the first big win I ever had."

Ward had no visions of winning when he decided to enter the tournament. The field was full of good golfers: Stranahan had won in 1946 and was generally considered the world's finest amateur (he would win the British Amateur

later that year) and Charles "Chick" Evans was returning for the first time in 37 years after winning the 1911 North and South. That was the year dare-devil pilot Lincoln Beachey, who was spending the spring at Pinehurst, promised the winner a ride on his airplane. Beachey would fly in his "weird collection of bamboo, wooden struts and a great deal of wire," according to one eyewitness, over the golf courses and terrify the caddies, and he scared Evans a good bit, too, when he was strapped in for his victory ride. "That was the only tournament I ever won with mixed emotions," Evans cracked. (Another rider was a Japanese admiral who commented that an airplane could be developed into a formidable machine of war.) But in 1948, Evans and his wife left Chicago at 1 p.m., changed planes in Cincinnati and were in Pinehurst in time for dinner.

Ward entered at the last minute and had to call his golf coach, Chuck Erickson, for permission to miss class on Monday for the qualifying round. He shot a 74 to make the field of 64 for match play but appeared to be headed home after five holes Tuesday morning in his match

THE ORIGIN OF THE COUNTRY CLUB

Author John P. Marquand spent many seasons in Pinehurst and eventually owned a home here. He was known for his love of Pinehurst golf and for his satirical spoofs of country-club life. From the jacket of Marquand's collection of stories about a fictional country club, *Life at Happy Knoll*, comes the following wisdom on the creation of the country club:

"Man's primitive desire to get away from woman originated golf. Woman's even more primitive desire not to let him get away led her to take up the sport. The children tagged along. Soon all over America country clubs sprang up in the wilderness. And lo, the cursing of middle-aged duffers, the screams of young girls being thrown into swimming pools, the clink of ice cubes, the conversational hubbub and shattering glassware of debutante parties was heard in the land."

against Charles Mulcahy of New York.

"I stood on the sixth tee and was four down," says Ward, who spent much of his adult life in California but now has "semi-retired" to Pinehurst. "I was playing bad; I was nervous. But I just kept plugging along, he started playing worse, and all of a sudden I was back in the match."

Ward tied it on 18 and won on the 19th hole and moved into the round of 32. He returned to his $7-room at Pope's Cottages in Southern Pines and called Erickson to ask if he could stay another day, then removed his tan gabardine pants, white shirt, maroon sweater and washed his clothes in the lavatory.

"See, I wasn't expecting to stay very long, so I didn't even take a change of clothes," he says. "So every night that I week I'd call Chuck and ask to stay another day and then I'd wash my socks and shirt and underwear there in the motel room. Then I'd show up the next day with my clothes half wet. By the end of the week those clothes could almost walk around without me in them."

Ward used his deft short game and the sound counsel on the greens of his stumpy caddie, 30-year veteran Barney Google, to

march through the field to Friday's semifinals; it took a nerve-wracking, downhill 15-footer on No. 17 on Thursday to dispatch long-time North and South challenger Dick Chapman of Pinehurst, 2-and-1. Then Ward faced an unknown sophomore from Wake Forest College with thick forearms and a gunslinger's golf swing in the semifinals. Arnold Palmer was no match for Ward that day, losing 5-and-4.

"I don't remember a thing about that match," says Ward. "I do have a picture of Arnold and myself taken before the match. One day I need to get Arnold to sign it for me."

(Two weeks later, Palmer would get a measure of revenge by posting a 145 total to edge Ward by a shot in winning the Southern Conference collegiate championship on No. 2.)

Grover Pope announced he'd feed Ward "the biggest steak in the house" that night and reminded the *Pinehurst Outlook* that Babe Didrikson Zaharias stayed with him the year before when she won the North and South Women's Amateur. "Good golfers stay at Pope's," he said proudly. Ward called a frat brother to bring him a change of clothes for the championship, and the helpful friend arrived Saturday morning with Ward's entire wardrobe.

"What the hell did you bring all these clothes for?" Ward asked.

"Well, I didn't know what you'd want to wear," his buddy responded.

Stranahan was the bettor's favorite—Ward confided to friends he just wanted to "make a good showing"—but Ward had the crowd on his side. His parents drove down from Tarboro for the match and Mr. Ward promised his son they'd talk about that new car Harvie had been wanting if he could beat the "Adonis from Ohio," as the papers took to calling Stranahan.

The match see-sawed throughout, with neither golfer gaining a commanding advantage. Stranahan's approaches were sharper, but Ward constantly got up and down from around the greens for halves or would drain a 30-footer for an occasional birdie. In the end, Ward's short game prevailed. The match arrived at its 35th hole, the par-three 17th, with Ward 1-up, but that looked like it could soon change when Ward was bunkered front right off the tee and Stranahan was safely on the green. Ward skinned his explosion into the back bunker; a

A Really Charming Suite at Moderate Cost

WHAT is your first impression of this suite? "Beautiful," you will say. While the outside beauty of the pieces is enough to recommend them to you; it is the inner beauty of the woods used and the fine workmanship that make them appeal to the most discriminating buyer.

With a Duco finish in Arcadian Green that will last down through the years, with panels of fine burl walnut, and with designs so beautiful that there is nothing left to be desired, they offer a harmony that builds rest into your room. Can also be furnished in Walnut with decorated panels.

double bogey was quite possible. But Ward exploded his third to within inches for a bogey, and Stranahan missed a three-footer for par. Ward remained 1-up and secured the championship with a par on 18.

The crowd and the dispatched Stranahan left the 18th green that day marveling over Ward's putting and chipping magic. And the contributions of old Barney Google weren't ignored. "Ward didn't beat Stranahan today," one spectator said. "Barney Google did." In all, Ward one-putted 18 greens in 36 holes, and Carolina roommate and tennis star Heath

Alexander, who'd been playing in a match at Davidson, remembered returning to Chapel Hill late in the night, finding Ward in bed and wondering who'd won the match.

"I crawled into bed and my foot brushed against something," Alexander told Ron Green of *The Charlotte News* years later. "I threw back the covers and there was the silver tray Harvie had gotten for winning.

"I went over and pulled the cover off Harvie to wake him and he was lying there hugging that old putter of his. He was just clowning, of course, but I couldn't much blame him for

From an early brochure for the Carolina Hotel (renamed the Pinehurst Hotel in the early 1970s).

sleeping with that club."

"Boy, could Harvie putt and chip," Cobb remembers. "Playing those bermuda greens was an art. A lot of people would get on those bermuda greens in Pinehurst and there's no way—they couldn't chip the ball on those grainy greens. Harvie had a little, short punch shot. It would take about two scoots and bite right at the cup. He'd pull the face down on a wedge and, boom, it'd take off with all kinds of

Arnold Palmer and Ward pose for Pinehurst photographer John Hemmer prior to their semifinal match in 1948. Ward won the match, 5-and-4.

backspin. You can't do that on bentgrass, it won't take the spin."

Ward won the qualifying medal the next year with a 69, defeated Chapman in the semifinals and was set for a rematch with Stranahan, who ousted Palmer 12-and-11. Stranahan had been exempted from qualifying at the last minute when he needed that Monday for a playoff against Bobby Locke in the Cavalier Invitational in Virginia Beach. The *Outlook* reported the events like this: "Walter Hagen Jr., who was associated with the Virginia Beach operation, called Richard S. Tufts, long distance, and inquired if Pinehurst would excuse Frank from qualifying."

Tufts responded, also long distance, in the affirmative.

Another huge crowd turned out, and a local radio station, WEEB, presented its first live, remote broadcast from the tournament. Gen. George C. Marshall was in the gallery and later awarded the championship and runner-up trophies. Ward's short game wasn't as precise this year and Stranahan's was. The latter holed a 40-footer for a birdie on the 27th hole for a 2-up lead and remained in control for a 2-and-1

triumph.

Stranahan, never shy with an opinion, recalls the two matches like this: "I remember that Harvie should never have beaten me in '48. I played much better, I missed a bunch of short putts, I was very unfortunate to lose. Then the following year in '49, I played him and I won and I played so poorly and I chipped and putted so well I didn't deserve to win at all. And it just shows how funny golf can be."

Ward would add to his amateur accomplishments with the 1949 NCAA championship, the 1955 and '56 U.S. Amateur titles and the British Amateur at Prestwick in 1952 (with a victory over Stranahan). Ward credits that latter title, in part, to his ability to hit the pitch-and-run shots required on the firm, crown-shaped greens of No. 2.

"You had to play a lot of bounce-up shots on No. 2," says Ward. "You couldn't play into the green. It was more like Scottish golf—you had to bounce it in there. I grew up on sand greens in Tarboro. You used to have to hit the chip-and-run or putt from off the green. There and playing at Pinehurst helped when I won the British Amateur. They were amazed over there how good I was hitting the pitch-and-run versus the flop wedge, where you hit it in the air and stop it by the hole. I adapted to golf over there very easily."

In later years Ward flirted with the idea of playing the Senior PGA Tour in the Super Seniors (over 60) division, but that division is closed unless you won a regular tour event or a senior tour event. "I haven't played competitive golf in 20 years, and there's no sense in my going out and banging my head against the Trevinos out there," he says.

Today he lives in Pinehurst with his wife, Joanne, and gives golf lessons at Pine Needles, plays at the Country Club of North Carolina and occasionally tours Pinehurst No. 2, which he still lists as his favorite golf course. He tootles around town in a black Jaguar with license plates that read, "Ol Harv." After 43 years, Ward is tickled to be back where he enjoyed so many fond memories. "I always said two places I'd love to live are Carmel in California and Pinehurst," he says. "Pinehurst reminds me a lot of Carmel. The city fathers have done a nice job over the years maintaining the ambiance and the feel of the place. I was just surprised to come back and find a stop light."

Collier Cobb says of his old friend: "Harvie Ward's in the briar patch now." ∎

BILL CAMPBELL

Amateur golf was in its golden era in the Forties through the Sixties. There were plenty of good players who wanted to compete but didn't want to turn pro. Bill Campbell was one of the best of that group, winning the North and South four times.

 orty-one years ago the "Long-knocker" hunched over a four-foot putt on the 17th green of Pinehurst No. 2. Bill Campbell needed to make the putt to remain even with Wynsol Spencer in the final of the 1950 North and South Amateur. Both golfers were tired—this was their 35th hole of the day. All Campbell needed was outside interference to cloud his concentration.

Then in the April twilight rang the chimes of the Village Chapel. They sounded for a few seconds. To Campbell it seemed like an hour.

It was six o'clock.

Unsettled, Campbell backed away from his putt. The gallery acknowledged the inconvenience. Some chuckled a little. Then Campbell hunkered down over his golf ball. He drained the putt and then won the match a few minutes later on the 37th hole; the victory was the first of four North and South titles he would win in 18 years.

One month later, the wind and rain were flying from the North Sea as Bill Campbell tried to concentrate on the five-footer on the 17th hole of the Old Course in St. Andrews, Scotland. This, too, was the sixth round of an important championship—the British Amateur. The water dripped from his cap. His hands were numb. The cup was blurred amid all the mist and gales.

Then from the one chapel in the nearby village came the haunting sound of church bells.

It was six o'clock.

"It put a tingle up my spine," says Campbell. "But I knew then I was going to make the putt, and I poured it into the hole."

The spell ended two holes later when Campbell missed a putt on the 19th hole to lose the match. But in 41 years, Campbell's never forgotten that little link between St. Andrews and Pinehurst.

"Short putts ... the 17th hole at No. 2 and the 17th at St. Andrews ... the bells chime six o'clock ... one month apart. It's kind of eerie, don't you think?" he says.

Eerie, indeed. And fitting, perhaps, given the high regard Campbell has for the game of golf, its Old World heritage of heather and gorse and the New World mecca that sits in the Carolina Sandhills. In more than four decades of amateur competition the world over, Campbell freely admits he's left part of his heart in St. Andrews and a part of it in Pinehurst.

"Pinehurst is more than good golf courses,"

Bill and Joan Campbell were all smiles in Pinehurst.

JOHN HEMMER

Campbell said in an April, 1990, speech to the Tin Whistles club in Pinehurst. "It is a state of mind and a feeling for the game, its aesthetics, courtesies and emotions."

Today William C. Campbell, former president of the USGA and recent captain of the Royal & Ancient of St. Andrews, is sitting in a wooden chair in his three-room suite on the second floor of a Huntington, W.Va., office building. Campbell has been on the same floor since he took over the family insurance business that his great-grandfather started.

On the walls of this and another office are

THE GAME IS GOLF
The following passage is displayed on a framed wall-plaque in Bill Campbell's office in Huntington, W.Va.:

"Golf is a science, the study of a lifetime, in which you may exhaust yourself but never your subject. It's a contest, a duel, or a melee, calling for courage, skill, strategy and self-control. It is a test of temper, a trial of honor, a revealer of character. It affords the chance to play the man and act the gentleman. It means going into God's out-of-doors, getting close to nature, fresh air, exercise, the sweeping away of mental cobwebs, genuine recreation of tired tissues. It includes companionship with friends, social intercourse, opportunities for courtesy, kindliness and generosity to an opponent. It promotes not only physical health but moral force."

David R. Forgan

dozens of framed photos of Campbell's storied amateur and administrative golf careers; one room has a large table stacked with golf and USGA correspondence. There's Campbell playing in the Walker Cup in Scotland. There he is, watching in the background as Curtis Strange hits his memorable bunker shot on the 72nd hole of the 1988 U.S. Open at The Country Club in Brookine, Mass. There's his old friend, fellow mountaineer Sam Snead. The stately Campbell is almost apologetic for all the fuss the game makes on his walls.

"Excuse all the pictures," he says. "I have no other place to put them, really, other than a closet, and that would be a shame. We don't get much traffic in and out of the office, so it's not like you're trying to impress people. I enjoy them."

Four photographs were taken at Pinehurst—in 1950, '53, '57 and '67 after his victories over Spencer, Mal Galletta, Hillman Robbins and Bill Hyndman, respectively, in the North and South Amateur. If ever there were good old days, those certainly were to Campbell.

"We hadn't reached the point yet where the better amateurs would routinely turn pro," says Campbell. "We weren't into the college golf syndrome where it was a scholarship leading to the tour. It was just the beginning of that. We had quite a number of people like myself who were fair players, who wanted to play competitive golf but had no intention of being professional golfers. The amateur game was pretty lively without being dominated by college golf. It was a fun thing. You'd run into the same people year after year. You grew older as they did. Over that period of the late '40s to the late '60s, I had the pleasure of being a part of that."

Campbell began playing golf at age three at Guyan Golf & Country Club in Huntington, where he's still a member. He was an accomplished player when he finished serving in the Army in World War II and graduated from Princeton with a history degree in 1947. Not yet married, Campbell joined the family insurance business and indulged himself in two hobbies—politics and golf. The former took him to the West Virginia state legislature, the latter to places like Pinehurst and Augusta. In 1951 he purchased interest in a four-seat, single-engine plane and would make his April pilgrimage to Pinehurst.

"By the time I got married, in 1954, Pinehurst was a habit," he says. "Joan, my wife, took to it very kindly. It was the only place I traveled for golf that she joined me. It was such a salutary experience for her as well as for me."

The Campbells would check in every year at the Holly Inn. They'd go for walks across the street in the Village Green, attend church at the Village Chapel. Campbell became friends with clubhouse institutions—caddies like Johnny and Junior, locker room attendants like Cliff. Campbell liked that the caddies called him "The Long-knocker," not because his tee shots needed canonizing but because it was just a neat thing to have Pinehurst caddies think of him on such familiar terms.

"And there was a sort of meeter-and-greeter named Brown," he says. "I can't remember full names. I'm not sure I ever knew their full names. They were there year in and year out and lent an aura of Old World to the place. You go to Augusta, and one of the nice features of the Masters for me is that over 25 years, you return and all the fixtures are the same, the people on the doors and gates, the Pinkertons. You got acquainted with people, the Browns and Cliffs. I used to like the relationships of the players and people running the tournaments. Those persisted through the years as if nothing ever happened between the tournaments. You shared a common denominator. You took up where you left off."

Only one man enjoyed more success in the North and South than Campbell—his four championships trail the seven won by George Dunlap. But when Campbell stood on the 15th tee of the 1948 tournament, no one had *ever* made a hole-in-one in the North and South in 47 previous events. Campbell, playing in his first North and South, was 1-down to Bill Klopman when he laced a four-iron on the 204-yard hole.

"The shot made a big noise," Campbell says. "It hit the flag and dropped in. That got me back to even, and I managed to win on the 19th hole. I was fortunate. I wasn't playing very well. But in those early years Pinehurst would be the first golf I'd play since fall. In '50 I qualified for the Masters— I'd made the finals of the '49 U.S. Amateur, so I was invited the next year—so therefore Pinehurst wasn't my first outing. I'd go to Augusta in early April, come home for a week or two, then go to Pinehurst. What a great combination that was—Augusta and Pinehurst."

The semifinals of the 1950 North and South were vintage amateur golf. In Campbell, Frank Stranahan, Wolcott Brown and Wynsol Spencer, you had an average age in the mid-30s and two insurance men (Campbell and Brown), a bank president (Spencer) and the heir to a spark-plug manufacturing plant (Stranahan). "I won't call them career amateurs," Campbell says, "because

that's a misnomer. They had careers other than golf. Golf was an avocation, and you developed a great rapport with these people."

Campbell beat Brown 6-and-5 in the semifinals, then endured Spencer, a 30-year-old from Newport News, Va., and the chimes in the final. Young and strong at six-foot-four, Campbell consistently outdrove Spencer and

---

THE CAROLINA
PINEHURST, N.C.

DINNER

~

Bluepoint Oysters on Shell or Cocktail

Spanish Gumbo   Consomme Calcutta

Olives   Cucumbers

Boiled Smoked Ox Tongue, Horseradish Sauce
Braised Loin of Pork, Southern Style
Baked Rice Cakes with Raisins

Roast Prime Ribs of Beef, Dish Gravy
Roast Stuffed Duckling, with Marmalade

Boiled and Mashed Potatoes
Stringless Beans   Buttered Onions
Steamed Rice

Plain or Dressed Lettuce   Salad Fruit
Mayonnaise, Thousand Island, French and Roquefort Dressing

Bread and Butter Pudding, Hard and Foam Sauce
Washington Pie
Vanilla Ice Cream   Assorted Cake

Oranges   Apples   Bananas
Mixed Nuts   Layer Raisins
American or Club Cheese
Tea   Coffee   Milk

November 9, 1922

A menu from the Carolina Dining Room in the 1920s.

was 25 yards beyond him on the first hole, their 37th of the day. Campbell arched an eight-iron to four feet, but Spencer, playing a much longer approach, missed the green and the match was over.

Campbell missed the 1952 North and South because he was running an unsuccessful campaign for Congress, but was back and won the '53 event with a 2-and-1 win over Galletta, a 42-year-old from St. Albans, N.Y. In 1955 he lost

BEMAN, BLANCAS IN NO. 2 MARATHON

Deane Beman forged a reputation for himself during a stellar amateur career and later on the pro golf tour as a lights-out putter. But the current commissioner of the PGA Tour lost that magical stroke during a 24-hole marathon against Homero Blancas in the quarterfinals of the 1962 U.S. Amateur on Pinehurst No. 2.

Beman and Blancas were two of the top names in amateur play at the time. Beman had won the U.S. and British Amateurs, and Blancas was runner-up in the NCAAs. They finished 18 square after a match that included Beman driving his tee shot on the 16th into the pond fronting the tee and Blancas missing a putt from 30 inches on 18 for the win.

Then it became Beman's turn to miss the short ones, according to *The Charlotte News*. He missed from five feet on the first playoff hole. After routine pars on the 20th, he missed from 15 feet on the 21st. He missed from four feet on the 22nd. He missed from three feet on the 23rd.

That brought the match to the long, par-three sixth hole. Beman drove between the green and a bunker, into high grass, and chipped to five feet. He marked his ball with a penny. Then Blancas lined up his 20-footer and stroked it toward the hole. As the ball neared the cup, Beman approached his penny and bent over to replace his ball. Just as he did, Blancas's ball tumbled into the cup for the win.

Beman's jaw hardened and he tossed his own ball at the cup—and missed. He shook hands with Blancas, then bent over, picked up his penny and pitched it at the cup—and missed.

He turned to walk away, but came back to the penny and swiped at it with his putter. This time, the penny fell into the cup.

Nearly 30 years later, Beman has few recollections of that match. "Those are the kind you try to forget," he says.

in the final to Don Bisplinghoff, 5-and-4, with his hands and face still salved in cocoa butter after a bad burn in late 1954. Three years later, he beat a 25-year-old second lieutenant from the Air Force named Hillman Robbins, 3-and-2, for another title. And he capped his title chase at the age of 44 with a 10-and-9 romp over Bill Hyndman in the 1967 championship.

A highlight of each year's visit to Pinehurst was Campbell's dinner at the home of Gen. George C. Marshall, who visited Pinehurst frequently in the 1940s and eventually purchased a home on Linden Road. Marshall wasn't a golfer, but he enjoyed riding his horse around No. 2 and watching the competition or having his sergeant drive him around in a Jeep. Campbell would always tip his hat to the general, in part out of the courtesy he would

show anyone and in part because Marshall was, at the time, quite famous and quite impressive to a young ex-soldier.

"One day I came off the second green and was crossing the little road to the third tee when General Marshall's man, Sergeant Hefner, approached me and said the General would like to have me for dinner that Tuesday night," Campbell says. "He said 'Six o'clock—sharp.'

"I'd heard he was punctilious, and I, having been a private up to a captain, was very careful. So I drove to his house and waited just down the street for a little while until my watch came around to six o'clock. Ten seconds before six I fired it up and drove up to the house. At that instant he came out the front door."

Marshall would delight Campbell year after year with fascinating stories and uninhibited answers about war and government and the military, often prompting Campbell to tell the General he should write a book on his experiences. "He said, 'I've been offered a million dollars by *Life* magazine, but I won't give my memoirs,'" Campbell remembers the General saying. "'Because if I did, I would want to tell the truth, and if I did that I would destroy the reputation of many people, living and dead, and I don't want to do that.' So I kept hearing these marvelous stories, year after year, that were unknown to the world."

Campbell's favorite story from his visits with Marshall involves the General chiding his wife on some small point and Mrs. Marshall looking to her guests and saying, "Poor George. He had 20 million men under his command and now he has only me."

"Those were fascinating times," he says. "Now I come back and see the big granite sign that says Marshall Park. That's a great tribute to a great man."

Campbell has returned to Pinehurst sporadically since his 1967 championship. The conditions of No. 2 aggravated him in 1971 after the sale of the resort to Diamondhead Corp., and his last round on No. 2 was in 1980. In November, 1990, Campbell was inducted into the PGA/World Golf Hall of Fame (in characteristic modesty, Campbell alludes to the visit by saying, "I had to be in the area last year") and he's inspected No. 2 on several recent occasions and has liked what he's seen.

"I think the people responsible today seem to be interested in restoration, not renovation," he says.   ■

PEGGY KIRK BELL

The Carolina Hotel and the inns in the village couldn't handle the demand for rooms during high season in the 1920s, so Pinehurst Inc. expanded its operations with the construction of Mid Pines and Pine Needles in Southern Pines. Both properties have exchanged hands several times since then. For nearly four decades now, the Bell family of Pine Needles has been a cornerstone in making the Sandhills a golfer's mecca.

wenty-year-old Peggy Kirk had heard about a golf haven known as Pinehurst and knew each spring it was the site of something called the North and South Women's Amateur. "I loved golf and I'd heard that Pinehurst was the golf capital of the world," she says. "I said, 'Gosh, I need to go play in that tournament.'"

So she bundled up some clothes in her dorm room at Rollins College in Winter Park, Fla., tossed her golf clubs into her '41 Packard convertible and set off for Pinehurst. Miss Kirk arrived without mishap, found the country club and presented herself at the tournament desk in the clubhouse.

"I'd like to play in the North and South," she announced.

"Fine," said the official. "Can I see your invitation?"

"Invitation?" Miss Kirk responded, her freckles turning bright red. "I'm sorry, gee, I'm just a college kid, I read about it and thought I'd like to play in it."

"Just a moment," said the official, who excused himself into a rear office. A moment later, while Miss Kirk was looking for a convenient rug under which to crawl, a distinguished looking man with wire-rimmed glasses presented himself.

"Hello," he said. "I'm Richard Tufts, and I'd like to extend an invitation to you to play in the North and South."

Nearly 50 years later, Peggy Kirk Bell is almost doubled over with laughter.

"My first trip to Pinehurst, and I *crash the party*," she says. "I was *soooo* green. I just thought it was a tournament, that you paid your five dollars and played. I was so embarrassed I could have died. There wasn't even an entry fee! I still have the little red billfold with the Pinehurst crest they gave to all the players.

"Two years ago the Silver Foils invited me to be an honorary member. I received the membership at a luncheon, and I'd never told that

Peggy Bell, Grace Lenczyk and Estelle Lawson Page during late 1940s North and South.

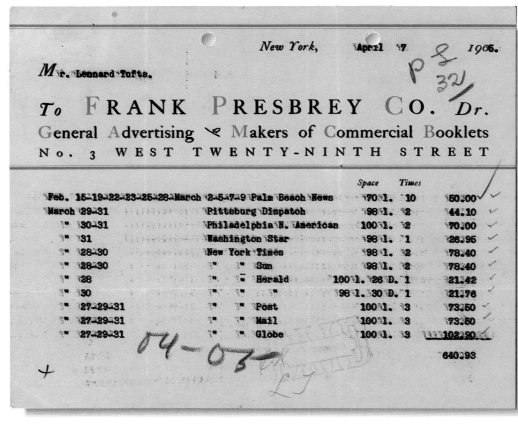

It cost Pinehurst $640.93 to reach readers of newspapers in Palm Beach and four northern cities during a late-March blitz in 1905, according to this statement from the Frank Presbrey Co.

story before. I told it and said, 'This time I was *invited*. The first time I crashed the party.'"

As Mrs. Bell speaks, there's a flurry of activity around her at the Pine Needles Resort in Southern Pines, where she, her late husband Warren and her family have welcomed guests for nearly 40 years. Her lunch is interrupted by the hostess bearing son Kirk's voice in a portable telephone. Six-month-old grandson Michael Warren McGowan is lollygagging underfoot. Son-in-law Pat McGowan is shaking his head over a practical joke waged the previous evening on him and his wife, Bonnie. Seems the McGowans arrived home from a stint on the PGA Tour around midnight and couldn't figure out why there was a half-eaten sandwich and a half-drunk glass of beer on the kitchen table.

Furthermore, McGowan wondered, why did he reach for a pair of shorts the next morning only to find his wife's panties where his underwear should have been?

"Don't look at me," said brother-in-law Kelly Miller, feigning innocence. In truth, Miller and wife Peggy and some friends had staged a nocturnal visit to the McGowans.

So what else is new where the Bells, McGowans, Millers and the venerable resort off Midland Road is concerned?

"That's pretty much the way it is," says

Miller. "You've got to have a thick skin to hang in there with them. I remember the first time I met the Bells. Mr. Bell used to have a group get together on the first tee at three or four o'clock every afternoon. Sometimes there'd be three or four, sometimes 10 or 12.

"The first time I ever played golf with Mrs. Bell, she walked right back to the back tee where the rest of us were. She ripped it out there, 235 yards or so. I said, 'What's this? Gee, I'm going to have to jump on it to keep up with her.'"

Peggy Bell has hit good golf shots nearly all her life and began hitting them at Pine Needles in 1953, when she and her newlywed husband—better known as "Bullet" Bell—pooled resources with Frank and Maisie Cosgrove and their son-in-law, touring pro Julius Boros, to buy the Donald Ross golf course from the Roman Catholic Diocese of Raleigh. The price was $50,000. For lodging, they leased one of two Army barracks that were built when the military used the land during World War II.

Two years later, the Bells bought their partners out when the Cosgroves and Boros needed funds to buy the neighboring Mid Pines Resort from Homeland Investment Co. of Durham. The Cosgroves, both former employees at the Carolina Hotel—he was a bartender, she was a waitress—began managing Mid Pines in the mid-1940s; now the bank wanted to sell, and they needed to buy it to protect their jobs.

"At the beginning it was room, board and golf for $15 a day," Mrs. Bell says of the early days at Pine Needles. "We'd have groups of eight or 10 or 12 guys ride the train from New York all night and go from the train to the first tee. It wasn't plush. You walked down the hallway to use the john."

Peggy Kirk had established a name for herself in Pinehurst long before joining the area's golf industry as a resort operator. She was a standout player as a youth in Ohio, played collegiately at Rollins and was a top amateur before turning pro in the fall of 1950.

She played annually in the North and South and developed a close friendship with Ann "Buttons" Cosgrove. Peggy spent several Decembers at Mid Pines playing golf between fall and spring semesters, when there was cold and snow at home in Ohio. She won the North and South in 1949, the first year it was played on Pinehurst No. 2 (previously, the No. 1 and 3 courses were used).

"I told them I had to get out on that big course and then I'd prove I could play," she jokes.

Kirk had won three Ohio Opens, been named to the 1948 and '50 Curtis Cup teams and won the 1949 Titleholders. She was fast friends with Babe Zaharias, the founding force behind the LPGA Tour who won the 1947 North and South and once hit a drive on Pinehurst No. 2 that was paced off by Dick Chapman at 290 yards.

Peggy had known Warren Bell since childhood in Findlay, Ohio. He played professional basketball for several years and was working for Spalding Sports Goods in Chicago when they were married in 1953. Both wanted to get into the golf business and were looking for a golf course to buy or property on which to build one in Florida when Buttons Cosgroves' parents suggested they go in together and buy Pine Needles.

Both Pine Needles and Mid Pines were built in the 1920s by Pinehurst Inc., which saw its facilities bursting at the seams in busy fall and spring seasons. Richard Tufts, grandson of Pinehurst founder James Tufts, noted in his unpublished history of the area that up to 15,000 people were being turned down for reservations during the months of February and March by 1920. That led to the inception of Mid Pines in 1921.

"The wonderful climate and the sporting facilities which these kindred resorts have developed in the last 25 years seem to have rendered the attraction of the section so irresistible that people are willing to go to almost ridiculous lengths to attain them," Tufts wrote. "The establishment of Mid Pines Country Club, Inc., by Knollwood Inc., is one answer to the problem."

With Leonard Tufts, Richard's father, serving as general manager, 300 shares of capital stock were sold for $2,500 each. That

The scaffolding still stands around the brand new Pine Needles Inn as Donald Ross tees off on the first hole in 1927.

bought 180 acres at $125 each and paid for construction of the golf course—designed, of course, by Pinehurst's Donald Ross—at a cost of $46,000 and the hotel and several outbuildings at $263,000. "The stock is not to be offered promiscuously, but to a clientele that will ensure congeniality and good fellowship, which is the club's ideal," said a 1921 memo on Pinehurst letterhead.

Mid Pines' opening helped ease the crunch, but by the middle of the decade the Tufts saw a need for more hotel space. "Pinehurst is anxious to see another hotel built in the area," Leonard wrote in a letter that outlined plans for Pine Needles.

Pine Needles was to be the area's first golf resort/real estate project and would be located across Midland Road from Mid Pines. Pinehurst bought 500 acres of Knollwood Inc., for $300 each, then spent nearly a half million dollars on a grand, 80-room hotel and a golf course. Three hundred lots were laid out around the course, and Edwin I. McKeithan was employed at $125 a week to "promote and sell real estate." Pinehurst Inc. was operating five hotels in 1927: the Carolina, the Holly Inn and the Berkshire

Inn in Pinehurst and Pine Needles and Mid Pines in Southern Pines.

The latter properties flourished through 1929, but when the Depression hit they fell on hard times. Pine Needles was owned in part from 1935 to 1948 by publishing magnate and Pinehurst winter resident George T. Dunlap, and both resorts were commandeered by Army Air Force personnel in the early 1940s. Then the church purchased Pine Needles in 1948 and decided after five years to get out of the golf business.

(The hotel was renamed St. Joseph of the Pines and was a hospital for years. Today it's a nursing and extended-care home. The Bells originally leased clubhouse and dining room space in the hospital. The course as Ross originally designed it began on the current 18th hole, then the current first hole was the second.)

The Bells soon found that one barracks wasn't enough.

"We thought we were getting into the golf business, we had no idea we were getting into the hotel business," says Mrs. Bell. "But we realized that just running a golf course, we'd be lucky to break even. There were very few motels in the area. The resorts were Pinehurst and Mid Pines and there was maybe one motel out in Pinebluff. So we had to get into the hotel business."

Bullet planned and supervised construction of what is now a sprawling compendium of Swiss-style chalets and supervised the construction. Meanwhile, Peggy continued her play on the fledgling LPGA Tour and the Bells started a family. Bonnie arrived in 1954, followed by Peggy in 1958 and Kirk in 1962.

Their young resort soon took a change of direction that would impact all of golf and golf instruction. Peggy Bell gave her first golf lesson and Pine Needles hosted its first golf school. The former was a disaster; the latter was a rousing success.

"Bullet pointed to a guest one day and said, 'That woman wants to learn to play golf, go teach her,'" Mrs. Bell says. "I said, 'I don't know what to tell her.' Bullet said, 'You know more golf than she does. Tell her *anything*.'

"It was awful. I told her *everything* I knew. We were out there for two or three hours. She'd hit it bad and I'd say, 'Try this.' Another bad shot. 'Try this.' I was going crazy trying to get her to hit it like I could. Finally, she said, 'Can we quit? I'm dead.' I would have stayed there until midnight. I often wonder about that poor woman. I'm sure she quit golf then and there."

That lesson piqued Peggy's interest in teaching, and she developed a close relationship with the late Ellen Griffin of Greensboro Women's College, a pioneer in women's golf instruction. The ladies were having lunch one day at Pine Needles in the late 1950s when Bullet bemoaned the fact that a business group, which had booked the entire resort one week the following month, had just canceled.

"Bullet, let's put in a golf school," Griffin said.

"We can't do that, no one will come," Bell responded.

"Well, let's try."

"So we took out an ad in *Golf World*," Mrs. Bell remembers. "We charged $105 for four days and three nights. We had video equipment, which was a brand new thing then. We sent out mimeographed flyers to all the country clubs in North Carolina. We had 53 people that first school."

That started the famed Peggy Kirk Bell "Golfari" tradition. Since then, thousands of women golfers have learned the game at Pine Needles, as have spouses during the annual family school held each summer. So noted in the world of golf instruction has Mrs. Bell become that she has won numerous awards. She points to a shiny new Rolex wristwatch she received in 1989 for the Ellen Griffin Award; she's also won the Bob Jones Award and is a member of the North Carolina Sports Hall of Fame and the Carolinas Golf Hall of Fame.

"I was really proud to win the Ellen Griffin Award," Mrs. Bell says. "She was a big influence on me early. She knew there was a vacuum of women teaching women."

Since that complicated and fruitless lesson some 35 years ago, Mrs. Bell has learned that simplicity works best in teaching golf. The basics count more than anything.

"You've got to work on posture and grip or you'll never get very good," she says. "You'll be lucky if you hit one. Your posture determines your swing. Once you get set up right and understand the swing, it's a matter of 'turn and return.' Every letter I get (from former students) comes from someone saying, 'I'm turning and returning.'"

Today Mrs. Bell is still active in teaching. Bullet died in 1984, but Pine Needles is still strictly a family affair. Bonnie and Peggy and their young families can often be found around the resort. Miller is general manager, and McGowan, who met Bonnie while staying at Pine Needles during a PGA Tour qualifying school at Pinehurst Country Club in 1977, promotes the resort while playing the tour. Kirk lives in Washington, D.C., working on the staff of Congressman Mel Hancock of Missouri.

"Golf has been my life," says Mrs. Bell. "It's taken me around the world, I've done all the traveling you could ever want to do. Golf is such an equalizing game, no matter where you come from you can relate to anyone on a golf course.

"Look at what the game's done for me: My husband probably wouldn't have been interested in me if I didn't play golf. All of my children have played college golf. Bonnie met Pat through golf. Peggy met Kelly through golf."

And now on a bright May afternoon, it's back to the practice range to teach more golf—and, if time allows, hit some balls herself and tone down a tendency to slide too far laterally at impact.

"She's got the best turn ever," says staff instructor Dr. Jim Suttie. "She looks like Sam Snead going back."

Mrs. Bell laughs. "And Byron Nelson coming down. I slide too much to the left."

"You swing better than any person your age," Suttie says.

"My age! Right!" she responds.

They say Peggy Kirk Bell still hits it sweet at 70 years. ■

Opposite: An aerial view of Mid Pines in the 1920s with the 18th hole in the foreground and Midland Road in the background. *Julius Boros was an accomplished amateur and an accountant by trade when he moved to Southern Pines in the late 1940s. In the 1948 North and South Open, he was low amateur and tied with Sam Snead for second place, two shots behind Toney Penna. At that tournament, he met Ann "Buttons" Cosgrove, whose parents managed Mid Pines. They were later married, and Boros and the Cosgroves were co-owners of the resort for several years in the 1950s. Boros's nephew, Jim, was head pro for many years at Mid Pines and now is pro at the Country Club of Whispering Pines.*

MAUREEN ORCUTT

Maureen Orcutt blitzed Pinehurst and its sand greens three times in the early 1930s. But that wasn't enough. She returned in the early 1960s and won three more times—on grass greens, of course.

aureen Orcutt was sipping cream sherry with her mother, Elizabeth, and a guest in the Orcutt home in Englewood, N.J., one day in 1960 when Maureen mentioned she was thinking of visiting Pinehurst soon for a golf tournament.

"The North and South?" Mrs. Orcutt said. "You've already won that three times. Isn't that enough?"

"Mother, this is the North and South *Seniors*," explained Maureen, one of the leading women's amateur golfers for nearly half a century.

"That's the trouble with Maureen," her mother said to their guest. "She thinks she has to win everything 10 times."

Winning was something that Maureen Orcutt did a lot of in her prime. And because her prime stretched from the 1920s through the 1960s, that meant some 65 victories. Six of those wins came in Pinehurst: three in the early 1930s in the Women's North and South and three more in the early 1960s in the Seniors tournament she was telling her mother about.

"I loved to play Pinehurst No. 2," says Ms. Orcutt, 84, who lives in Durham in a townhouse alongside the sixth green of Croasdaile Country Club. "I could *hit* the ball. I used to be a *hitter*, they'd say, and I loved to let out, and you could let out on No. 2. We didn't get to play No. 2 in the North and South. It was always played on No. 3."

She pulls out some old scrapbooks filled with clippings about her 10 wins in the Metropolitan Amateur; her seven titles in the Eastern Amateur; her playing on four Curtis Cup teams. The only clippings lacking are ones telling of a win in the U.S. Women's Amateur— she made the final in 1927 and 1936, but lost both times—and of winning money playing golf professionally. But there wasn't any money for women pros and little competition, so she remained a lifetime, career-girl amateur.

"I was looking at one old clipping the other day about Pinehurst," she says. "I was amazed at how often I shot in the 70s. I had no idea."

Several clippings from *The New York Times* are of particular interest. From the October 28, 1960, edition, there is a one-column headline, "Maureen Orcutt Wins Senior Golf," followed by a three-paragraph story telling of her one-stroke win over Estelle Lawson Page in the North and South Seniors. On October 27, 1961, the same amount of coverage declares, "Miss Orcutt's 153 Wins By 3

Galleries delighted in watching the big-hitting Maureen Orcutt.

TUFTS ARCHIVES

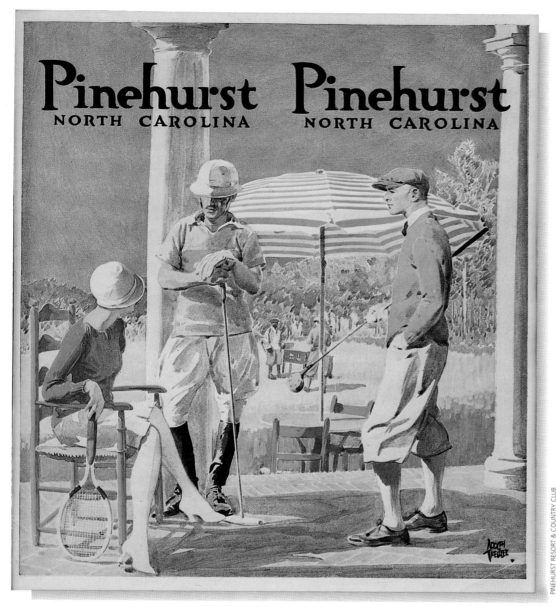

The cover of a Pinehurst brochure from the early 1930s. The introductory copy on the third page reads: "Pinehurst is built for pleasure. The kingdom of happiness lies within, but the kingdom is appreciably enhanced by a good table, good bed, perfect service, and congenial people to share a wide range of entertainment indoors and out, in beautiful surroundings and a satisfying climate."

Strokes." And then on Oct. 26, 1962, an eight-column headline shouts, "Maureen Orcutt Wins Third Consecutive North And South Seniors Title." She battled cold and wind to shoot an 80 and overtake Mrs. John Pennington, who shot an 85, to collect the victory.

(The article beside it, for what it's worth, reported that Wimbledon tennis officials had ruled that white—and *only* white—panties could be worn by women competitors, who had turned up spectator interest recently with panties of varying length, color and design.)

What none of the stories mention is that Ms. Orcutt was a staff sports writer of the *Times*. After beginning her newspaper career with the *New York Journal* and the *New York World*, she joined the *Times*' sports staff in 1937. She spent much of her career on the desk, but ventured out as much as her bosses would let her to

cover local golf and top women's events such as the Curtis Cup. And why not? Usually she was there as a participant anyway. She was the only woman on a staff of nearly 50 and was affectionately dubbed "The Duchess."

"My brother and I started writing a column for the local paper when we were in high school," she says. "We were paid by the inch, 15 cents an inch, so we wrote *long*. I was covering the Metro one year and playing in it, too. I got to the finals and told them, 'You need to get someone else to cover the finals.' I didn't go to Pinehurst after winning in the '30s until they'd started the Seniors tournaments. I'd take a week of vacation, drive my mother to Durham, where my brother was living, then go on to Pinehurst. I'd play and then write down all the scores and phone in a story."

Maureen was athletically inclined as a child

Pinehurst, N.C.
November 26, 1927

Mr. S.G. Rosson
Roland Park Apartments
Baltimore, Md.

My dear Mr. Rosson:

Mr. Fitzgerald has handed me your letter of the 21st in which you suggest that we should have grass greens here. Such letters as yours are very very gratefully received and are of great assistance to us in shaping our policies—I want to thank you most sincerely for writing us and only wish we received more such letters.

There is no difficulty at all about making grass greens and we would use them except for the fact that the play is so heavy here in the cold weather that the growth of the grass isn't sufficient to take up the wear during that time. Of course we keep in pretty close touch with the conditions at other places and we hear considerable complaint of the grass greens and I feel sure that 90 percent of our guests would say that our good sand greens are much preferable to any grass green that can be grown north of Florida. Mr. Donald Ross, Secretary of our Club, and as you probably know, the best known golf architect in the country, was the first to build grass greens in Florida and in fact built some of the grass greens in Georgia. New methods of handling grass are continually coming up and it may be that the time will come when we can safely use it for our putting greens but our present knowledge would indicate that it would be a mistake.

Very truly yours,
Leonard Tufts

and had no problem picking up golf's difficult nuances. Often Elizabeth would take her three children with her to their club, White Beeches Golf Club in Haworth, N.J., to play golf. Once Maureen ridiculed her mother's swing. "Okay," Elizabeth shot back. "If you think you're so hot, I'll tell you what we'll do. If you can beat me you can have my club membership."

Maureen borrowed her father's clubs and did just that. Elizabeth kept the bargain, turned her membership over to Maureen and gave up the game for good. Maureen won the New Jersey State title at age 17, and, as a senior at Englewood High the following year, got special permission to postpone her final exams so that she could play in the Women's Eastern Amateur. She studied history between rounds and beat Dorothy Campbell by several strokes for the title.

In the following decades, Ms. Orcutt would be one of the game's highest profile amateurs, duking it out with the likes of Virginia Van Wie, Glenna Collett Vare and Helen Hicks as the "Big Four" of women's golf. Her North and Souths were over Van Wie, 1-up in 1931; Opal

Hill, 1-up in 1932; and Bernice Wall, 5-and-4 in 1933. Her bright personality was a crowd favorite as she charged around the golf course in the day's attire of broad-brimmed hats, white knickers, billowing dresses, long socks and white shoes.

She had been playing golf in Florida in 1931 before traveling to Pinehurst for her first North and South. And what a surprise she found.

"It was very strange: they had *sand greens*," she says. "I'd never seen sand greens before. All the courses in Florida even had grass greens. It was an entirely different game. We used what we called the 'Texas wedge'—the putter—from 50 yards in. You couldn't hit the ball to the green because it would bounce over on those hard greens.

"If you could hit a straight putt you'd be a good player. There wasn't any break at all to the putts. When you finished a man would come by with a carpet and drag it around to smooth it over for the next group."

Ms. Orcutt's heyday in Pinehurst came at a time when technology and knowledge of growing various grasses hadn't yet advanced to where grass greens could be planted. Richard Tufts explained those early greens in this passage from an article on golf in the early 1900s he wrote for the *Pinehurst Outlook*:

"Until 1935, we did not have sufficient knowledge to build and maintain a satisfactory grass putting surface for greens in this climate. Consequently, all the greens were what was then known as 'sand greens.' Actually, the name was a misnomer as the greens consisted of a sand-clay base four to six inches thick which was packed hard by rolling and provided a surface much like a clay tennis court. This surface would have been too 'fast' for a putting green and consequently a light sprinkling of sand was spread over the clay in order to slow down the speed of a rolling ball. These greens were originally about 50 feet square with the hole permanently located in the center. They were subsequently built nearly round and reduced in size as we learned how to maintain better turf conditions on the grass immediately surrounding them.

"Naturally, these sand greens did not have to be mowed, but they had to be maintained. The problems were to maintain an accurate putting surface as the greens were scratched up from play, to replace sand blown off the greens by wind during dry weather and to repair washes caused by heavy rains. To take care of these problems, an old oil barrel was sunk in the ground near each green and kept full of water supplied by a mule-drawn watering cart. There was no water piped onto the course then. There was also a convenient small pile of sand for replacing sand blown or washed from the clay surfaces. Shovels were used to spread this sand over the greens and it was then worked into place by scrapers made like a rake with a wooden board about three feet long and four inches wide taking the place of the teeth on a rake.

"To give a final finish to the surface of the green, a carpet, roughly four-by-two feet, was fastened to a narrow board and dragged around the green. A green could essentially be maintained by one man, who first drew some water from the barrel and sprinkled it, principally around the hole, using a watering can. He then dragged the carpet around the green, starting at the hole and working out. To keep the greens in top condition for tournament play, it usually required one man for each three greens."

Sand greens were taken for granted around Pinehurst during that era. Another part of the game encountered often in the 1930s was the stymie, a part of golf that today is just a vague memory.

"I was playing Virginia Van Wie in the North and South finals in 1931 and I had six stymies," Ms. Orcutt says. "I was two-up after 16, and on the 17th I had another stymie. Virginia's ball was in my way. I didn't have to go straight at the hole, I could have gone in a roundabout way. Darned if I didn't hit her and knock her *in the hole*, for a win. I was 1-up with one to play."

Ancient rules of golf stipulated that you never touched your ball from the time it was teed to the time it was holed out. The rules were modernized somewhat in 1787 to allow one to mark his ball if it sat within six inches of another or if it was within six inches of the cup. That's why scorecards were six inches long; they served as rulers to determine if a stymie was in effect. Otherwise, you didn't clean it. You didn't mark it on the green. And so if your ball came to rest 15 feet from the cup and your opponent's or playing companion's ball was 10 feet away, directly in your line, you had to putt around it. Or you chipped over it, and it was quite an art to maneuver one's golf ball around another's. Many golfers felt this rule was unfair, and in 1833 a motion was carried by the Royal and Ancient of St. Andrews to abolish the stymie. This lasted only one year, however, and the stymie was back in force in 1834. It survived another 117 years, until it was finally abolished in 1951.

"Those were very interesting situations," Ms. Orcutt says. "You'd take a niblick and hop and jump over them. Sometimes it worked, sometimes it didn't."

Today Ms. Orcutt is still an avid golfer as she juggles a schedule that's full of hospital volunteer work and assorted other activities. The feisty octogenarian recently whipped off an angry letter to the editor of the local newspaper over a column that made fun of golf, and she laments the paper's lack of coverage of women's golf.

"They'll run the first-round scores but won't run the final results," she says. "It makes me so mad. I still try to play two or three times a week. I can't hit it as far as I used to, and I'm fussing about that all the time. It's amazing how far these young girls hit it today. Of course, they play a shorter golf course than we did. We always played from the front or the middle of the men's tee."

She was a crowd favorite in Pinehurst, as an *Outlook* story in 1933 attested. The previous year, she made a dramatic rally from 1-down through 16 to beat Opal Hill. She made a 22-foot eagle putt on the old par-five 17th of the No. 3 course and a 20-foot par putt on 18 for a win.

"Maureen Orcutt is a colorful personality," the story said. "Her game, as everyone in Pinehurst knows, is brilliant and attracts the largest galleries in any event except the North and South Open. In any competition the crowd is with her because she always comes through from the most difficult situation to a flying finish. The tournament which she has just recently won again—for the third consecutive time—permanently marks her ability to get out of difficult spots successfully." ■

Babe Didrikson Zaharias won the Women's North and South Amateur in 1947. She also teamed with Ed "Porky" Oliver in the Pro-Pro competition of the Mid-South Open in November, 1937 at Pinehurst. They shot a 68-72—140, eight shots behind Tony Manero and Mike Turnesa.

PETER TUFTS

The great grandson of Pinehurst founder James Tufts was jack-of-all-trades during his years around the resort and club. There wasn't much he didn't see as he carried the golf torch into the family's fourth generation.

Peter Vail Tufts experienced a little of everything during his years growing up in Pinehurst and working for the family business, Pinehurst Inc. He was master to Lucy the beagle, Joey the black bear and Mister Mack the monkey. He fixed the town's plumbing. He put out fires. He refereed golf tournaments. He managed the country club. He reroofed Gen. George Marshall's home on Linden Road while listening to the general tell war stories. He hustled caddie Jimmy Steed to the hospital once after Steed broke his leg in a golf-cart accident during a match against Tufts.

Once Tufts even applied mouth-to-mouth resuscitation to a preacher in the men's card room at the club. The Reverend was ignoring his doctor's advice not to play bridge and suffered a heart attack after drawing a nice hand. Amid the flurry of activity around the fallen man at the bridge table, Tufts overhead two members wrapped up in their game of gin rummy: "Let's go in the next room," said one. "How the hell are we supposed to concentrate with all this commotion?"

Tufts shakes his head and laughs. "You name it, it happened," he says. "The strangest things happened around that hotel and those golf courses."

Tufts represents the fourth generation of Pinehurst Tufts and is the closest link to the family's golf heritage. Great-grandfather James knew nothing about the game when he founded the resort in 1895. Grandfather Leonard shepherded the resort's early expansion into golf and recognized it had a future, but he wasn't an avid player. His special interest was in his herd of dairy cattle and in hunting (he bagged 30 quail on a single day's outing in 1906). Leonard took golf lessons from Alex Ross, Donald's brother, but never got very far. Said one wit after watching Tufts cold-top his drive on the first tee: "Well, if I owned a golfing resort and couldn't play any better than that, I'd quit the game." Tufts took that advice.

All three of Leonard's sons played golf but only one adopted it as his chief interest. That was Richard, the oldest. Albert was a hunter and fisherman; James loved playing polo and raising bird dogs. "We all played golf," says James, who was born in 1903 and lives with his wife, Helen, and two dogs in Little House, halfway between the Pinehurst Hotel and the clubhouse. "You couldn't much work at Pinehurst and not play. But I didn't enjoy it especially.

Tufts (L) and frequent Pinehurst guest Billy Joe Patton.

TUFTS ARCHIVES

Richard became the golf expert in the family."

And he passed that interest along to his two children, Peter and Sally, though with Peter the interest came gradually. The Tufts lived near the second hole of Pinehurst No. 2, and often in the summer, when the golf courses were closed, Richard would get young Peter and say, "Let's go play golf."

"By that he meant he'd hit and I'd chase. Dad had a built-in golf-ball retriever: me," says Pete. "He'd hit balls and tell me to try and catch them on the first or second bounce. He encouraged me to play; he wanted me to play. One day he said, 'The day you beat me, I'll buy you a new set of irons.' That got me all fired up, and I worked my tail off trying to beat him. But I never could. In exasperation he gave up and just bought me a set anyway. I guess I had a letdown after I finally got those irons, and I quit playing for a while.

"Then my mother decided she'd start

playing. So Dad bought the irons off me and gave them to Mom. He wouldn't just take them. 'That would be wrong' (he'd say). He had to buy them off me, since they were mine. Mom didn't play golf any time at all and she quit, and about a year later I decided I'd start back again. So for the third time he bought those irons. He bought them off Mom and gave them to me. That was probably the most expensive set of irons that's ever been sold.

"That's the kind of guy he was. He thought it only proper that he buy them from me. He was a very odd individual. If they had perfectionists clubs, he would be the president or the chairman of the board."

Peter Tufts was born in 1926 and, once he finished school, spent nearly two and a half decades in various capacities with the resort and the village. As Richard became more and more involved with national golf competitions through his roles with the USGA, Peter took

Donald Ross (standing, far right on the front row) played Jack Jolly (at Ross's right) in a legendary "Moonlight Match" in January, 1905. The match started at 8 p.m. and, with forecaddies spotting their shots, Ross and Jolly played in two hours. Ross shot an 88, Jolly a 93. Neither lost a ball.

over more responsibilities around Pinehurst.

The famous guests Tufts got to meet were legion: Everhart Faber, the pencil magnate; John Philip Sousa, the musician; Randolph Scott, the actor; Richard Nixon, the politician who would one day be President; Chick Young, creator of the Blondie comic strip; Julie London, the actress and singer. Tufts remembers a visit from President Harry Truman, who was in Pinehurst to see a most memorable man, Gen. Marshall.

"There was a motorcade a block long when Truman came," Tufts says. "I thought it interesting that Truman came to see Marshall. Marshall didn't go to see him."

Tufts was working in the village plumbing shop once when Marshall had a leak in his house. It took Tufts about two days on Marshall's roof to complete the repair, and Marshall would spend hour after hour on the roof with Tufts, just talking.

"What a great experience that was," Tufts marvels. "He would just sit on the top of that roof, talking about his experiences and about people."

Marshall told Tufts of a little test he'd devised to determine whether a person was genuine or was fake.

"General Marshall would ask someone, 'When does a fly when?' That doesn't make any sense," Tufts says, then slowly repeats the question. "'When ... does ... a ... fly ... when?' It makes no sense at all. Usually, the person would say, 'I don't know.' The General would say, 'The higher the fewer.' That doesn't make any sense either. He said he'd know if the person laughed and carried on like they understood it, they were fakes. He'd have them pegged. But if they rippled their brow and said, 'I don't understand,' they're genuine.'"

Pinehurst during its first 50 years or so used to be home to a variety of animals. There was literally a zoo for many years in the area between Hwy. 2 and the clubhouse, known today as Marshall Park. In 1906 there were lions, tigers, yaks, a leopard, an ocelot, monkeys and camels on which you could ride. Razorback hogs wandered around wild, and the village

had a fence around it to keep them out. "When someone left a gate open and a family of razorbacks came in, they could root up a shrubbery bed like a herd of bulldozers," Richard Tufts once wrote. "They could run like deer and it took the entire labor force to drive them out. It was great sport." In his day, Peter can remember seeing such varmints in the zoo as boa constrictors, rabbits, deer, porcupines, owls and raccoons.

Tufts was fond of these animals and spent much of his time looking after the zoo and whatever pets he had at home at the time. One year he was officiating a match in the Women's North and South when a golfer, getting set to putt, was disturbed by a ruckus in a greenside bunker. Lucy, Tufts' beagle, was scampering through the sand, churning her legs and creating a mess.

"I had to go in there and get her," he says. "I was manager of the club at the time, and I had to climb into a bunker to get my dog. You talk about embarrassing."

Tufts acquired a 200-pound black bear from some soldiers at Fort Bragg in nearby Fayetteville and named him Joey. The bear would spend his days in a cage and was the frequent target of abuse from caddies, who whiled away their time in the caddie yard where the tennis courts now sit, near the Members Clubhouse. Tufts would come by for Joey's daily walk, wrap a strong leash around his neck and let the bear out.

"The first place he'd go, every time, was to that caddie yard," Tufts says. "You should have seen those caddies move. There were caddies in the clubhouse, under cars, on top of cars, in cars. I never could figure out why that bear went after the caddies like that. Unbeknownst to us, they would tease him when he was in his cage. He'd get out and go after them."

Tufts' favorite pet, though, was a monkey named Mister Mack. Tufts bought him as a teenager from a girl in Sanford for $25 and kept him for a dozen years or so. "Most people didn't know him by his name, though," Tufts says. "They just called him 'Pete's damn monkey.' He was the talk of the town. Until the day I gave him away, I thought he hated my guts. He loved Dad. Dad would go out to his cage and scratch him on his way to work. But me, I'd take him for a walk and the first thing I know I'd feel something warm running down the back of my shirt. He'd done his job. I'd knock him on the side of his head, and he'd

---

"YOU BIG BOHUNK"

Sam Snead and Clayton Heafner were hitting balls on the practice range late in the day after the second round of the 1948 North and South Open had been postponed because of rain. Snead was hitting shots that landed within a foot of each other when Heafner had something wise to say.

"What's wrong with that?" Snead said.

"Nothing, you big bohunk," Heafner responded. "Except that you ought to be down on the putting green instead of up here."

Snead was having problems dropping putts and had resorted to running his right forefinger down the shaft to guide the putter.

show his teeth at me and growl."

One time, a houseguest of a Cherokee Road resident was in the bathroom when she thought she saw a monkey climbing around the trees. She didn't say anything to her host because she didn't want to be thought daffy, but the woman was relieved when the *Outlook* ran an article a couple days later about one of Mack's exploits. "That woman knew she wasn't crazy, after all," Tufts says.

Tufts was called home one day by his mother, who was aghast that Mister Mack was going nuts in her kitchen. "She had an old-fashioned kitchen with shelves all the way around with pots and pans and vases on the shelves," Tufts says. "Mack was up on the shelves, knocking everything off. You've never seen such a mess in your life. There were pots and pans everywhere, broken glass all over the place. It's a wonder she didn't shoo him away that day."

Several years later, Tufts had married and moved out, but Mister Mack remained. One year Allie Tufts was preparing for vacation and told her son that she wanted the monkey gone by the time she returned. "Either you take him or give him away," she said. Tufts called an acquaintance who had a monkey and asked if he'd like a second.

"I found out that day he didn't hate me, after all," Tufts says. "I went into the cage to get him, and that monkey knew right off something bad was happening. He wrapped his arms and legs around me and used his tail as another arm. When we got to the man's house I really had to tear him off of me. He started to scream bloody murder. He threw a tantrum, shook the cage. It really broke me up.

"A week later, he was dead. He died of a

broken heart. There wasn't anything wrong with him. The guy couldn't get him to eat anything. Then Mom got back from Florida and looked in the cage and said, 'Where's Mister Mack?'

"I said, 'He's gone, you told me to give him away.'

"I'll never forget what she said. She said, 'I really didn't think you would.'"

While working his way up the corporate ladder during the 1950s and '60s Tufts looked forward to the day when his generation could begin to implement new ideas. As respected as the regime of Richard, Albert and James was, as

---

A SANDHILL EPIC

Rare is the visitor to Pinehurst who's not been confused and befuddled by the street patterns of the village. There's not a single right angle, just a series of curves and three-way intersections that emanate from the Village Green. Clyde L. Davis moved to the area after growing up in Kansas and graduating from Harvard in 1913 to become secretary of the Sandhill Board of Trade. This verse from *Kansan at Large* pokes fun at the frustration of negotiating village traffic.

The mule at eve had drunk his fill,
Where danced the brook a-past the still,
And in the stable's stench and shade
His weary bones to rest had laid.
But ere the sun a Pekin red
Had kindled all the East, from bed
The Deacon rose, his figure gaunt
Dressed with more care than was his wont.
Then strode afield, his blade took out
And cut a hickory, tough and stout.
A hand of fodder from his crib
He took, and roughly in the rib,
The slumbering mule he smote. I wat
The beast awoke as up it got.
The harness rattled on o'er bones
As rattled Ford o'er paving stones.
Ere scarce that mule his paint-brush tail
Could switch he felt the hickory flail
And straining forward, mad and grim,
Drew cart and Deacon after him,
Whose children beamed both old and young;
Whose spirits far outflew the pace.
The Fair their goal; Pinehurst the place.

The way was long, the sun was hot,
That mule the slowest e'er begot.
His shambling sole remaining gait
Was slow as Woodrow's watchful wait.
But now fair Pinehurst domes and spires
The fretting heart with hope inspires.
And now they pass the castle great
Wherein Lord Leonard* sits in state.
On, on they urge, but wonder, when
They pass the castle soon again.
Another road they try. Once more
They pass the castle full before.

Again, again, full ten and twain,
They try but find them back again.
Then drew he rein
As one in pain
And o'er the drawbridge sprang amain.
Flashed lightning from his steely eye,
In thunder tones: "Lord Leonard, why,
I prithee, didst thou build this town
With corkscrew streets both up and down
As winds the smoke from chimney fork,
When dames at morn are frying pork,
Wouldst though make sport of country guy?
If so, my Lord, prepare to die."
Lord Leonard turned. Kind was his eye;
His face was calm as apple pie;
"My streets are curved, as you're aware,
But all else here is on the square.
Credit indeed the man deserves
Who can get on to all my curves.
As for thy fury, 'tis but purr,
At storming you're an amateur.
My life-boat every season sails
Through blowing schools of angry whales.
Here calm I sit and bravely smile,
Howe'er their lashing tails may rile;
The man who could not smile through hell
Will never run resort hotel."
He waved his hand. From office new,
Came John McCaskill, son of Hugh.
A goodly youth of ample fist
Whom love-lorn maiden ne'er hath kissed.
"Squire John, be thou of use this day.
Go, set Sir Hayseed on his way."
The squire withdrew, went boor along,
Full soon Clan Deacon joined the throng.

* Mr. Leonard Tufts.

the 1960s unfolded Pinehurst was seen in some circles as clinging too tightly to its elitist heritage. Golf was becoming a game of the masses—Arnold Palmer and television had become the game's marketing lynch-pins. Hilton Head and Myrtle Beach were growing as golf destinations, and northerners could now fly to Florida easier than they could board a train to North Carolina. Many of Pinehurst's long-time regulars simply ran out of life, and there were too many options

sell Pinehurst for $9.2 million to Diamondhead Corp., headed by Malcom McLean, a native of nearby Maxton and founder of McLean Trucking in Winston-Salem and Sea-Land Services Inc. The papers were signed on Dec. 30, 1970.

Peter remained on staff under the new management, but soon after he had seen enough new ideas imposed on the hallowed No. 2 course and resigned.

"Pinehurst had been in my family for generations, I'd grown up living for the day I could run it," he says. "Then I wake up one day and they bring in a golf pro who knows less golf than I've forgotten, and I have to answer to him. Would you like that?"

Tufts quickly moved full-time into the golf-course design business, having honed his craft by tagging along behind Donald Ross as a child and then fine-tuning the Pinehurst courses under his father and architect Ellis Maples. He built Seven Lakes Country Club in West End, which opened on July 4, 1976, and operated it for eight years. He still lives in the Seven Lakes community. He currently has several golf-course projects across the state—mostly remodels and additions—and was disheartened to learn in early May of 1991 that his High View Farms Country Club course in Salisbury would never see its first birdie.

"It's been planted over with pine trees," he says. "The owners just had financial problems. It breaks my heart. I think that course would have been in the top 10 or 15 in the state if it had opened and matured. To have all of it go to seed makes you sick."

Tufts turns 65 his next birthday and now is gradually cutting back on his design business. "It's time to fish and play golf," he says.

Though Tufts takes into retirement bittersweet memories of his Pinehurst experience, he takes comfort knowing what a positive influence the resort had on so many people.

"I think of something Clyde Mangum once said," Tufts says. "I hired him as director of golf at Pinehurst, and he used to say, 'Every time I go to the pay window I feel guilty. Working here is such a pleasure.'" ■

Upon close inspection, this Pinehurst pooch rules that Bobby Dunkelberger has hit his ball into the bunker and must play it as it lies.

for their sons and daughters.

"The company was in the process of changing from the older management to the younger crowd," Tufts says. "These were concerns we were beginning to address."

More than 80 percent of the company's stock had been controlled by four men—the three third-generation brothers and Isham Sledge, a trusted and loyal friend of Leonard's and a long-time hotel manager. Sledge died in 1958, and soon after Richard proposed that all the stock be merged and redistributed equally among the fourth generation, which included Richard's offspring (Peter and Sally), Albert's children (Leonard and Emily) and James' three sons (Robert, Tim and Fred). Sledge's son, however, wanted to liquidate his interest and vetoed the proposal. All of the stock-holders recognized that a prolific infusion of cash was needed to renovate the facilities, and concern gradually arose among James and Albert that, in the event of their deaths, the inheritance taxes would bankrupt their families. Those factors led the controlling interests to vote to

PETE AND ALICE DYE

In their early years together, Pete Dye looked at Pinehurst No. 2 until he was "blind," and his wife won the 1968 North and South championship. That grounding in Donald Ross's handiwork influences their golfing lives today.

I t's late one April evening on Kiawah Island, off the South Carolina coast near Charleston. Pete Dye has just returned from Harbour Town, a course two hours south on Hilton Head Island he designed in the late-1960s that on this day hosted the first round of a PGA Tour event. He's loaded with groceries: carrots and yogurt and grapefruit and all the staples of a man who watches his health religiously. Several miles from the townhouse that's been home for two years now is a golf course he designed and built entirely along the Atlantic Ocean that would, in September of 1991, challenge golf's finest players in the Ryder Cup Matches.

It's a golf course Dye designed for the 1990s and beyond, with par-fours of 475 and 478 yards, par-threes of 222 and 227 yards, par-fives that are legitimate three-shot holes and not the cheap birdie factories that so many of today's par-fives are. It's a golf course built to stand all the icosahedron dimple patterns and cavity-backed irons and graphite shafts and steel clubheads that modern technology has pumped into the venerable old game.

Dye slumps into a couch and, late into the night, talks about this subjective business of creating golf courses. He talks of the many times as a soldier in the 1940s at Fort Bragg in nearby Fayetteville he took a back road to Pinehurst to play No. 2: "I've been

lucky; I've played No. 2 more than the law should allow," he says.

Of the North and South Amateurs he's entered: "I never got past the third round. Maybe I made the quarterfinals one year, I can't remember. I do seem to remember playing with Jack Nicklaus one year. Nicklaus beat me in the semifinals of the first tournament he ever won, the Trans-Mississippi. I said if I couldn't beat that little fat boy I ought to quit. He dusted my ass off. He said, 'Go on home, boy.'"

Of the many daybreaks he's spent wandering Donald Ross's *tour de force* for inspiration: "I've looked at that thing 'till I'm blind," he says.

He takes a while in his own, meandering style, but Dye weaves a scenario linking Pinehurst No. 2 to the 1991 PGA Championship at Crooked Stick Golf Club in Indianapolis and poses an interesting question.

"I built Crooked Stick in 1964, and all anyone could do at that time was build a golf course that was right for the time," Dye says. "When I built those greens, the only thing I could envision was how professional golfers would play it at that time. Those greens were built to putt at a seven or eight (on the USGA's Stimpmeter, an apparatus that measures green speed).

"So in 1985, Mickey Powell of the PGA goes up there and starts talking about bringing a PGA Championship to Crooked Stick. I realized then that what I envisioned in '64 would not *remotely* challenge these golfers. So the club went into debt; they never knew what hit 'em. I went in and rebuilt that golf course, every hole, every green, every tee, all the bunkers, the irrigation. When I built the greens I built them for the speed I knew in '64.

"Now hang on a minute, I'm getting to Pinehurst. I tore that course up and put it back together. I knew players were hitting the ball farther, so the golf course now is 7,500 yards long. I knew they weren't cutting the greens anymore at seven or eight, they're cutting them at 11. You try putting those severe greens at 11 and the ball will roll off the green and those pros will be coming after me with a shotgun. So I had to soften the greens.

Dye on the Ocean Course, site of the 1991 Ryder Cup.

MARK PERMAR

"It killed me to go in and have to soften those damn greens, but I thought the club would be totally ridiculed if I didn't. I added 500 more yards, bunkered the hell out of it. And if you asked me, 'Do I think the golf course is harder today than it was for the pros 30 years ago?,' the answer is no. I don't think there's enough I can do to give them the same challenge I envisioned in '64.

"Now I always thought Pinehurst No. 2 was a great golf course. I thought it was the greatest thing in the world when I was getting started. It hasn't changed much in length since it was built, in 1935 or so. The first hole is still 400 yards or so, the second around 430, the third 350, the sixth over 200 yards. Now I've been wondering what Mr. Ross would do if today he woke up and knew that the pros were coming. When he built it in 1930, or whenever he finished, he had to envision it, I would assume, as the players played at that day and that given time.

"I wonder about all this talk about the 'subtleties' of Mr. Ross. I don't think when he built this thing in the early '30s that he felt the golf course was *subtle* at all. I think he thought he built a golf course that was *severe* and challenged the hell out of the great professionals at that time. I know he was very upset he couldn't build a golf course for Bobby Jones at Augusta.

"If he woke up and saw Brandie Burton, that young girl, stand on the first tee and knock a drive down there and hit a wedge to the first green, I wonder if he wouldn't take the first tee, pick it up and put it in the parking lot. I wonder if he was alive today, and he could see the great players play and how they play, if he thought a *challenge* was a drive and a long iron to a par-four, if he wouldn't do like I did at Crooked Stick and modify the whole damn thing, to try to give these guys the same challenge that their peers had 50 years ago. I always wonder what he would do."

The next morning, Dye is wearing a rain slicker and tan pork-pie hat as he wheels around the Ocean Course in a golf cart. Usually he walks—this 65-year-old is in better physical shape than many teenagers. A strong breeze is blowing off the ocean. A slight drizzle is falling as he stops occasionally to confer with workers and makes mental notes on further refinements.

"Now, Mr. Ross might have done this green," he says, pointing to the second green. "It has that upside-down look to it." He points to a wide apron around the green. "This will be maintained like a collar. You can run the ball up or putt it or whatever, like he did at Pinehurst."

A few moments later: "This is more of a Mackenzie green."

Still later: "This is kinda like a green Tillinghast might have built."

And then a bit later: "This is just a damn green. I don't know who did this."

Dye smiles. He's one of the most talented, opinionated and outspoken men in all of golf. And he's funny as hell.

He points down the 11th fairway, a par-four of 470 yards, and explains how the hole might play in September. "For Greg Norman it's still a 300-yard drive and maybe a six-iron," he says. "For some of the shorter players, it might be a long iron, a long iron on a par-four like Mr. Ross envisioned. You see pictures of Hogan hitting a two-iron at Merion and a two-iron at Oakland Hills on a par-four. You'd never see that happen today unless there's a windstorm. It's changed a lot even in 10 years. I remember when TPC opened, in its early years, I can still see Ed Fiori hitting a three-wood on the sixth hole and bitching like hell. Today those kids hit six-irons.

"Is this a good golf course? I don't know. That's in the eye of the beholder. But this golf course is *right* for 1991.

"That's what I was saying last night," Dye says, his voice climbing an octave or two and his arms beginning to flail around a little. "Mr. Ross never envisioned Brandie Burton hitting a drive and wedge to the first green of Pinehurst No. 2. That old man would have jumped out of that box and come out fighting and put that tee back in the parking lot."

Pete Dye gets riled up talking about Pinehurst No. 2 because it's his favorite golf course, because he and his wife, Alice, have enjoyed so many North and Souths over the years and because both feel that advances in technology over the last several decades are antiquating too many of America's classic courses. They're both strong supporters of reigning in the golf ball and making sure that 7,020-yard classics built by people such as Donald Ross don't become pitch-and-putts in 2010.

The Dye perspective on No. 2 is particularly fascinating given the reputation he developed in the early 1980s for building courses with greens bulkheaded into water, for putting a green in a lake at the Tournament Players Club at Ponte Vedra, Fla., for building PGA West, a golf course in the California desert that touring pros hate. All seem to fly in the face of the staid, button-down legacy of Pinehurst No. 2.

In truth, Dye was building courses to his clients' wishes and within the confines of the land he had to work with. The 17th at the TPC was built for spectator interest. PGA West was intended to be a bear because its owners, Joe Walser and Ernie Vossler, said they wanted the hardest golf course ever. Interestingly, his listing in the 1976 book, *Who's Who In Golf* by Len Elliott and Barbara Kelly, mentions Dye in these terms: "He leans heavily toward the Scottish school of natural design and does not turn out the clean-cut, manicured course that has become conventional in America today. The result is a course that looks as though it just happened to grow there ... He doesn't build outsized greens, claiming that a 95-foot-putt is not part of the game; a chip with finesse to a small green is more interesting, he says. He doesn't like elevated greens and water, either."

"You take a golf course like No. 2," Dye says. "The first hole you've got a nice little change of elevation downhill. The next hole, a little down. The fourth hole, a *magnificent* natural elevation change. Down on five, then back up. Nice roll on eight. Nine and 10, *wonderful* changes of elevation. Eleven, nothing. Twelve, nothing. Thirteen, you get a break. Sixteen, 17 and 18—wonderful natural elevation. With all due respect to Donald Ross, I never in my *life* ever had a piece of inland ground like Pinehurst or remotely like Pinehurst. Pinehurst must have 30 or 40 feet of change. It's very subtle. I mean, not subtle. I hate that word. It's just the *right* change of pace for a golf course. And the drainage. Hell, that sand is perfect for a golf course. Early in my career, I tried to do some of those hollows and dips around a green, but they won't drain in

clay like they do in sand. Ray Charles could have built a course in Pinehurst.

"TPC is two feet under sea level, and people say, 'You sure got a lot of lakes and a canal,' and I kinda laugh. If you're working with something two feet under sea level, what else can you do?

"Crooked Stick was just a cornfield with absolutely zero change. PGA West didn't have a foot change of elevation. It was all *manufactured.* Tom Watson came up to me and said, 'That's the most manufactured looking golf course I've ever seen.' I said, 'Truer words were never spoken.'

This ad from 1911 that appeared in "Scribner's" magazine boasted of Pinehurst's three golf courses "in the pink of condition."

Ethel Gray handled much of the resort's early printing, and Donald Ross, in this 1926 telegram, provides some fodder for brochure copy for the coming season.

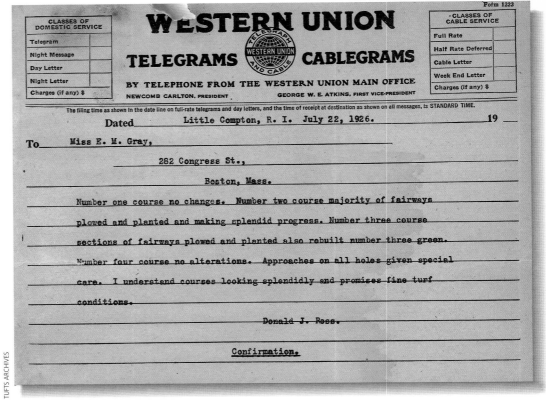

"PGA West, the pros can't play it. It gets more play from members than any course they've got. You can't get on it. Five courses, and the first one that gets filled at PGA West is my course. The old women get around it better than any course there. But the pros will not play it. They hate it. The members love it. Isn't that something? That's the ultimate compliment in golf. The pros hate it; the members love it. I always thought that was the idea.

"My wife loves No. 2. She can play it. You can dribble it on one, dribble on two, dribble on four, dribble on five, dribble on six, dribble on seven, dribble on eight, half-ass on nine. It's that way all the way around.

"Par-threes are the only holes you block the green with a hazard, with water. Everybody starts from a given point of ground, and everyone puts it on a tee. I never put a hazard in front of a green on a par-four or par-five. *Never.* I've been accused of everything, and on par-threes I've put everything but the damn kitchen sink in front of a green. But if you have a pond in front of a green on a par-four, Marie Fudd has got to dribble the ball right up to the edge to get across. On a par-three, you tee her up right there on the edge."

***

Golf has been the Dye family's common denominator since Pete and Alice met in the 1940s when she was a student at Rollins College in Florida. They'd both played in several North and South Amateurs by the time they married in 1950, and Pete was already a successful insurance agent before deciding he might enjoy golf-course architecture more. They began a family—sons P.B. and Perry are now in the golf-design business, too—with Pete designing courses and Alice assisting, always with input from the perspective of the woman golfer. She won the 1968 North and South with a 1-up victory over Connie Day after spending the winter revamping her game under the tutelage of the famed Tommy Armour.

"I had a putt of about a foot, foot-and-a-half on the last hole," Mrs. Dye says. "I was shaking so bad I could hardly hold my putter. But Connie gave me that putt. If she'd known how nervous I was she'd probably have made me putt it."

They live today in Delray Beach, Fla. Alice continues to play almost annually in the North and South, as she did in June, 1991. Mrs. Dye lost her first-round match to Marion McInerney after qualifying with an 82, but returns on a bright Wednesday afternoon to follow the results of several traveling companions with whom she'll leave Pinehurst in a couple days and move on to the Western Amateur. She relaxes on the porch outside the pro shop and talks about the things that have made Pinehurst special. She decries some of the lengthy wire grass that borders the left of the 18th fairway and the fact that modern maintenance practices make soft, lush courses play longer for women. But like her husband, Alice Dye has a revered spot in her heart for Pinehurst, the No. 2 course and the late Richard Tufts.

"You think of some of the fine old golf courses, say an old course that's maybe had the U.S. Open a few times," she begins. "Say you're going to one of these courses for the first time and you see the quaint old clubhouse and all the huge trees and the ambiance of wealth. You go through the gate house and before you get to the locker room you're impressed. By the time you get to the first tee you're in awe. Sometimes I think we get our clubhouses and golf courses mixed up.

"At Pinehurst, in spite of the fact they had a very nice clubhouse, there still was nothing to impress you until you got to the first tee. Everything started with the golf. There's never been a clubhouse to impress you. There used to be a little shack to get something to eat. The caddie area was dirty and dusty.

"It all started on the first tee. What you had was a golf course that was really fun to play. Everybody loves it. It's a wonderful, fun golf course. It's not as much fun for the women any more, the higher handicap women, because you don't get the roll you once did. The turf is much lusher, it's softer now that everyone waters their golf courses so much. You've got to go to England and Scotland to get the roll, and they're starting to water over there now."

The Dyes were like so many people who came through Pinehurst regularly: they developed a close kinship with Tufts, one of the game's premier guardians.

"Mr. Tufts was a very special person," Mrs. Dye says. "I remember once he told me, 'Alice, there are no bad people in golf. The game itself drives them out.' The fact that you're your own scorekeeper, your own referee … Bad people don't stay in the game. It doesn't suit them, it doesn't work for them. They're unpopular, no one will talk to them, no one will play with them, they feel out of place because everybody abides by the rules and everybody's their own referee."

Mrs. Dye then mentions a recent incident at the Byron Nelson Classic in Dallas, when Tom Kite was overruled on where to drop his ball by a PGA Tour official watching on television.

Coincidentally, the topic comes up at Pinehurst No. 2, where, in 1978, Kite called a penalty on himself on the fifth green in the last round of the Colgate/Hall of Fame Classic. Kite said his ball moved a fraction of an inch at address. No one saw it but Kite, but he assessed himself an extra stroke and eventually tied for second with Hale Irwin and Howard Twitty, one painful shot behind Tom Watson. "It was the only thing to do," Kite said. "I've got to live with myself the rest of my life, and when you break a rule in golf, you suffer the consequences." Watson won $50,000; Kite won $19,333.33.

"Everybody in that (Byron Nelson) field, if Tom Kite said his ball didn't cross the water, then it didn't cross the water. Not one person argued," Mrs. Dye says. "Maybe it did cross; but the point is, no one questioned his judgment. The guy playing with him agreed. There's something about cheating in golf you can't handle. Cheating just doesn't work in golf. I don't know why. You *know* you did it. There's something physical that happens when you cheat. You can't play. It's an enzyme or something. To play good golf you've got to concentrate. When you cheat it ruins your concentration. You know you did this. You think, 'I should have called it.'

"Mr. Tufts was the spirit of everything good in golf. He really was. He was the spirit of good sportsmanship. His portrait hung on the far wall in the clubhouse. Every time you walked in you stopped and looked at it. It was like a picture of Lincoln or something. You looked at it with a sense of awe. The kind of man he was inspired that feeling in you.

"The very first golf course we did, Pete and I did it together, it was south of Indianapolis, called Eldorado. I did the routing. It was very amateurish. There was a creek that ran through the property, and I drew these holes. We had it put on a Christmas card and sent it out. Mr. Tufts wrote back to say how delighted he was to hear we're going into golf, that we'd do a great job, that we'd be a credit to the game, that kind of thing."

Alice Dye smiles and leans forward. "Then he said, 'Don't you think that crossing the creek 13 times in nine holes is a little too much?'"

"PLAY IT WHERE IT LIES"
A finalist in a 1917 Pinehurst tournament chipped a ball that caught in the cuff of a spectator's trousers. There was a hurried conference. Finally the referee announced his decision: "You'll have to play the ball where it lies."

"Not on your life," protested the spectator. "I'm not going to have a divot taken from my leg."

The referee stood his ground, and the player tried to persuade the reluctant onlooker to stand still so he could play his shot. At last the two went into a huddle and came up with a solution.

The spectator removed his trousers and held them at arm's length as the golfer neatly lofted the ball onto the green. Amid cheers the spectator replaced his pants and the golfer sank his putt.

ARNOLD PALMER

For all his worldwide golf success, "The King" was merely a commoner in 1940s competition on Pinehurst No. 2. But that didn't dampen Arnold Palmer's love for the Sandhills one bit.

un down the members of the PGA/ World Golf Hall of Fame, and their Pinehurst highlights could fill up a book (and they do, thanks to the three pounds you're holding): Hogan and Snead each win three North and South Opens. Nicklaus wins as an amateur and as a pro. Vardon and Ouimet play here. Watson and Evans are champions. Palmer loses a match 12-and-11. Career amateur Bill Campbell wins four ....

Whoa.

Arnold Palmer loses *12-and-11*?

Indeed he did, in the semifinals of the 1949 North and South Amateur. Frank Stranahan applied the plaster. In fact, for all the glory he would later achieve at the Augustas and Cherry Hills and Royal Birkdales of golf, Palmer was surprisingly ordinary in competition over Pinehurst No. 2, a golf course he grew to love during his three-plus years at Wake Forest College in the late 1940s and early '50s. Sometimes, in fact, he was downright bad, as he was on April 22, 1949.

Palmer's problems began the afternoon before, when he labored to defeat teammate Frank Edens in the quarterfinals. Palmer, a sophomore at the Baptist college some 90 miles north, was hooking the ball off the tee. At Pinehurst, that meant trouble as the hot golf ball would scoot through the thin rough into wire grass, sand and, eventually, pine trees.

Teammate and best pal Buddy Worsham—younger brother of touring pro Lew Worsham— figured he could help Palmer, so they retired to the practice tee for a lengthy session.

"Your problem," Worsham said, "is your grip's too strong. That's why you're hooking."

So Palmer moved his left hand around the club. The weakened grip worked. Palmer practiced until dark—hitting nearly 400 practice balls—and nearly all of them went straight.

The next day against Stranahan, the 26-year-old who'd already been in three North and South finals (winning in 1946), the tonic was still working. Through three holes, Palmer had won one and the ball was splitting the fairway.

"Then on the fourth hole, I hit what I thought was a good drive," Palmer said afterward, "but I looked up and saw the ball slicing into the trees."

The gremlins of the mind started stirring at that point. Palmer lost the hole, then adjusted on the fifth tee.

"I moved my hands back into a strong position, and duck-hooked it," he said.

The gremlins were prancing around now. Palmer lost the hole, then adjusted again on the sixth tee.

"I moved my hands back to a weak position and I pushed it out to the right," he said.

Now the gremlins were raising hell. Palmer lost another hole, and his opponent's miracle recovery twisted the knife a little more. Stranahan hit his long tee shot on the 211-yard par-three to the right, so far that it landed in the adjoining third fairway. But he lofted a sand wedge over the trees to two feet and made par.

"After that, my game collapsed," Palmer said.

"I don't think Arnold was too good at the time," Stranahan says today. "He was a little nervous, it seemed. He gripped it too tight, was getting nowhere off the tee. He left a couple in the bunkers. On about 14 or 15, I was killing him, and I said, 'Arnie, when we get in I'll give you some help in the bunkers and stuff.' He had a bad day against me. He was a hero at his school already. But it was like he was going against one of the pros."

Stranahan closed him out on the seventh hole of the afternoon round after Palmer hit another of several poor bunker shots for the day. Stranahan climbed into the bunker and began tutoring the 19-year-old on proper sand play.

"That really burned me up," Palmer said at the time. "Here my game is in a state of collapse and Stranahan is giving me lessons."

Forty-two years later, Arnold Palmer gives golf-course design associate Ed Seay a wry grin in his office at the Bay Hill Club in Orlando.

WHAT DID ARNIE HIT?
This has nothing to do with Pinehurst, but Charlotte's close enough.

Once Billy Joe Patton was playing at Charlotte Country Club the day after Arnold Palmer visited. Faced with a long shot to a green fronted by a hazard, Patton turned to his caddie.

"What did Palmer hit?" Patton asked.

"A five-iron," the caddie said.

So Patton drilled his five-iron and landed in the water.

Patton eyed the caddie. "*What* did you say Palmer hit?"

The caddie was nonplused. "A five-iron, and he landed about where you did."

"That's true," he says. "There we were on the seventh hole hitting shots out of the bunker.

"He only beat me 11-and-9 or something. I didn't think that was very decisive, what the hell," Palmer says, rolling his eyes.

Seay laughs heartily.

"But I'll tell you something else, for whatever it's worth," Palmer says. "He beat me again, in Minneapolis in the Amateur championship there. But in the most important one, I beat him. Nineteen fifty-four, I won the Amateur championship. That's the end of my story."

But that really is the beginning of the Arnold Palmer story, as the raw and unpolished collegian at Pinehurst would one day sparkle for all the world to see. Even Richard Tufts, the Pinehurst president and noted golf administrator, had trouble in those early years seeing any potential in the muscular kid from Latrobe, Pa., who chain-smoked, walked fast and kept his swing thoughts simple: "Keep your head still, stay over the ball all the time and then *bust* it." A year prior to Stranahan's ambush, Harvie Ward had ousted Palmer 5-and-4 in the North and South semifinals.

Peter Tufts, Richard's son, recalls that Palmer's mother approached Richard, a USGA tournament official, at the U.S. Amateur in 1954 at the Country Club of Detroit.

"Oh, Mr. Tufts, I'm worried to death," Mrs. Palmer said. "I'm afraid Arnold's going to turn pro after this."

"I'm sorry to hear that, Mrs. Palmer," Tufts replied. "With that swing of his he'll never make it on tour."

Palmer won at Detroit, turned pro and proceeded to make hash of his critics. Palmer and Tufts were reunited 14 years later in Charlotte, when Palmer spoke on Tufts' behalf at the latter's induction ceremony into the North Carolina Sports Hall of Fame. They shared a laugh over Tufts' snafu.

"There were numerous people, he was just one of a few, who got in line to say I shouldn't have been a golf pro," Palmer is saying now, just an hour before teeing off in the Nestle Bay Hill Invitational. "(They said) I didn't have the game, and my game wasn't suited. Some of that came from his knowledge of my playing in the North and South. Mr. Tufts was my friend, and a nice man, but he didn't know there was more to playing golf on the tour than what was visible as an amateur. That means mentally, physically, as well as whatever golf swing you

might have.

"Granted, my golf swing has never been one that anyone would take to an exhibition and show off. It wasn't meant to be something that was a thing of beauty. It was meant to be effective and accomplish something. I like to think it did accomplish something."

A little something, maybe: 61 PGA Tour victories, four Masters, one U.S. Open, two British Opens, 12 Senior Tour victories and a business empire that stretches worldwide. And

Arnold Palmer and his father, "Deacon," in Pinehurst around 1950.

one victory at Pinehurst: the 1948 Southern Conference championship, one week after losing to Ward.

Palmer and teammates such as Jennings Agner, Dick Tiddy and Edens would pile into a Desoto station wagon for the drive to Pinehurst. Even as a youngster, Palmer displayed the brashness that later would lead to his epic charges. A curly lock of hair often fell into his eyes after a robust whack at a drive, a shot that likely would outdistance anything his team-

Johnston entered private business.

Palmer remembers Pinehurst as being the number one place in golf in the 1940s. He wasn't as enamored in the 1970s with the changes made to No. 2—much of the older, natural look was plowed under by new owners who wanted green. Much of that natural look has been restored, but that didn't help Palmer then. Perhaps his play during the old World Open underscored those feelings, as Palmer missed the cut in 1974 just days after being inducted into the World Golf Hall of Fame. He also missed the cut in 1975.

"Pinehurst was the most elite spot in the world as far as I was concerned," Palmer says. "It was the golfing capital of the world. No. 2 was the best golf course I had ever played. I was very disillusioned over the years with all the changes they made to No. 2. I just thought as that golf course stood in the '40s when they had the North and South Open and North and South Amateur, that it was impeccable—it was perfect.

"Then people came in and changed it. I was just very, very sorry to see that happen, and I'm sorry today it happened. I think it's still a wonderful golf course, but I think it lost some of the charm."

Palmer and Jack Nicklaus share a laugh on the dais during the 1974 World Golf Hall of Fame induction ceremonies. They were among the 13 charter inductees, but it wasn't a good week competitively for Palmer in the World Open. He missed the cut.

mates could hit.

"He was awfully long and was a great putter," says Tiddy, the head pro at Bay Hill. "He had an advantage because he could reach all the par-fives and the rest of us were laying up. Four, eight, 10 and 16, they were a piece of cake for Arnold. The golf course was long and it was tailor-made for Arnold back then."

Palmer was an intense golfer who practiced constantly and chided his teammates for anything less. He talked then about winning pro golf tournaments. Wake Forest athletic director Jim Weaver used to say, "He had more guts than a second-story burglar." He spent three years at Wake Forest, then dropped out for a three-year stint in the Coast Guard following the tragic and jolting death of Buddy Worsham in a car accident. Palmer returned to Wake Forest in 1953-54, played for the Deacons and even served as golf coach when Johnny

Palmer's golf-course design business has ties directly to Pinehurst, as Ed Seay cut his teeth under Ellis Maples. Seay lived in the Pinehurst area from 1964-68, spent two years in Augusta building two of Maples' last projects, West Lake CC and Goshen Plantation, then started his own business. He and Palmer joined forces in the early '70s.

"There very definitely is a connection to Donald Ross, Ellis Maples and Pinehurst," Seay says. "Arnold and I and all the guys on our staff are traditionalists. We believe there's a very soft element to the game of golf. Every architect tries to use the land to the best of his ability. But what happened in the '80s is that a lot of designers got to change for change's sake or at the client's request. That's where such terribly difficult terrain developed.

"There are limits to what a player can do with a golf ball given a certain set of circumstances. It's asking too much to hit off a downhill lie onto a green that slopes away, that's 30 feet wide, that falls off severely into a body of water. In order to keep it on the green, you've got to mis-hit it."

And as Seay runs through his ABCs of golf-course architecture, remember that on Pinehurst No. 2 it's difficult to incur a penalty stroke or hit one out-of-bounds. Moreover, it's not too difficult a golf course for the average player.

"'A,' is the golf course fun?" Seay asks. "Can people play this course, does it have a measure of forgiveness? If a man hits the ball 96 times and scores 103, you figure he's left a couple in a bunker, hit one OB and a couple in the water somewhere. But if hits it 96 times and scores 110, then the golf course has got him. There's something physically beyond him. It's above his skills. He doesn't have an out.

"'B' is beauty. It's gotta be pretty. It's a measure of 'Wow-ness.' You stand up on the first tee, see everything groomed and pretty and say, 'Wow.'

"'C' is difficulty and challenge. That's easily taken care of and satisfied nine times out of 10 with the placement of tees and hazards. Where do the hazards fall in relationship to the tees and skills of the players where they play from?"

Palmer and Seay began putting those principles into the ground in Pinehurst itself in 1987 with the design of Pinehurst Plantation, the cornerstone to a planned club and residential community on Midland Road between Southern Pines and Pinehurst. The course was designed and shaping was under way when the project's original developers went bankrupt in 1989. Seay was back in Pinehurst in the spring of 1991, optimistic that the property was going to be resurrected and the course completed.

"Knowing what kind of golf course it's going to be, knowing where I started and knowing Arnold's ties to Pinehurst, there's nothing we'd like better than to see that golf course be completed," Seay says. ∎

"Briggs" was a popular cartoonist for the "New York Herald-Tribune" in the 1920s and occasionally penned several panels about Pinehurst.

BILLY JOE PATTON

Billy Joe Patton never met a crooked shot he didn't like—or at least one he couldn't recover from. He won three North and South Amateur championships and delighted thousands with a brand of "happy golf" all his own.

Jerry Boggan witnessed some miraculous golf shots in the 35 years he caddied at Pinehurst Country Club.

Once his boss appeared dead on the sixth hole at Pinehurst No. 2, his golf ball sitting to the left of the green. A bunker between the ball and green prevented a bump-and-run; overhanging trees prevented a wedge shot. So the golfer invented a bump-and-pop. He took a four-iron, punched his ball at the slope above the bunker leading to green, then watched it hit, pop into the air and finish six feet from the cup. "If it hadn't hit the bank, that ball would have

been in the next county," Boggan says.

Another time Boggan's boss hooked his tee shot on the par-four 18th hole into the driving range. Too many pine trees prevented a straight approach shot. "He asked me, 'What would I hit if I was in the fairway?'" Boggan remembers. "I told him a seven-iron. So he takes a five-iron, aims it up the tree-line along the driving range and slices it onto the green."

Still another time this golfing adventurer hooked his tee ball on the par-five fourth hole into the trees, to the left of a service road and below the fifth fairway. Conventional wisdom called for a safe punch shot back to the fairway,

but there was nothing conventional about this golfer.

"I think I can take a five-iron, hit it through that gap in the trees and fade it back to the fairway," the golfer told Boggan and anyone around him listening. This golfer was like that; he liked to talk his shots through, sometimes barely shutting up in time to strike the ball. He did just what he'd said he'd do. Then he wedged up close, drained it for a birdie and won the hole when his stunned opponent three-putted after reaching the green with two drivers.

Boggan laughs and shakes his head one afternoon as he sits on the porch outside the Pinehurst CC clubhouse.

There was no doubt: Billy Joe Patton was a mess.

"To tell you the truth, I'd rather see him hit the ball off bare ground in the woods than from the middle of the fairway," Boggan says, delighted at the thought.

Perhaps no one more exemplified the essence of Pinehurst—the quest of great golf and good times—more than William Joe Patton, the pride of Morganton, N.C. One of the country's finest amateurs through the late 1940s and all of the '50s and '60s, Patton played great golf: he won three North and South Amateurs, one Southern Amateur and made the semifinals of the 1962 U.S. Amateur, all on No. 2. And he had a good time: Patton never met a stranger and played a scrambling brand of golf that delighted the galleries.

Ron Green, who covered dozens of tournaments in Pinehurst for *The Charlotte News*, once put it quite well: "Patton played swashbuckling golf, happy golf, splendid in its result; golf that substituted soul for mechanism, golf that had dramatic uncertainty to it, golf to which

Fairway? What fairway? Patton scrambles out of the pine straw after an errant drive. More often than not, his recoveries solved whatever problem he'd been facing.

bystanders could relate."

Former U.S. Open champion and current golf commentator Ken Venturi takes it a step further: "If they locked the gates at Augusta and didn't let anyone watch, Billy Joe wouldn't break 80."

It was at Augusta in 1954 that the golfing public hugged Patton to its bosom. Born and raised in the western North Carolina town of Morganton, Patton graduated from Wake Forest in 1943, served in World War II and returned home and started a career in the commercial lumber business. There was no lure of riches in pro golf at the time, so Patton and his wife, Betsy, started a family and Patton played as much golf as he could.

He was invited to his first Masters Tournament in 1954 by virtue of being an alternate for the Walker Cup. Patton spent every spare moment that spring honing his game, and felt confident enough in early April that he had his tailor make him a new sports coat so he'd look spiffy at the presentation ceremony. He came close to never needing the new jacket— and getting a green coat instead—but gambling wood shots on the par-five 13th and 15th holes found water on Sunday and left Patton in third place, one stroke behind Sam Snead and Ben Hogan.

Two weeks later, he began building a legend in Pinehurst.

Patton first gained a measure of notoriety in Pinehurst for a match he didn't win: the 1951 North and South final against Hobart Manley. Patton was 2-up through 13 holes, then played one-under-par from there but lost as Manley made five straight threes, closing him out with a 30-foot birdie on 18.

Then in 1954, Patton won his first North and South, edging Alex Welsh 1-up in 37 holes. And in the early 1960s, Patton put a streak of golf together that's never been matched in North and South history.

> **April 17, 1922**
>
> Mr. Frank Maples
> Pinehurst
>
> Dear Frank:
>
> I wish you would not take any of the Bermuda off of the pastures around the dairy. This we have been doing for years and with the result that we are helping the golf links $.10 and hurting the dairy $1.00.
>
> There is enough pasture there for about fifteen head, practically all summer, which would save the dairy about $7.50 a day and we have taken that away a couple of times a year so that it has left the pasture practically valueless and the loss to the dairy, as near as I can estimate, is about $400 a year for what would cost about $45 to buy outside.
>
> Yours very truly,
> Leonard Tufts

He beat Manley 7-and-6 in '62, the key shot being the aforementioned scramble from the woods on the fourth hole. "You know, that's a birdie when I was almost dead, a hole I'll always remember, a hole that might just have meant a golf match," Patton said afterward.

The following September, he won six matches in the U.S. Amateur, losing in the semifinals to eventual champion Labron Harris Jr. Patton had battled back to even the match by winning 13 and 14, but a horrible iron on the 15th tee put him one down and he soon lost, 2-up. That Amateur was special to Patton because it was on one of his favorite golf courses, was in his home state and because he'd helped convince Pinehurst's Richard Tufts to offer No. 2 as a venue. Tufts, a long-time USGA official, had refused to use his connections to bring events to Pinehurst. But a group of players, led by Patton, approached him at the 1960 Amateur in St. Louis and persuaded him to relent.

Then in 1963, Patton won the North and South by defeating Bob Allen 7-and-6, but he lost in the '64 final to Dale Morey of High Point, 3-and-2. Over that period of 25 months and in four tournaments, Patton won 25 of 27 matches, including 19 straight in the North and South.

Patton was a member of the 1963 Walker Cup team that was captained by Tufts. Played in wind and rain at Turnberry, the Americans fell behind 6-3 after the first day's play. That night, Tufts adjusted his lineup—which included current PGA Tour Commissioner Deane Beman—and told his team he didn't want to be the captain of the first American team to lose in 25 years. With Patton leading the way, the Yanks won four morning foursomes the next day, then took five of eight singles in the afternoon to win, 12-8. There wasn't a dry eye on the American team at the awards ceremony.

And then in 1965, when Patton was 43 and figured he didn't have many more wins left in him, he won the Southern Amateur at Pinehurst.

"Pinehurst has added more to my life than any other place I ever played," Patton once told the *Greensboro Daily News'* Irwin Smallwood. "I played there when I was younger, when I was in my prime, and when I was not. It was something more than my favorite place to play. I mean, I just held Pinehurst on a pedestal, and I am not just speaking of the golf course, but the peace and quiet, the atmosphere, the people. For me it was like walking down main street

back home.

And alongside every step of the way was the colorful caddie, Jerry Boggan, a man who stands only five-foot-four but carries a heart the size of a boulder. During Patton's heyday, Boggan would begin his day at 2 a.m., delivering newspapers, then be at the golf course by 7, wearing who-knows-what.

Boggan became a flashy dresser after being impressed with the wardrobe of Jimmy Demaret in the 1951 Ryder Cup. His closet included seven hats: white, yellow, black and several plaids. He had six pairs of Footjoy golf shoes and a variety of colors of plus-fours, shirts and sweaters. The first day of the tournament, he'd wear tan or khaki—"Nothing too spicy," he says. By Friday Boggan would sport a green suede sweater, green alligator shoes, yellow pants and a yellow and green plaid cap. Then for the finals, he'd pull out the red pants, white shirt and shoes and a special Italian hat.

"It looked like a ladies hat, but it wasn't," says Boggan, who wears mostly green today as he tends to yards and gardens around the Pinehurst area. "It was a wide hat, kinda tan in color, with a red ribbon that ran around it. Billy Joe would say, 'I'm ashamed, my caddie looks better than me.'"

The combination of personalities as well as Patton's brand of golf made them a crowd favorite. Tag along with Billy Joe, they said, and there's no telling what you might see or hear.

Like the time in the late 1950s when Patton was on the second hole of a playoff with Dr. Bud Taylor. Patton had hooked his tee shot onto the lip of a bunker bordering the long par-four. A hundred or so people watched as he addressed the ball awkwardly with a four-wood, his right foot in the bunker, his left foot maybe 18 inches above it and the ball in the high grass. Meanwhile, a motorist who'd probably been trying to figure out Pinehurst's curious maze of streets, stopped her car on the road next to the gallery and asked, to no one in particular, "Does anyone know where I can get a room for the night?"

Patton continued waggling. "If you can wait a few minutes you can probably get mine," he said.

The gallery erupted. Then Patton punched out, en route to a bogey. Taylor, safely in the fairway, parred the hole and won the match.

Boggan says: "I declare, I'll never forget that. 'If you can wait a few minutes you can have mine.'"

The little man laughed. "That's why people enjoyed following him. Yes, sir. He was something *else*."

***

Billy Joe Patton has been sitting in his living room on Riverside Drive in Morganton one February morning for about an hour, talking about playing golf at Pinehurst. He's dressed casually in a navy sweater, khakis and white golf shirt. Retired now, what Patton does most

This scene from the fifth green of No. 2 is from a calendar published by Pinehurst in 1951. If you look closely on the right, you can see a golfer kneeling in a light blue shirt and a caddie in yellow pants. That's the Billy Joe & Jerry Show.

is play golf. He spends much of the winter in Florida and can be found daily at Seminole Golf Club in North Palm Beach. Now he's back home for a few days, but tomorrow it's on to Augusta for a round with his son and then back to Florida.

His thoughts and memories of Pinehurst are filled with emotion, animation and vigor—just as his golf was three decades ago.

On Pinehurst No. 2:

"When I think of Pinehurst, I think of No. 2. If I listed the five best golf courses I ever played, it would never leave my hand. I don't know if I ever thought any course was any better. I think Donald Ross just took what he had. It was a desert of sand and scrub oak and pine, and the fellow just built a golf course on it. He didn't build it around a lake because there wasn't a lake there."

On Donald Ross:

"I'm kind of partial to Donald Ross golf courses. We have one here (Mimosa Hills CC).

Patton was all smiles most of the time in Pinehurst, adding a Southern Amateur title to his North and Souths. The one that got away, though, was the 1962 U.S. Amateur.

I'm a member of a Donald Ross course in Florida (Seminole). I'm fond not only of Pinehurst but all these courses.

"On at least 13 of the holes, he'd give you a place to drive the ball. It was unusual on his better courses where you'd have to hit an iron off the tee. He gave you a driving avenue where you could stand on the tee and knock the hell out of your driver. If you could put the ball in the fairway, you had a decent shot at the green. He normally gave you a flat landing area, a place to play a decent shot from."

On his 1954 North and South win that followed his epic charge to near-victory at Augusta:

"I'd been on a roll that particular year, but I should have lost that championship match. On the 18th hole, Alex Welsh was on the right fringe, five or six feet off the green, and he elected to chip rather than putt. His chip rolled some four feet past and he missed the putt. If he'd two-putted from the fringe, he was the champion. We went extra holes, I parred the first one and won the match. Alex and I became great friends."

On his four victories at Pinehurst:

"I've always felt it's not what championships you won, it's *where* you won them. I have won in various cities, but winning at Pinehurst meant more to me. It was something entirely different. You just feel you have to play a match of your life."

On avenging his 1951 North and South loss to Hobart Manley's string of threes with a win in 1962:

"I don't remember much about my victories. But I remember every match that I lost. That's just way I'm wired. That loss was in my craw for a long time, the way I lost the match. Even though Hobart and I were great friends, I was delighted for the opportunity to play him again. I was kinda having one of my days getting up and down. But it didn't mean the same thing to win that it meant to lose. I don't know what's wrong about me, I never got much kick out of winning, until I got older. I just expected it, I reckon. To lose tore my innards. It really grabbed me to lose, and particularly if I lost something in unusual fashion. He played great golf to win that tournament. He deserved to win. Like maybe I deserved to win years later. But I never got the pleasure out of winning like the displeasure of losing."

On never turning professional:

"I couldn't have made a living. Hogan was

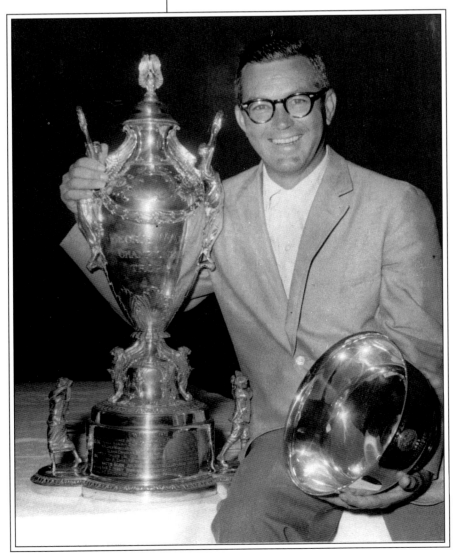

the leading money-winner in '40, and I think he won $10,400. You get the wife in the car and drive around the country and buy hamburgers and hot dogs and not a whole lot of filets. You pay for gas, oil, caddies and your hotel room, and there's not much left. It wasn't something I wanted to do. By the time I got to my first Masters in '54, I was married, had three children, was 32 years old. I wasn't a kid. I'd been to college, the service, then came home to get my feet on the ground and make a buck and get started in something. I never thought at the time of turning pro. The money just wasn't that much. I was making as much or more doing what I was doing as I could make playing golf. There was no TV, the purses were small, it was a different ball game.

"Now, look at flip side of the coin. If I'd won the Masters I might have turned pro, but that's hypothetical. I think there would have been so much money available, an amateur winning the tournament like that, it probably would have been available and I might have gone for the bucks. But I don't know that."

On urging Richard Tufts to allow the USGA to bring the U.S. Amateur to Pinehurst in 1962:

"I just felt the players wanted to go. I'd played in enough Amateurs, knew enough people, it was like a fraternity. You knew the people well. And I knew everyone wanted to play at Pinehurst. It was a difficult thing for Pinehurst: they had to open the hotel early, get the golf course ready early. It was quite an undertaking. We were delighted when he agreed."

On the 1963 Walker Cup, which Tufts captained:

"That was a moving week. I can't talk about it. It meant so much to the two of us. Charlie Smith from Gastonia was on that team. They were beating the hell out of us that first day. It was damn close. We barely won."

Patton excuses himself for a moment. Regrouped, he continues.

On losing in the semifinals of the Amateur:

"That one hurt. *What* it was, *where* it was, made it very disappointing. The Amateur, the National Amateur, on one of my favorite golf courses ... if you were going to have an examination of your golf game, it suited me fine to have it there. Back then we weren't smart, we didn't know you could win on and on. By then I was about 40, and I kinda felt it was my last chance."

On his last major win at Pinehurst, the 1965

Southern Amateur, at age 43 when he knew twilight was coming.

"I won by a stroke. I was to the left of the 18th green in two. I had a bare, sandy lie. I can't remember if I was in a cart path or what. I pitched the ball onto the green, and it stopped six or eight inches by the cup and I tapped it in.

"After I accepted my trophy, I got in that car and drove out of Pinehurst. When I got on the highway and there was just me and the pine trees shooting by, I let out the damnedest yell you ever heard. I kept shouting and driving. I let it all out."

On Jerry Boggan:

"He must have caddied for me a dozen times—10 anyway. We were a team. He was the best. He was just such a pleasant person. And those clothes. He'd start off Tuesday dressed about like I am. By Thursday he'd be spruced up a little. By Saturday he looked like a peacock ..."

A tear or two is welling up in Billy Joe Patton's eyes about now.

"You're hitting all these subjects ... I just can't stand it ... The things we went through together ... It was a very special time ...

"I'm sorry. You get older, you get emotional about things. They meant so much to you. It was just a big time in my life." ■

Francis Ouimet played in several North and South Amateurs, winning the title in 1920, seven years after beating Harry Vardon and Ted Ray for the U.S. Open title at Brookline. He was revered by Richard Tufts for his strong amateur ideals. "With Francis Ouimet, golf has always been a game," Tufts said.

CLYDE MANGUM

The former club manager worked under Richard Tufts at Pinehurst and joined Peter Tufts to offer golfers "the best dog-and-pony show" in town during the 1960s. They were, Mangum says, the best days of his life.

 lyde Mangum has spent more than 30 years in golf administration. He's penalized Ben Crenshaw for slow play and told Jack Nicklaus where to drop his golf ball. For 17 years, from 1971 to 1988, if a ruling was needed on the PGA Tour, Mangum was just a walkie-talkie away.

But over the years Pinehurst and its curious amalgam of competitors of varying abilities has challenged rules officials like a 75-yard bunker shot from a fried-egg lie tests the golfer. Sometimes it's almost an impossible job.

Mangum spent 12 memorable years in Pinehurst from 1959-1971—for six he was executive director of the Carolinas Golf Association and the next six general manager of Pinehurst Country Club.

The N.C. Women's Amateur was once being held on No. 2 and Mangum was called to the 11th hole to give a ruling. He arrived to find two middle-aged women confronting one another in the woods to the right of the hole.

Another match was playing through.

"Can I be of any help?" Mangum asked.

"My opponent isn't keeping score properly," one of the ladies huffed. "As a matter of fact, she's drunk. Look in her golf bag and you'll find a pint. She thinks she's one up, I say she's one down."

Mangum knew a loaded gun when he saw one—not to mention a loaded golfer. He knew Rule 18-1 talked about an "Outside Agency." But he wasn't about to search a woman's golf bag for an outside agency made of malt or potatoes.

"Sorry, I can't rule on that," he said. "I will meet you ladies at the scoreboard after the round and I expect the winner to come and report the match."

Mangum laughs.

"That's the first and only time I was ever asked to give a ruling and couldn't," he says. "Or *wouldn't*."

Once Mangum watched in amusement as an

Mangum (R) chats with Pinehurst pro Lionel Callaway (L) and sports writer Ken Alyta on the tee.

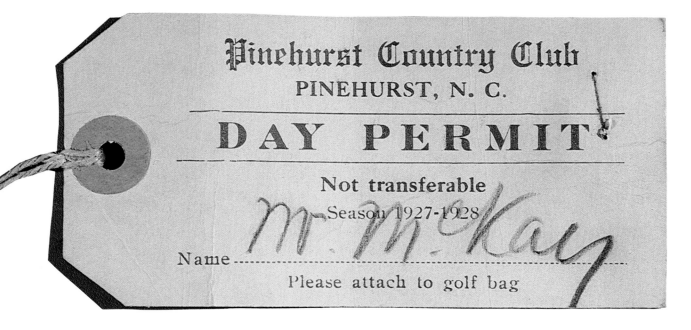

elderly competitor in the North and South Women's Amateur had fellow official Hale Van Hoy squirming over a decision. The woman reported that she'd picked up on one hole, leaving the ball on the edge of the cup, and figured she had a penalty coming.

"Here we are, the protectors of the game, and the rules say if you pick up in stroke play, it's disqualification," Mangum says. "This woman's in her 70s, in the last flight. How are we going to impose such an awesome penalty?"

Van Hoy considered his options, then said to the woman: "Well, if you won't tell anybody, we won't."

That wouldn't do.

"Young man, I insist on being penalized," the woman said.

"All right. In that event, you're disqualified," Van Hoy said.

"That's ridiculous," the woman shot back.

"All right. I'll waive the disqualification and penalize you two strokes," the rules official offered.

"That's too much. I'll take one stroke," the woman said.

You kind of had to be there, Mangum says, to see the expression on Van Hoy's face as the shrewd negotiator signed her scorecard and left. "Hale was begging for mercy by the end of

that exchange," he says.

Mangum left Pinehurst in 1971 when he became deputy commissioner of tour operations for the PGA Tour. He spent 17 years running tournaments from Pebble Beach to Hilton Head, from Doral to Hartford, before retiring in 1988. He took with him to the tour a solid foundation in golf administration honed by his boss, Richard Tufts.

"He was my mentor as far as a basic education in golf goes," says Mangum. "He was also my hero. My greatest days were at Pinehurst. I've traveled all around the world officiating golf tournaments, but I never enjoyed those times as much as I did Pinehurst. Golf was number one in those days. We weren't in the real estate business."

Mangum and Peter Tufts, Richard's son, were contemporaries in those days and played a lot of golf together, often teeing up after work. In order to play more holes, they'd sometimes ride the golf carts that Richard Tufts abhorred, and Mangum was always careful to walk the second hole of No. 2, which skirted past the Tufts home. "Clyde didn't want Dad to chew him out the next day about riding a golf cart," Tufts says.

Today they volley stories back and forth about one another, Mangum from the Greens-

Note that such items as bag tags were always dated by the season—not the calendar year—when Pinehurst was closed during the summer. This bag tag is from the 1927-1928 season.

The Donald Ross Memorial, held annually the week after Christmas, was a big event for a busload of juniors from Florence (S.C.) Country Club. Seven-year-old Jack Lewis would later win the North and South and become a golf pro. Today he is a golf coach at Wake Forest.

boro townhouse he and wife Eileen have moved to and Tufts from his home alongside the Seven Lakes course he designed after leaving Pinehurst.

Says Mangum: "Playing golf with Pete was life-threatening, to say the least."

Responds Tufts: "Clyde was one of the biggest characters I've ever known. It's too bad more people didn't appreciate Clyde's humor."

For an objective opinion we offer Downing Gray, the 1962 U.S. Amateur runner-up to Labron Harris on No. 2 who's played a half-dozen amateur events at Pinehurst: "Clyde and Pete had the best dog-and-pony show in town," he says. "One of them couldn't *wait* to get an audience around him and tell a story on the other. It was worth coming up here just to sit

around and listen to those two go after each other."

Mangum is a kindly sort who looked after stray animals around the premises. He once risked life and limb driving from his home in Southern Pines to the club in an ice storm to check on an alley cat that he'd seen underneath the clubhouse. Mangum reached under the club-house in an attempt to comfort the cat, who promptly clawed a half dozen gashes in his arms and hands.

Mangum could take a hint, so he left to return home, but not before stopping at the post office to pick up the mail for neighbor and friend Van Hoy, thus saving him a drive in nasty conditions. Mangum appeared at the Van Hoy residence bearing the mail, only to have his pants ripped by Luke, the Van Hoys' chubby beagle.

"The good Samaritan tries to do two good deeds and the cat scratches him to pieces and Hale's dog bites him in the leg," Tufts says.

Mangum revels in the tale of holing a 40-footer for birdie on the 18th of No. 2 to put the match and the press on the line with Tufts, who responded by missing a five-footer to lose both bets. Tufts' face turned beet red. He glared at Mangum. "I'm quitting golf. I'm never playing again—at least not with you," he said.

Tufts was the volunteer fire chief and ran the Pinehurst auto dealership in the 1960s and had just gotten a brand new Chevrolet. The antidote to his golf misery, he decided that afternoon, was to take up fishing. So he went to the village hardware store, bought a rod and reel and stuffed them into the trunk of the car with the rubber boots, shovels and other fire department paraphernalia. He set off for a bass-stocked pond on the site where the No. 6 course sits today.

"He's all alone up there with his new fishing gear, and he casts his line and the rod and reel separate and go flying into the pond," Mangum says. "So he takes off his clothes and tip-toes around, looking for his new equipment, and about now has decided this is the end of his fishing career. Finally he abandons the search and runs to the car and puts his clothes on."

Next Tufts tried to drive out on the sandy, dirt road and got stuck. So he took his shovel out, dug the tire out of its mess and got back in the car. Then he gunned it and got stuck again.

"Picture this," Mangum says, giggling. "Pete's lost to me on the golf course, he's lost his brand new rod and reel and now he's stuck for the second time."

Pete Tufts will deny this, Mangum says. But he swears Tufts' brand new Chevrolet was seen the next day with one side bashed all to hell with a heavy instrument—a fireman's shovel, perhaps.

Tufts hears that one and sniffs: "I can't even *recognize* my own story after Clyde gets through with it."

Then he assures one and all that good friend Clyde had a few bats of his own loose in the belfry.

"Clyde went through a bad period where he couldn't get out of a bunker," Tufts says. "He'd hit it fat and leave it in the bunker, then he'd hit it thin and knock it across the world."

Tufts was marking his ball on the 11th green of No. 2 one day when he looked up in time to see Mangum skin it out of the bunker in front of the green, across the putting surface and into the trees behind the green.

"Then Clyde disappears," Tufts says. "All I could see was dust coming out of the bunker. I walked over there, and there's Clyde, laying on his back in the bunker, taking sand and dumping it all over his chest and legs."

Tufts has about lost it by now.

"Clyde said, 'If I can't get out of one of these things I'm going to bury myself in one.'"

Says Mangum: "True story."

Another time Mangum and Tufts were on the seventh hole of No. 1. Mangum hit safely to the green, about 12 feet away. Then Tufts' ball landed right on Mangum's and caromed off the green, into the woods.

"What's the ruling?" Tufts asked, figuring he had some recompense coming from the sorry luck of having his good shot land in the garbage.

"I repair my ball mark and replace it," Mangum answered. "You play from the woods. It's called 'rub of the green.'"

Tufts stalked to the golf cart, jumped in and drove off, "leaving Clyde all by his lonesome," Mangum says. "I had to catch a ride on a pickup truck back to the clubhouse."

"Clyde likes to tell stories about me, but I bet he didn't tell you any about *him* throwing clubs," Tufts snarls. "Well, I've got a bunch.

"We were on the 12th hole of No. 1 one day. We both hit our approach shots close, I was about nine to 10 feet away, Clyde just inside me. Clyde used to have this beautiful old mallet-head putter with a wooden shaft. He could putt the eyes out of it with that putter. He was a great putter. I made my putt, then Clyde, on the same line, missed his. So he throws this beautiful putter up in the air.

"About the time he lets go he remembers that putter had a wooden shaft in it. If you've never seen a fat man chase a thrown golf club, let me tell you, it's a sight.

"And then we're on the 13th tee of No. 2 one day. Clyde hits it bad and throws his driver. It gets caught in the branches of a cedar tree, 15 feet off the ground. Clyde finds this lead pipe, a six-foot piece of pipe that's heavy as hell. He throws this pipe into the tree trying to dislodge his driver.

"I can still see him sweating and heaving over that."

And then there was the time the Mangum-Tufts team entered the annual Pine Needles Four-Ball, which was played at Pine Needles and Southern Pines Country Club. On the 15th hole at Southern Pines, Tufts hit a four-wood poorly, then picked up on the hole. His playing companions later wondered what was keeping Tufts as they teed off on the 16th.

"Where's Pete?" they wondered.

Moments later, Tufts returned and they resumed their round. On the 17th, Tufts eyed a long shot.

"What should I hit?" he asked Mangum.

"Hit your four-wood," Mangum said.

"I don't have a four-wood," Tufts replied.

"What do you mean? You've always carried a four-wood."

"I said, I don't have a four-wood," Tufts said, sternly this time.

Several weeks later, Southern Pines pro Andy Page called Mangum and asked if he knew of anyone missing a four-wood.

"The greenkeeper was mowing out around 15 this morning and this four-wood fell out of a tree," Page said. "I just wondered if you knew who it belonged to."

Between fits of laughter, Clyde Mangum said he knew exactly who it belonged to. ■

NELSON ACES, CAMERA FLUBS
Byron Nelson was making instructional movies at Pinehurst after winning the Masters one year. He holed a tee shot on the par-three 15th of No. 2 only to have the camera run out of film when the ball was 12 feet from the hole. He said he pitied the poor guy who had to kiss a movie queen time and again until everything was right.

JACK NICKLAUS

Golf's Golden Bear grew up on a Donald Ross golf course and became further enamoured with the Scotsman's work over 26 years of playing and watching in Pinehurst. He's a three-time winner on No. 2—as an amateur, professional and father.

Jack Nicklaus has won three golf tournaments in Pinehurst. As a stocky 19-year-old with a crew cut in 1959, he beat Gene Andrews to win the North and South Amateur. With a trim waistline and stylishly long blond hair in 1975, he beat Billy Casper in a playoff to become the World Open champion. And as a 45-year-old with a few creases around the eyes and an intestinal tract on roller skates, Nicklaus watched as eldest son Jack II won the North and South Amateur in 1985.

That creates a new category in the Pinehurst record book: Most victories, combined, as an amateur, a professional and a father.

Which brings up the obvious question: Which of the three meant the most?

"I don't think there's any question, winning there as a father was by far the most special," Jack Nicklaus says today.

Nicklaus left Pinehurst that week in May, 1985 and traveled to Dublin, Ohio, to administer and participate in his Memorial Tournament at the Muirfield Village course he designed. He shot 71-76-74-78—299 and finished two miles behind champion Hale Irwin.

Nicklaus laughs. "I was so emotionally drained after watching Jackie all week I didn't have anything left by the time I got to Muirfield."

"Dad got to Pinehurst in time for my second-round match," Jack II says. "I think he thought he'd watch me in a couple matches, I'd lose and he'd go on to Muirfield. He got to Muirfield a little later than he planned, but I know he didn't mind. I felt kind of bad because he did so bad the next week. He said he'd never been that drained after winning a tournament himself. He was grinding with me every hole."

Nicklaus, Pinehurst No. 2 and the game itself had evolved eons from the time Nicklaus first visited Pinehurst 26 years earlier. The player had become the best ever. The golf course was softer and lusher. The equipment was better. Consider that Nicklaus, who would win 20 major championships, shot 76-79 in ousting Andrews in his 36-hole final in 1959. His son, who won't win any majors, was under par all week during his triumph and made eight birdies in his win over Tom McKnight of Galax, Va., in the final.

Nicklaus didn't appear overwhelming as a 19-year-old Ohio State golfer and member of the Walker Cup team. Peter Tufts, son of Pinehurst President Richard Tufts, was an accomplished player and administrator in his own right and didn't think too much of the kid in the wrinkled sweater. Nicklaus weighed 190 pounds, prompting one newspaper reporter to term his physique "the kind football coaches covet for halfback duty." His plans at the time were to join his father in the drugstore business and remain an amateur, which seemed like a smart move to Tufts.

"I'd heard a lot about this guy, Nicklaus," Tufts says now. "I told my Dad I didn't think this fat kid from Ohio would be much of a player. I was pulling against him in the finals. I wanted a 'name player' to win the North and South. I didn't want someone winning who wouldn't amount to anything. I wasn't impressed at all."

Tufts laughs. "Shows how much I know."

Pinehurst's Dick Chapman was the defending champion, and the field included eventual four-time champion Bill Campbell. Nicklaus, Campbell and Andrews shared the qualifying medal with a four-over-par 76. Nicklaus quickly got the attention of first-round opponent Harry Welch of Salisbury, N.C., a North and South regular, with his drive on the second hole.

"He put it about 70 yards by me," says Welch, who was 42. "And I was pretty long myself at the time. On the fourth hole, a par-five, he was on in two with an iron. On five, a long par-four, he hit an eight-iron. He was just awesome with his driving. He was exceptionally long."

Nicklaus closed Welch out on the par-five 16th with an eagle and a 3-and-2 victory, then marched through three more rounds and into the semifinals. He was the only youngster of the four remaining golfers. Bob Cochran, 46, was a St. Louis paper-company executive. Jack Penrose, 44, was a Miami insuranceman, and Andrews, 45, was in the insurance business in Pacific Palisades, Calif. Nicklaus beat Cochran 2-up, and Andrews beat Penrose 3-and-2,

Three generations of Nicklauses: Charlie Nicklaus (right, inset) shares 1959 North and South victory with young Jack. Twenty-six years later, Jack was beaming over Jack II's Putter Boy.

George T. Dunlap Jr. watches the flight of his ball during one of his all-time record wins in the North and South Amateur. Dunlap won seven times: 1931, 1933-1936, 1940 and 1942. His father, a founder of the Grosset & Dunlap Publishing Co., was a long-time seasonal resident in Pinehurst and got young George started at golf early. In 1926, Dunlap won the North and South qualifying medal at the age of 17. Seven years later, he set new amateur scoring standards on No. 2 with a 65 during qualifying and a 64 during a quarterfinal win.

setting up the final. Andrews wore a straw hat throughout the week, chatted with anyone within earshot and exuded confidence. "He was a breed of cat who wasn't afraid of anything," remembers longtime Pinehurst tournament director Ken Schroeder. "I was working at the desk when we registered him. He said, 'When are the finals?' I said, 'Saturday.' He said, 'Fine, register me through Saturday.'"

Nicklaus took a 3-up lead after 19 holes but then missed five greens in a row, bogeyed each of them and fell behind by one hole. The match see-sawed until the 36th, where Andrews drove into the bunker to the right of the 18th fairway. It took him four shots to reach the green, and Nicklaus made a six-footer for par to win the match.

"The golf course was hard and fast," says Nicklaus. "The ball would hit the fairway and run right into the trees if you didn't hit it straight. There wasn't any rough, as it relates to grass. It was very thin around the greens. You couldn't use your wedge because you couldn't get your club under the ball. So you hit a lot of bump-and-run shots. There weren't really many good scores back then. I didn't feel I played all that badly, but I wasn't near par when I won."

When Nicklaus returned to Pinehurst in 1987 to work on his design for Pinehurst National Golf Club, he noted the difference in course maintenance standards over those three decades. "This isn't a slight to No. 2 or Pinehurst, but I'm not sure golfers today would stand for the conditions back then," he told

charter members of the new club at a luncheon and press conference in the spring of '87. "People today demand lush green turf on their golf courses."

No. 2 could look brown, too, because so much of it was left in its natural state through the Tufts era until the early 1970s. Then the new owners wanted that lush, green look as well and planted bermuda grass in the sandy waste areas. The greens were converted to the softer bentgrass surfaces, so it was a much different course which Nicklaus teed up on for the 1974 World Open.

"You'd hit the green and it went 'Splat,'" Nicklaus says. "It was a completely different golf course, much greener and softer."

The changes notwithstanding, it was still a fascinating test to Nicklaus and the rest of the field. Nicklaus, Frank Beard and Bob Murphy lost in a playoff to Johnny Miller, but Nicklaus shrugged afterward to Dan Jenkins of *Sports Illustrated*, "So I lost another golf tournament, but I never enjoyed playing a golf course more. Pinehurst No. 2 is fabulous. I learned about five things about design this week—on a course 50 years old."

Nicklaus elaborates today:

"I've always thought Pinehurst to be one of my favorite designed golf courses in the United States. And the reason I say that is there's not any water on the golf course—well, there is on 16 but it's not in play—and there's not a tree in play on the golf course. It's a tree-lined golf course but the trees aren't a strategic part of the golf course."

The 1975 World Open field included 11 of the 13 golfers who'd won more than $100,000 that year, among them Weiskopf, Hale Irwin, Bob Murphy, Lee Trevino and Raymond Floyd. Nicklaus had won four times (including the Masters and PGA Championship). He shot a first-round 70 to trail Lee Elder by five shots and said, "I'd love to see a golf tournament here every year. I'd like to win here because the golf course is so much fun to play."

He did just that three days later, charging from five shots out of the lead after three rounds to tie Billy Casper at 280. Third-round leader Tom Weiskopf skied to a 75 and missed a six-foot putt on 18 that would have tied Nicklaus and Casper. Nicklaus played a steady, two-under round of 69 with no bogeys and birdies on the par-five fourth and 16th holes (No. 2 was played as a par-71 throughout the tour's 10-year run from 1973 to '82, with the eighth hole being played as a par-four).

On the first playoff hole, Casper drove in the thick bermuda rough, missed the green and Nicklaus won the $40,000 first prize with a routine par. He was the tour money-leader for the year with $298,149 and was in a seven-year streak when he finished first or second in winnings.

Pinehurst was the site of another Nicklaus milestone, but it's one he'd just as soon forget. He returned in 1976 as defending champion of the World Open and brought with him a string of having made 105 consecutive 36-hole cuts in PGA Tour events. He was closing in on the 111 straight that Byron Nelson set in the 1940s, but Nicklaus shot 72-74—146 and missed the cut by one shot. He found all manner of places to hit his golf ball that week, with one approach on the seventh hole landing in a woman's purse.

"If anyone told me I could shoot 146 at Pinehurst and miss the cut, I'd have said, 'You're crazy,'" Nicklaus said.

Nicklaus's fondness for No. 2 wasn't lost on his son, who figured Pinehurst into his reasons to attend the University of North Carolina on a golf scholarship beginning in 1980. Chapel Hill is only a 75-minute drive away.

"No. 2 was one reason I went to Carolina," Jack II says. "Whenever we'd have a free weekend we'd go to Pinehurst and play No. 2. I remember my Dad saying that the more he learns about golf course architecture, the more he becomes a preservationist of Donald Ross courses. He grew up on a Ross course (Scioto

CC in Columbus, Ohio). He thinks Donald Ross was a genius."

The younger Nicklaus was more of an all-around athlete as a youngster, playing football, basketball and baseball as well as golf, so he was hardly the accomplished golfer when he arrived at Carolina that his father had been at 19. He was red-shirted one year and didn't become a consistent member of Carolina's first team until his final year. He averaged 77.9 shots in competition his first three years, then improved to 74.16 as a senior. He was playing well when the North and South arrived.

"Our team had won seven of eight tournaments that spring, and I was playing much better," he says. "I wasn't doing anything super-fantastic, but I think I'd learned to chip and putt a lot better."

Nicklaus's success that week and the ensuing arrival of his father created a buzz around the North and South that hadn't been heard in years. The gallery for the championship match swelled upwards of 2,000, prompting comparisons to the famed matches between Harvie Ward and Frank Stranahan in the late 1940s. Pinehurst officials even dusted off the "Quiet Please" signs. Bill Lovett, a Greenville, S.C., dentist, was ousted by Nicklaus in the quarterfinals and asked for an autograph from opponent and Pop before departing. Peter Persons was Nicklaus's victim in the semifinals and felt the Golden Bear's shadow as he lost, 4-and-3.

"It wasn't the gallery that bothered me, it was one person in the gallery," Persons said.

"I was nervous playing *behind* Nicklaus," said McKnight, the other semifinal winner.

With a gallery including father, mother Barbara, a contingent from Chapel Hill and still others who flew up from North Palm Beach, Fla., where young Jack grew up, Nicklaus played steady golf against McKnight and collected a 2-and-1 triumph.

Now both knew the glory of victory on Pinehurst No. 2. "On the third tee one day, Dad came up to me," Jack II said, "and I said, 'This is a good golf course, isn't it?' And he said, 'No, it's a marvelous golf course.'"

The Nicklaus family beamed over the Putter Boy trophy. The elder Jack unleashed a few tears. Barbara Nicklaus told her son that the old man was so nervous he'd been stepping all over her feet without realizing it.

"It's not easy being a father to a famous golfer," Jack said to Jack II. ∎

QUIET, PLEASE
It was against the law in Pinehurst in early days to own a rooster. It might crow and wake people up too early.

HALE IRWIN

Bentgrass and August served up some mind-boggling scores when the PGA Tour played Pinehurst in the late 1970s. Just ask this three-time U.S. Open champion who carved out a 62 in 1977 and followed with a 63 the next year.

he PGA Tour came to Pinehurst in August, 1977, and it was not a pretty sight. They raped and they plundered. Women and small children cried. Dogs cowered and hid their tails. Brave men grieved that they could not put up a fight as General Hale Irwin and the rest of his troops dropped bomb after bomb on a defenseless Pinehurst No. 2.

Pin on hole number two sighted, General. One hundred and seventy-six yards. Six-iron. Ready, fire. *Splat.*

Pin on number 18 sighted, sir. One hundred forty-four yards. Eight-iron. Ready, fire. *Splat.*

And on and on it went for four hot, humid days. When the tour troops mercifully retreated late that Sunday afternoon—Irwin took with him a booty of $50,000 and a death count of 20-under-par—the survivors wept.

"Pinehurst Pounded," screamed *Golf World* magazine on its cover the next issue. "Wethersfield South" was the tawdry moniker applied to the golf course in the locker room in honor of the old Hartford, Conn., site that the pros demonstrated annually was ready, willing and able.

And in the wake, they remembered a comment that Irwin made in the press room after his five-shot victory over Leonard Thompson: "No. 2's playing about as timid as we'll ever see it."

What a storm Hale Irwin and his mates created during that 1977 Colgate/Hall of Fame Classic. Irwin doubled in strokes-under-par the previous 72-hole tournament record, shooting rounds of 65, 62, 69 and 68. His 264 total was 10 strokes lower than Raymond Floyd needed the previous year. Thompson tossed in two 66s and a 64, including a 29 on the back nine Sunday with seven birdies. J.C. Snead shot a 63. Forty-one players broke par for 72 holes, compared to 25 in 1976, five in '75 and eight in '74.

Today those are merely scores in a faded record book. But at the time they ushered in an important transition in Pinehurst history. Combined with the fact that Pinehurst No. 2 had fallen from the Top 10 rankings in *Golf Digest's* semi-annual ratings, the scores proved to management that maybe the old days

weren't the bad days, after all.

"Everyone involved with Pinehurst at the time realized something was missing," says Lou Miller, the director of golf at Pinehurst from late 1975 to the end of 1980. "Something had to be done. Falling out of the Top 10 was the worst thing in the world to happen to it. No. 2 was always the pride and joy, and it was an advertising thing, too: 'Come play one of the Top 10 courses in the world.' There are only two you (the public) can play, No. 2 and Pebble Beach.

"When the Tufts family sold Pinehurst in the early 1970s, the whole concept of the people who came in was, 'Hey, we've got this vehicle and we're going to bring in California, La Costa type ideas.' That was the whole thing. They planted tree-line to tree-line in grass. They were literally burning memorabilia. They didn't want history. They wanted the future. They wanted the glitz and glitter of Doral, La Costa, those kinds of places."

Many tour players had no historical reference to compare No. 2 with when the tour returned to Pinehurst for the 1973 World Open. Some were still in swaddling clothes when the North and South Open was discontinued in 1951. Irwin didn't know what had been, he just knew what he found was pretty good.

"I've always thought Pinehurst one of better golf courses in the country, and long ago I stumped for having the tour look at making Pinehurst our home," he says. "I felt it was that good a golf course, and it's certainly in a great golf area with all the golf courses and the history and tradition. How could you go wrong? But that wasn't what the commissioner had in mind.

"I remember feeling I was in over my head the first time I played there. You first look at No. 2 and you think, 'This is not all that difficult.' It's not until you start playing it and trying to post a score that you realize there's a lot of little intricate things about it that at first blush you don't see, such as the balls that just roll off the green five or six feet.

"Then you look at the little pitch shots that you have. You look at the putting. It's very deceptive putting. The greens aren't particularly highly banked with a lot of pitch and roll in them, but they're very difficult to putt. I just liked a lot of—I suppose you could say—the innocence of it. You knew it wasn't innocent. It doesn't get its reputation and the scoring you generally have without it being difficult."

Irwin, the 1974 U.S. Open champion, found an inviting golf course August 25, 1977, when he arrived in Pinehurst. And that suited his ornery frame of mind just fine, too.

He'd been told earlier in the summer that he had earned a spot in the World Series of Golf, scheduled for early September at Firestone CC in Akron, Ohio. So he arranged his summer schedule accordingly. But a teen-aged mathematics whiz from California informed the tour that its intricate computer calculations were off—that Graham Marsh, and not Irwin, was actually the winner of the spring quarter and thus entitled to that automatic exemption into the World Series. The tour sharpened its pencil, found the lad was correct and told Irwin just before going to Pinehurst that he was not yet in the World Series. Irwin wouldn't have quarreled had the error been caught immediately and had he not taken time off during the summer, thinking he didn't need to grind out a spot in the World Series.

"To qualify I had to win at Pinehurst," he says. "I was aggravated by the timing of the whole thing. Given the circumstances, I felt they should have allowed a special exemption. But they didn't see it that way. So I get to the golf course for the first round, I had an afternoon tee time, and already there's a 63 and 64 on the board.

"I'm thinking, 'Great, I've got to win and already I'm looking at a 63 and 64.'"

So Irwin goes out and fires a six-under-par 65 of his own and the race is on. Tom Watson adds a 65 in round three and says: "The No. 2 course is playing easier than I've seen it. There are two reasons for it. First of all, the fairways are in the best shape ever. More important, the greens are like dart boards. Anything you throw on them will hold. The greens were sure a lot firmer in 1973 when Gibby Gilbert and I shot 62s. The hot summer has taken its effect. The bent greens needed a lot of water and now they're so soft they're fragile."

The worst time of the year to play competitive golf on Pinehurst No. 2 is July through mid-September. Remember, when Donald Ross completed in 1935 laying the holes out as we know them today, Pinehurst shut down for the summer. All the major competitive events were held in March, April and November. The greens had been converted to bentgrass in the early 1970s, but the substructures of the putting surfaces weren't rebuilt to strengthen the roots and accommodate all the water that the more fragile strain needed to survive the hot summers.

A jubilant Irwin marches toward a 20-under-par triumph in 1977.

The rough provided the final kicker in 1977—or, ironically, the *lack* of rough. When bermuda rough was planted in the natural areas of hardpan sand and pine needles several years earlier, good players were able to become more aggressive off the tee. If their tee shot went slightly askew, the rough was less a penalty than the previous fine of seeing the ball, with nothing to stop it, roll into the trees where the only option was to pitch back to the fairway. But the area had received little rain that summer of 1977, so the rough wasn't thick at all. There was enough grass to stop a ball from bouncing into the trees, but there wasn't enough to stop a pro from spinning his ball from the rough and having it check up on the soft greens.

That's what Irwin was talking about: "When

you can rip an iron from the rough and know it will hold, there's no fear off the tee." Of course, a man wearing light green, sans-a-belt pants and a white shirt with green flowery designs—as Irwin did on Saturday—isn't scared of *anything*.

"Any ball that landed on the putting surface stayed right there," Irwin continues. "It essentially took away the fear of missing a green and having those funny little chip shots. I don't remember having any of those shots that week."

"The low scoring is not a disgrace," said Leonard Thompson, whose 15-under total beat the previous 72-hole record by five shots. "It's a compliment, a tribute. We don't shoot good scores unless it's perfect. Our higher scores come on ratty courses. When on No. 2 the greens are like this and every lie is perfect in the fairway, it lets you do whatever your abilities let you do."

Pinehurst retained architect Tom Fazio, who was designing the new No. 6 course, to help restore No. 2 over the next year. Fazio asked columnist Charles Price, who had lived in Pinehurst in the 1940s and had played No. 2 in the North and South Open and Amateur, to assist. Among their missions, Fazio says, was to remove much of the bermuda grass that was flourishing amid the trees and hand-plant tufts of wire grass in its place.

The course still had bermuda rough in many places around the fairways and greens the following August, and plenty of rain leading up to the tournament left the grass lush and thick. Tournament officials let it grow long, and players sometimes took several minutes to find their ball. "It's like hitting a brick wall. I've already hurt my hand trying to hit out of it," said Lou Graham. "I'm weary. I just keep chopping away at it. Hitting it in the rough is just like a penalty stroke because you've got to hit a wedge to get it out."

Thompson, a native of nearby Lumberton and a devout No. 2 fan, shot a 69 in the opening round and winced: "You miss a fairway and you just have to blow the ball toward the green. The rough should be difficult, not impossible."

The scores the first day were significantly higher than a year before. Where 48 players opened with sub-par rounds in 1977, only 14 did in 1978. Then on Friday, Irwin did the unthinkable:

He shot 63.

"If I'd made a couple more birdies I might have shot 62 again and I'd have been shot or someone would have committed hari-kari," he joked afterward.

August in the late 1970s continued to spawn scores in the low 60s. Dana Quigley opened with a 63 in 1979, then Johnny Miller followed with a 63 of his own on Friday. Which just goes to show you: scores and golf courses by themselves don't mean much without knowing the month they were shot.

"Look at what Johnny Miller did at Oakmont, one of the hardest, most difficult golf courses in the world with terribly fast greens," says Fazio, referring to the final-round 63 that won Miller the 1973 U.S. Open. "They had a big rain storm and the greens were soft. And No. 2 was not designed to be played with soft greens.

"Even though there might have been some panic on the part of Pinehurst's owners at the time—and it was legitimate panic, because how can you have such a great golf course if all those low scores were being shot?—my belief would be if Donald Ross was alive and knew the best golfers in the world were going to play No. 2 in July or August on soft greens, he would have done something to adjust or meet those conditions."

"I've always felt that No. 2 is the type course that ought to host the national Open some day," Irwin says. "You're looking at the middle of June, and I think that would be a great week, a superb week. You haven't had the summer build-up of heat and humidity. Whatever kind of grass you had on the greens would still be doing well. I think it would be a fantastic time of year to play. I've never played Pinehurst in June and would love to."

Pinehurst officials hope that landing the 1994 U.S. Senior Open—open to golfers 50 years and older—will lead to making Irwin's wish come true and the Open itself will come to Pinehurst later in the decade.

"Nineteen ninety-four, how old will I be then? Let's see ..." Irwin muses, counting the years from his June 3, 1945 birthday. "Shoot. I'll be 49. I'll miss by a year. That's a shame. It would be a lot of fun to play my first Senior Open on Pinehurst No. 2."

∎

ONE GREEN, THREE BUNKERS

There are three bunkers to the left-front of the ninth green on Pinehurst No. 2. One day in 1980, Hal Sutton found all three of them.

Playing in the World Amateur Team Championship, Sutton pulled his tee shot into the far left bunker, and the ball came to rest under the back-left lip of the bunker. He had no backswing if he aimed at the green. His only shot was to address the ball sideways and hit it into the middle bunker.

He got an indentical lie there, too, and had to play into the rightside bunker. Finally, he had a shot at the green, blasted out and two-putted for his six.

Sutton overcame that hole, however, to win the individual title and add it to previous Pinehurst successes that year. He won the North and South and the U.S. Amateur (played at the Country Club of North Carolina, with qualifying rounds on Pinehurst No. 2).

THE MAPLES

The legacy of the Maples clan cuts a wide and prominent swath through the Sandhills. From golf-course design to construction to maintenance, the Maples have been there from the beginning.

Dan Maples has built a par-three over marshland on the Atlantic Ocean to a green surrounded by oyster shells. He's built a golf course around an ancient lava field beneath a vanquished volcano in Hawaii and has fashioned 18 holes around 17th century stone walls and buildings on the island of Majorca, off the coast of Spain. He's got 27 holes waiting to be cut outside Hanover in West Germany, and in the summer of 1991 he began melding golf holes amid Japanese gardens near Tokyo.

Yet no matter where Maples travels to design golf courses, the umbilical cord still stretches back to the village of Pinehurst, back to the days when his ancestor worked alongside Donald Ross to carve Pinehurst Nos. 1, 2, 3 and 4, Pine Needles, Mid Pines and Southern Pines Country Club.

Maples points to a large, framed black-and-white photograph on his office wall taken in the early 1900s. It shows two mules dragging an apparatus along the ground as two men follow behind and use their strength to guide the tool through the dirt. Absent from the picture in body but certainly present in spirit are Ross, who designed the golf hole, and Frank Maples, the Pinehurst course superintendent who executed the design.

"Several years ago, when we were building the Pit (golf course), I got to thinking about rigging up this thing to float out (shape) ground. I got a couple pieces of railroad iron and showed the guys how we'd do it. We'd drag this thing behind different kinds of machinery to get a certain look," says Maples.

"After we'd done about half the golf course, I had that picture in my office, and I got to looking real close at it. I said, 'God almighty, my grandfather already invented it.' I thought this thing up, but he'd done it 85 years ago. Only his was adjustable—you could adjust the pitch. These kinds of apparatuses give you a certain look when you do a golf course. It's not just how you draw it—it's how you implement it. I'm not afraid of trying something different, but we've been very steadfast in maintaining the old traditions and methods of building golf courses."

Those traditions are important to the Maples family. James Maples Jr. was born in 1856 in Pinehurst, and, of his nine children, three of them, Frank, Walter and Angus, made at least some part of their living in golf-course construction and maintenance and have spawned sons and grandchildren who've carried the golfing torch. The offspring of Frank and Angus, in particular, have been prolific in extending the Maples golf heritage.

Angus was born in 1882 and helped construct Pine Needles in the late 1920s and later was course superintendent. Son Palmer was a lifetime golf pro—noted most in the Carolinas for the 28 years he spent at Benvenue CC in Rocky Mount—and Palmer's three children, Palmer Jr., Nancy and Willie, grew up with the game as well. Palmer Jr. is superintendent at

Dan Maples carries on Ellis's tradition as golf architect.

MCKENZIE & DICKERSON

Summit Chase CC outside Atlanta, Nancy is an avid amateur in Charlotte and Willie is a former pro who now works at Trump Plaza in Atlantic City, N.J.

Frank had two sons, Ellis and Henson. Ellis designed some 70 courses throughout the region, including the Cardinal Course at the Country Club of North Carolina, Whispering Pines CC and Woodlake in the Pinehurst area and Grandfather Mountain in Linville. Henson was course superintendent at Pinehurst for 30 years. Both were instrumental in the development of bentgrass in the South. Ellis was the first to plant bent on greens in North Carolina east of the mountains (at Pine Brook CC in Winston-Salem), but his interests were more in design than turfgrass research, so Henson took the baton and further developed the research in Pinehurst.

Ellis's two sons are Dan, the Pinehurst architect, and Joe, the head pro and superintendent for 33 years at Boone Golf Club, another Ellis creation. And Henson's two sons

GRAY DAY IN THE PINES

One of the first things Downing Gray (inset, opposite) did upon arriving in Pinehurst for the 1991 North and South Amateur was to see if his old nemesis pine tree was still standing to the right of the fourth fairway of No. 2. Alas, it's no longer there. But Gray's memories certainly are.

Labron Harris Jr. (below) beat Gray, 1-up in 36 holes, in the 1962 U.S. Amateur finals in Pinehurst. Harris was a 20-year-old Oklahoma State University graduate and Gray a 24-year-old insurance man from Pensacola, Fla. Gray apparently had the match well under control until his escapades in the pines. The photo at right ran across two pages in *Sports Illustrated*. Gray describes the scene, 29 years later:

"That was the beginning of the end. I lost five in a row after lunch. I was 5-up with 15 to play. You'd figure a cripple could get to the clubhouse with that kind of a lead. I pushed it and put it under that tree. There was a big, low-hanging branch with a fork on it. You're allowed to take your stance, and the only way I could get my stance was to get my neck under that fork and push up. I was trying to hold that pine bough up with my shoulders and hit that shot. *Oh boy*. I made six and lost that hole and the next four in a row. He made two birdies and two pars, and I made two pars and two bogeys."

Harris, who would go on to a career on the pro golf tour, took a 2-up lead through 16 and held on for the win. Gray never turned pro and has played in several North and Souths and is a regular in top amateur events around the country. "The sleepy, quiet atmosphere of Pinehurst is special to begin with," Gray says. "Combined with my own special memories, it makes Pinehurst very close to my heart."

R. HUNTSINGER/SPORTS ILLUSTRATED (2)

are Gene and Wayne. Gene was long-time super at Pine Needles, following his uncle, and Wayne has worked at Pinehurst CC and now works for Dan as superintendent of the three courses Dan owns: the Pit and Longleaf in Pinehurst and the Sound Golf Links on the North Carolina coast near Hertford. Gene now is executive director of the Turfgrass Council of North Carolina.

Dan and Wayne both are carrying the Maples and Pinehurst traditions into the next generation, Dan with architecture and Wayne with construction and maintenance.

***

The temperature is inching toward 90 degrees late one May morning as Wayne Maples sits on a picnic table in the maintenance building at the Pit. Around him are the bells and whistles today's "super" uses to manicure velvet golf courses: $40,000 hydraulic fairway mowers, a staff of 10 workers, newfangled systemic fungicides that actually enter a blade

of grass to ward off disease instead of fighting it from the surface.

That's light-years away from the way golf courses used to be maintained. Pinehurst Country Club, where father Henson was course superintendent and where Wayne worked as a teenager and again in the early 1980s, was always known as the golf capital of the world.

Donald Ross (L) and Frank Maples.

But even Pinehurst's course maintenance standards would be vilified by today's practices.

"We only had five or six people working on two-course," Maples says (there are three times that number today on the No. 2 staff). "There weren't weed-eaters, things like that. None of the golf courses were irrigated, except for two-course, and that was just down the center lines. The water didn't get thrown very far. The traps wouldn't get any water, so hardly any grass grew around them. All the outlying areas were scrub rough.

"That wouldn't be accepted today. You can't find many golf courses maintained today like they were back then. You'd have to go to Europe to find them. When irrigation started, the whole deal changed. Golf courses turned green, we started trimming and manicuring the whole course. Golfers expect it to be that way now. You could please a small percentage of golfers by maintaining courses more or less like we did then, by leaving them natural except for greens, tees and landing areas. But that small percentage won't pay the bills. They want to see green, tree-line to tree-line."

Maples knew from childhood that he liked to be outdoors and he liked to be around golf. So it's no surprise that he chose the career path of his father. In addition to working at Pinehurst

CC, he's worked at Foxfire, Lake Surf in Vass (now Woodlake CC) and spent several years in Birmingham, Ala., helping build and working on a golf course owned by former touring pro Mike Souchak. He joined Dan's team in 1985 and, like his cousin, takes pride and accepts the responsibility his heritage brings.

"By all accounts they were in the right place at the right time," he says. "They were exceptional people in the jobs they did. I made a decision that if I was going to do it, I had to do as good a job or better. I had to be a superintendent as good as any and better than most. It's a competitive type thing. Someone will take your job if you're not careful.

"I was bound and determined from day one that just because my name was Maples, that wouldn't open doors. My work would open doors and keep them open, whether my name was Maples or Smith. If you're good, you're good. If you're not, you're not. With what my grandfather and father did here, you sure wouldn't want to be a dud, so to speak, if you did the same thing."

Maples acknowledges that his job today is comparatively simple to those of his ancestors. They didn't have the seed, the chemicals, the equipment and the technology to groom and maintain courses that Maples has at his fingertips. He rummages through a bookshelf in his office for an old USGA publication. He finds the September, 1964, issue of the "USGA Green Section Record," with a photo on the cover of a man kneeling on a golf course green. The caption reads: "Henson Maples, golf course superintendent of Pinehurst, N.C., Country Club, examines a green planted in Nimisila bentgrass. Mr. Maples is one of the pioneers of bentgrass in the South."

"That was his big contribution," Wayne says. "No one had bentgrass in the South. People said you couldn't grow bentgrass in the South. But he did, and pretty successfully. He convinced others and got the breeders involved. Two courses at Pinehurst were bent at the time, then eventually all of them were changed to bent.

"It's all been a natural evolution process. Sand greens to bermuda to bent. Two-course would have evolved that way if Donald Ross was alive today. People say that two-course isn't the same without bermuda greens. That's junk. It would have evolved just like all the others. We've got it lucky today. We're just fine-tuning what my Dad and others before us did. They were the pioneers. They took the chances.

You couldn't move much earth in the early 1900s when golf courses were built by mule and man and a few hand-made apparatuses.

Feb. 17, 1922

Mr. Frank Maples,
Pinehurst

Dear Frank:

Have you thought of suggesting to Mr. Caddell that he buy a tractor to use down at our place this year instead of two mules? You know the International people have a tractor that they sell at a very cheap price now and they will allow from one to three years to pay for it.

The Fortune tractor is selling at a very cheap price now, but of course they want spot cash for that. I believe an International tractor would be almost as cheap as a good pair of mules, and I am sure we could get better terms on this than on a pair of mules. I don't believe the operating expense would be as much either.

This is only a suggestion, however, and not to be considered unless you think it advisable.

Very truly yours,
Isham C. Sledge
Pinehurst Inc.

It took guts, I'll tell you that."

***

Along with the vintage photography in the conference room of Dan Maples' office across the street from the post office in the village is a huge color print of the 17th hole at Marsh Harbour, a course Maples built near Myrtle Beach in the early 1980s. The contrasts in the old and new are striking.

And in the competitive world of golf-course design, those contrasts are where Maples looks for an edge. The industry is saturated with great players who see design as a natural evolution of playing careers that slip with age. Design is in Maples' blood. And instead of winning the U.S. Amateur at 19, he was driving a bulldozer or tractor on his father's courses.

"There's no other golf course architect who can bring a client into a room, show him those pictures and say, 'That's where I come from,'" says Maples associate Larry Craft.

By the time Maples was born in 1947, his grandfather had built seven courses in the community, and his father would soon design Pinehurst No. 5. So it's no wonder young Danny popped into the world hauling a golf bag loaded not only with clubs but blueprints and grass seed as well.

"My mother gave me a drawing I did when I was 6 or 7 of a golf-course routing," he says. "I was on a driving range in diapers. But with golf in the family and growing up in Pinehurst, that's about what you'd expect."

Maples was a good player from childhood and worked long hours on his father's golf courses. He inherited his father's ability to play (Ellis once shot 62 at Raleigh Country Club), and made all-conference on the golf team at Wingate College in the late 1960s before entering the School of Design at the University of Georgia.

"I've always loved design," he says. "It was creative, it was an art. I've always liked to build and make things. Those years flew by. It wasn't like going to school. It was something I was fascinated by every minute."

Maples graduated in 1972 and returned to join his father's business. Father and son designed a number of courses together, then Dan began taking over more of the work as his father slowed down. Maples and Larry Young built Marsh Harbour on the North Carolina coast in Calabash, then followed with Oyster Bay, with Maples often climbing on a bulldozer himself to shape greens. When they opened in the early 1980s, both courses were acclaimed for their innovation and beauty.

His name quickly spread throughout the Carolinas, and hundreds of thousands of golfers enjoyed his two dozen works over the 1980s—from the Pit to the Pearls to the Witch. Maples is particularly proficient at building different styles for different purposes. The Pit, located on an abandoned sand quarry off Hwy. 5, just a few miles from the village, offers postcard views and demands some heroic shots; it's ideal for a resort course, but some might find it too demanding to play every day. For contrast there's Longleaf, located on Midland Road between Pinehurst and Southern Pines. Built on the former site of Starland Farms, a thoroughbred training center, Longleaf is an entertaining design that isn't so testing as to ward off potential members and buyers of surrounding property.

Maples wants players to have fun, and his courses are noted for their innovative cosmetics. In keeping with its equestrian heritage, Longleaf opened with little jockey statues on every tee. Unfortunately, they've been stolen, but the tee markers are replicas of fence posts. One par-three is even played over a steeplechase hedge, and part of the original race track is intact. At the Pit, tees are marked with old railroad spikes, except for the far back tees, which are old wrought-iron screws. "Dan's sending you a little message if you play from back there," says Craft. And at the Witch, golfers warming up aim at wooden "witches" 100, 150 and 200 yards from the practice tee, and you play either the black, orange or white tees.

Maples' business has thrived so much on word-of-mouth advertising that it wasn't until recently that he broke down and had a slick company brochure produced.

"Nearly all of our clients are golfers who've played our courses," Maples says. "I like it that way. I like for someone to think one of our courses is memorable enough that they'll hire us. That's what we're trying to accomplish, anyway. There's nothing worse than playing a round of golf, then afterward somebody says, 'What did you have on five?' and you've got to think hard to remember what the fifth hole was. A well-designed golf course will let you remember that hole right off without much trouble."

Those new clients have flung Maples from his office in the village to Spain and Hawaii, where new courses have recently opened; to Germany, where 27 holes have been designed but construction is held up because of red tape; and to Japan, where Maples signed a deal in the summer of 1991 to build a course. The foreign adventures can be gruesome at times—try spending 24 hours on a plane to Tokyo or losing your way in Paris' subway system, as Maples did once en route to Majorca.

But they're exciting challenges to a man who gets a rush talking about a former professor who taught his students to build cameras out of ladies' pocketbooks.

"We're really spoiled (building courses) in the Carolinas," Maples says. "I can pick up a phone, get equipment, no problem. Grass? No problem. Scheduling? No problem. If we need irrigation equipment, we call the suppliers and have it the next day. Europe's not that way. Majorca is just an island, it's very limited. We were working with old equipment. If we wanted grass, we'd have to send to the mainland. So we're used to scrapping in the trenches, working with something else.

"It's like a photography course I took one time. This guy built pinhole cameras. He could take a ladies' pocketbook and make a pinhole camera out of it. He's traveled all over Europe and taken pictures with that. He said you don't have to have $2,000 worth of equipment to have quality. He was right. You don't have to spend

$10 million to have quality. He sent you home and said, 'I want a picture back tomorrow.' You've got no darkroom and a homemade camera. You have to improvise. So when I go to Europe, I'm great at improvising. I can get there 10 different ways. I'm not street smart, but I'm what the equivalent would be in the woods,

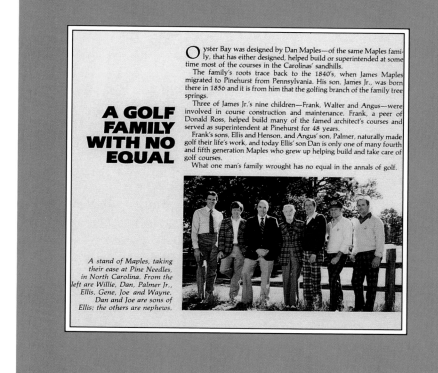

A GOLF FAMILY WITH NO EQUAL

Oyster Bay was designed by Dan Maples—of the same Maples family, that has either designed, helped build or superintended at some time most of the courses in the Carolinas' sandhills.

The family's roots trace back to the 1840's, when James Maples migrated to Pinehurst from Pennsylvania. His son, James Jr., was born there in 1856 and it is from him that the golfing branch of the family tree springs.

Three of James Jr.'s nine children—Frank, Walter and Angus—were involved in course construction and maintenance. Frank, a peer of Donald Ross, helped build many of the famed architect's courses and served as superintendent at Pinehurst for 48 years.

Frank's sons, Ellis and Henson, and Angus' son, Palmer, naturally made golf their life's work, and today Ellis' son Dan is only one of many fourth and fifth generation Maples who grew up helping build and take care of golf courses.

What one man's family wrought has no equal in the annals of golf.

A stand of Maples, taking their ease at Pine Needles, in North Carolina. From the left are Willie, Dan, Palmer Jr., Ellis, Gene, Joe and Wayne. Dan and Joe are sons of Ellis; the others are nephews.

grading and working the land and things. I don't have to have everything to get something quality."

Quality is something important to his hometown, too, as Maples globetrots to build golf courses. As much as he clings to his heritage and time-honored methods of polishing golf courses, Maples accepts that times change and towns grow.

"Things can't stand still—nothing can. A golf course can't stand still, a community can't stand still," says Maples. "The thing about growth is to try and control it the way you want it. They've done a nice job here in Pinehurst. They've kept the atmosphere of the village. It hasn't been harmed by the growth. People have been moving here ever since it started because it's such a clean, nice place to live. There's nothing here but pine forests and sand. Quality is what I'm most concerned about. As long as the growth is quality, I'm not worried." ■

"Golf Digest" featured the Maples in 1984, shortly after the opening of one of Dan's most acclaimed courses, Oyster Bay.

JOHNNY MILLER

Johnny Miller's three-wood on the 16th hole that beat Jack Nicklaus and Frank Beard in the 1974 World Open was one of the best shots he ever hit. Not as well remembered—but just as significant—were the 272 shots he hit in 1979.

Johnny Miller is perhaps best remembered around Pinehurst for his stirring playoff victory over Jack Nicklaus and Frank Beard for the 1974 World Open title. That was the year the blond bombshell from Northern California scorched the PGA Tour with wins in three straight tournaments to open the season, took first in five others and banked $353,021. He drove the ball long and straight, smothered flagsticks with his irons and seemed to have magnets drawing his putts to the cup.

Yet perhaps more significant but virtually forgotten is that Pinehurst, in a sense, gave the world of golf the second coming of Johnny Miller. Four nostalgic days in the Colgate/Hall of Fame Classic in 1979 helped Miller shake a three-year slump and rebounded him into a stretch in the early 1980s when he won five tournaments and finished among the Top 30 money earners four times. Miller didn't win (Tom Watson beat him in a playoff), but he left town a champion in his own mind.

"That tournament single-handedly got me out of my slump," says Miller. "It was like signaling to the rest of the PGA Tour that Johnny Miller could play golf again. It was a weight off my shoulders. Pinehurst's been very good to me. I haven't played it that many times, but it's the kind of course I wish we played every week on the tour if I was still active."

Miller, 44, has retired from active competition on the PGA Tour to concentrate on his golf-course design business and his color commentary position with NBC Sports' golf team. Today standing atop the tower behind the 18th green at Bay Hill Club in Orlando, Fla., preparing for NBC's telecast of The Nestle Invitational, Miller relives fond memories of Pinehurst—of one big tournament he won and another he didn't.

"The World Open in '74 was the biggest money tournament of the year," he says. "First prize was $60,000, which was unheard of at the time. Obviously, it was a big tourna-

ment and had a tremendous field. It was like a Players Championship of today."

The tournament format had been revised from the previous year, when it lasted two weeks and 144 holes and such notables as Nicklaus, Tom Weiskopf, Lee Trevino and even Miller, the reigning U.S. Open champion, didn't play. It was shortened to 72 holes in 1974, and the tournament coincided with the opening of the $2.5 million World Golf Hall of Fame. President Gerald Ford attended induction ceremonies, and among the 13 original inductees were eight still living: Ben Hogan, Sam Snead, Byron Nelson, Arnold Palmer, Gary Player, Gene Sarazen, Patty Berg and Nicklaus. Honored in memory were Bobby Jones, Walter Hagen, Francis Ouimet, Harry Vardon and Babe Zaharias.

"I feel lonely up here," Sarazen said from the dais, reflecting on the absence of Jones, Hagen and Ouimet. "All of my colleagues are gone. They're waiting on the tee in another Hall of Fame, expecting me to complete the foursome. But I keep telling them, 'You better go ahead and start without me, boys. I'll catch you on the back nine.'"

(Seventeen years later, they're still waiting. Sarazen was sighted in April, 1991, once again hitting the ceremonial first ball off the first tee at The Masters. He was 89 years old.)

No. 2 had been seared with 62s the previous year by Gibby Gilbert and Tom Watson, although the field as a whole had difficulty with the course and the generally chilly, windy November conditions. No one, not even champion Miller Barber, finished under par (and two of the eight rounds were played on No. 4). But the 62s stood out and Pinehurst responded with a golf course the following September that featured heavy, gnarly rough, which prompted enshrinee Sam Snead to grouse: "I've been coming here for many years, and I've never seen anything like this rough. You don't need rough on this golf course. There won't be any 62s shot this year."

He was right. But there was a 63—by Johnny Miller.

The first two rounds were split over courses No. 2 and 4, and Bob Murphy led after 18 holes

SIDEHILL PUTTS AND HOGAN
A reporter at the 1951 Ryder Cup matches in Pinehurst asked Sam Snead if his team's chances would be hurt by the cold, freezing weather that suddenly descended the first day of the matches.

"Nope," said Snead, "we ain't gonna be bothered by no weather. We ain't afraid of nothing."

Porky Oliver overheard and added, "Ole Sam's afraid of only three things on a golf course: lightning, a sidehill putt and Ben Hogan."

Miller hit the ball long and straight and right at the flag during his glory years in the early 1970s. He seared Pinehurst No. 2 with a 63 in 1974 in his first competitive round on the course (his first round of the World Open was played on course No. 4).

with a 65 on No. 2. New Hall of Famers Palmer and Player shot 78-72 and 74-77, respectively, and missed the cut, and Miller opened with a 73 on No. 4. Then in round two, he staked himself to a one-shot lead with an eight-under round that included a missed six-footer on 18 that

OFFICIAL PROGRAM

PGA

Championship

PINEHURST
COUNTRY CLUB
November 16-22, 1936

PRICE
15¢

Denny Shute won the PGA Championship in 1936 when it was played at Pinehurst, beating Jimmy Thomson 3-and-2. The PGA was played at match play from its inception in 1916 until 1958.

would have tied the course record 62. The round featured five birdies on the first six holes (including a 60-footer on the fifth hole) and could have been a shot better if not for a jungle of spike marks around the cup on 18.

"It looked like someone did some kind of an Indian dance around the hole," Miller said after his 63.

"It was like one of those old Johnny Miller blitzes," he remembers. "I dominated the course and scored a fairly easy 63, if there is such a thing. I went from darn near missing the cut to leading."

Miller and Nicklaus were tied at 209 after

three rounds, with Charles Coody and Bruce Devlin two back and Murphy and Beard trailing by three. The 27-year-old Miller, winner of $256,383 that year, reveled in the challenge of going head-to-head against the 34-year-old Nicklaus, who had earnings of $208,307 and a Tournament Players Championship that year.

"I wouldn't be surprised if both of us shot in the 60s head-to-head," Miller said. "I've held him at bay recently and I've had a lot of success against Jack, but I don't talk much about it. I know he's a better player than I am, but I'm not afraid of him. He's going to try to beat my brains out, but he's got to respect me because I've had such great success against him."

Miller and Nicklaus had been partners in the World Cup in Barbados the previous summer, with Miller winning the individual trophy and the duo winning the team title. "I played with Jack five straight days, and it was then I realized I could play with Jack Nicklaus," Miller says today.

It turned out that Miller and Nicklaus each shot one-over 72s, allowing Murphy and Beard to force a four-way playoff with 69s and 281 totals, three-under for 72 holes (only eight players beat par for the tournament).

The playoff started on 15, where TV cameras were set up. Beard scored a routine par on the par-three, leaving a birdie putt dead short that could have ended it there. Miller and Nicklaus got up-and-down from the fringe, and Murphy was eliminated after his tee ball found a greenside bunker.

Miller won the tournament with a two-putt birdie on 16 after Beard three-putted and Nicklaus missed a 12-footer for birdie. Miller hit a three-wood to eight feet—"The best shot under pressure I've ever hit," he says—and went from thinking he had to make an eagle to simply needing to two-putt.

"Nicklaus hit a huge drive and was last to hit," Miller says. "Beard hit his second to the front edge, then I hit my three-wood to eight feet. Nicklaus, knowing he had to hit it good, came over the top of, I think, a two-iron and pulled into the left rough. Then Nicklaus hit a weak chip. Then Beard did something I'll never forget. He putts by about 12 feet, then misses for his birdie. *Then he picked the ball up.* He didn't finish it. I guess he said, 'John's never going to three-putt from there.'

"Nicklaus missed his birdie putt and now all I had to do was two-putt from eight feet. I'll never forget the feeling. 'Geez, I don't even know how to two-putt from eight feet. How hard do you hit it to get close from eight feet?' I ran it by two and a half feet. So now, if I miss this coming back and Beard had finished with his par, he ties me. He made a real mental error. Of course, I made the putt, but by no means was it a gimme.

"To beat Jack Nicklaus in a playoff sort of capped off the year for me. I enjoyed playing No. 2. It was perfect for my game. It gave you enough room off the tee, you had extremely difficult approach shots, and if you hit it real bad off the tee, you had broom grass, sand and trees. To me that course is the perfect course for my game. It's the kind of course I like to design. It's the perfect test of golf because it's got difficult putting, it accepts the approach shot fairly and it penalizes the poor shot. It gives you enough room off the tee, versus U.S. Open courses, which give you only 25 or 30 yards."

A different Johnny Miller came to Pinehurst in 1979. He had been the talk of the tour in the early 1970s for his good play but now had become the talk of the tour for his bad play. He slid to 48th on the money list in 1977 and 111th in 1978, with only $17,400 in winnings. Miller hadn't won a tournament since early 1976.

"What's wrong with Johnny Miller?" the world wanted to know.

Miller responded that there wasn't anything wrong that a bunch of birdies and a little confidence couldn't solve.

"Before Pinehurst I played in the Lancome in Paris and won against a good field, and that signaled that maybe I was ready to play well again on the U.S. tour. I came home a week or two later and continued my good play," he says.

Miller opened with a 69 and then equaled his 1974 heroics with another 63. "It was amazing. It was like it was '73 or '74 all over again." he said. Watson moved into contention after three rounds, shooting a 65 to stand at 203, one behind Miller. The leaders talked about the confidence Miller was gaining on the eve of the final round.

"Confidence isn't something you get from reading a book," Miller said. "You can't have confidence if you've just hit four bad shots in a row. It comes from hitting a lot of good shots. Confidence is Seve Ballesteros hitting all those shots from the trees and making pars because he knows he's going to. That's the way Arnold Palmer used to be.

"The difference between 63 and 73 is so little it's scary. It may be the distance between the ears."

Said Watson: "What Johnny Miller has gone through the last three years is something every golfer hopes he won't have to suffer. But I think he has worked it out and will be up there. He just needed to regain some confidence in his swing. That 63 Friday helped. Confidence. That's all it takes."

Miller hit a three-iron on the 17th hole to one foot away and went one ahead of Watson, but a hooked tee shot on 18 led to a bogey and a playoff after a closing round of 70 and a 272 total. Watson won on the second playoff hole after Miller's approach went over the green.

"The three-iron on 17 was probably the best long iron I ever hit under pressure," he says. "On 18 I was pretty sure I was going to win and I hooked it off the tee. Unfortunately, I was in a spot where I was just dead. If I'd hooked it a little more it would have been fine, just a touch less I'd have been fine. But I stymied myself dead behind a pine tree, tried to hook it around and went in the bunker and made bogey. Watson parred two and I bogeyed. He's a tough guy to be in a playoff with. He's really tough."

But Johnny Miller was back. Pinehurst will always be special to him for those weeks in 1974 and 1979.

"I almost can't tell you how good the golf course is," he says. "It might not be the hardest golf course in the world, but for pleasure, for going out and having a pleasurable time with a smile on your face, it can't be beat. It's hard to get mad when you play Pinehurst.

"It reeks of golf, it has a definite golf spirit, very similar to a Pine Valley or Augusta National or Cypress Point. It's very blessed with that golfing spirit." ∎

HAPPY 50TH TO PINEHURST

What's this? Have fifty years gone by
    Since Pinehurst first was made
And almost thirty years since I
    Tin Whistle matches played?
It seems but yesterday, I'll swear,
    Those grand old friends of mine
Bade me to join a foursome there
    Upon the tee at nine.

Has Donald Ross for fifty years
    Been placing pits and traps
To punish with a thousand fears
    Both hook and slicing chaps?
For half a century can it be
    So fine a gentleman
Has labored spreading misery
    For all the golfing clan?

How long has stood the Holly Inn
    With welcome warm and true
To shelter those not taken in
    The Carolina new?
Those putting contests round the clock!
    Are they still going on?
What of that "snow-bird" golfing flock?
    Are all now dead and gone?

Well here's a toast to one and all,
    The ancient and the new;
To all the friendships I recall,
    And here's to Pinehurst, too!
Long may good fellows gather there
    (Come drain the cup that cheers!)
And find in golf release from care
    Another fifty years.

© 1945 by Edgar A. Guest

TOM WATSON

Tom Watson shot a 62 at Pinehurst in his second full year on the pro golf tour, 1973. Then the last three rounds of the World Open did him in. By 1978, Watson had learned how to win—and he collected two triumphs to join the ranks of the greats who'd walked before him.

om Watson knew how to play golf when he came to Pinehurst for the first time in 1973. But he didn't know how to win. There was still something separating him from all those magical golfers whose huge photographs graced the hallway leading toward the pro shop.

"I was very young when I played Pinehurst the first time, I guess it was my second full year on the tour," he says. "I can still see all those pictures in the clubhouse: Billy Joe Patton, Charlie Coe, Sam Snead, Byron Nelson, all those people who won the North and South when it was considered a major tournament."

The North and South Open was long gone when Watson was introduced to Pinehurst (it was discontinued in 1951, but the North and South Amateur has run continuously since 1901). Having grown up in Missouri and played golf collegiately at Stanford, Watson never had the opportunity to visit Pinehurst until the tour brought him here. Wake Forest golfers had Pinehurst No. 2; West Coast golfers had Pebble Beach. And though it wasn't a major tournament that ushered No. 2 back into the pro spotlight in 1973, it was a special one. The World Open lasted two weeks and 144 holes and offered a cash bonanza unheard of at the time: $100,000 to the winner.

It also produced some golf never before seen on a course that previously had yielded competitive course records of 65s to Ben Hogan and Johnny Palmer.

On the first day of the tournament, played in early November, Gibby Gilbert constructed a nine-under-par 62 with eight birdies, one eagle and one bogey, setting back for the moment his earlier plans that year to retire from the tour. He was playing horribly after the old American Golf Classic at Firestone in Akron, Ohio, and had lined up a job back home in Florida as a golf manufacturer's sales rep. But a lesson with noted instructor Jack Grout, he of Jack Nicklaus fame, put Gilbert's game together and helped him scorch No. 2, which now was played with bentgrass greens.

"It was certainly the greatest round of golf I've ever played," Gilbert said. "By far the greatest. It was just one of those days. It was a freak round. It was one of those rounds you dream about."

His peers dropped their jaws like Gilbert was dropping 20-foot birdies.

"I played 18 holes out there and I haven't seen a birdie hole yet," said Bobby Mitchell, who shot a one-over 72. "And he shoots it nine-under?"

"No way to shoot that kind of score out there," added Leonard Thompson.

World Golf Hall of Fame official John Derr was equally impressed. He interviewed Gilbert for a tape to be shown in the yet-to-be-completed shrine and concluded by predicting, "This record won't be equaled for 50 years."

He was wrong. It didn't last one week.

The year had been a good one for Tom Watson so far. He married childhood sweetheart Linda Rubin in July and had won nearly $58,000—44th on the money-winning list, guaranteeing his spot among the 60 players who would retain their cards for the following season. He shot lackluster 74s in the opening two rounds at Pinehurst and then retired to the practice range, where eight buckets of balls and some adjustments in his takeaway and set-up helped him improve to 69 and 68 and survive the cut.

Wednesday, Nov. 14, dawned warm and sunny (temperatures would hit an unseasonably warm 80 degrees). Watson turned in three-under, made a 12-foot putt on the par-five 10th to go four-under but three-putted the 13th for his only bogey. He then unleashed an assault that eclipsed the heroic stretch of four-under golf that Hobart Manley played on 14 through 18 in the 1951 North and South Amateur.

It began with an eight-iron on the 438-yard 14th that bounced into the cup for Watson's first career eagle on a par-four. "I was in a daze after that," Watson said. "I felt I could make everything after that."

He did. Ten-foot birdie on 15. On 16 green in two, two putts for birdie. Twenty-foot birdie on 17. Twelve-foot birdie on 18.

Another 62. John Derr had to update his videotape.

"You can't explain a round like that," Watson said after bolting to a six-shot lead at

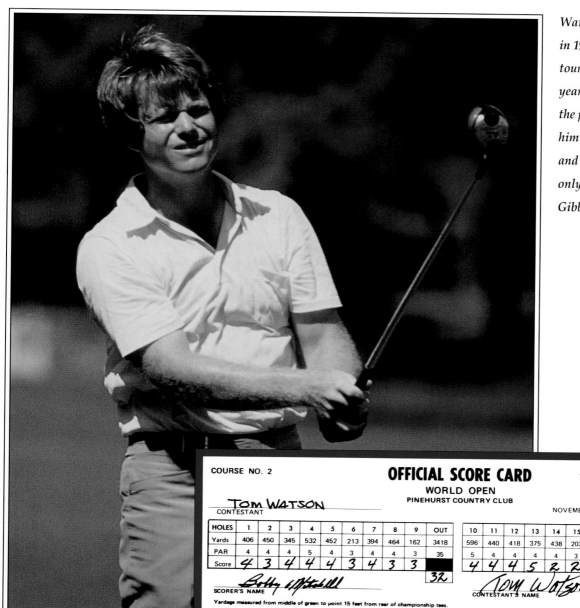

Watson shot 277 over 72 holes in 1978 to win his first tournament in Pinehurst. Five years earlier, an eagle-two on the par-four 14th hole helped him shoot a nine-under-par 62 and tie the course record set only days before by Gibby Gilbert.

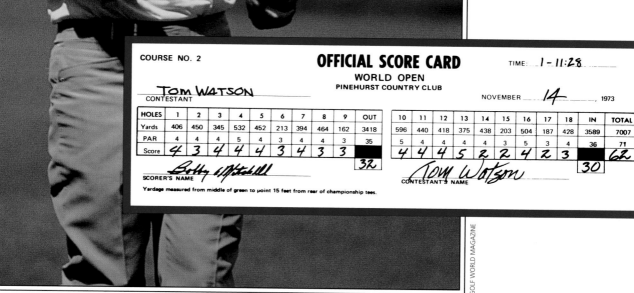

COURSE NO. 2									OFFICIAL SCORE CARD WORLD OPEN PINEHURST COUNTRY CLUB								TIME: 1 - 11:28		
TOM WATSON CONTESTANT															NOVEMBER 14, 1973				
HOLES	1	2	3	4	5	6	7	8	9	OUT	10	11	12	13	14	15	16	17	18	IN	TOTAL
Yards	406	450	345	532	452	213	394	464	162	3418	596	440	418	375	438	203	504	187	428	3589	7007
PAR	4	4	4	5	4	3	4	4	3	35	5	4	4	4	3	5	3	4	36	71
Score	4	3	4	4	4	3	4	3	3	32	4	4	4	5	2	2	4	2	3	30	62

SCORER'S NAME *Bobby Mitchell*

CONTESTANT'S NAME *Tom Watson*

Yardage measured from middle of green to point 15 feet from rear of championship tees.

347 (Gilbert was his nearest competitor, at two-under 353). "It just seemed to happen. Everything fell into place. I didn't work hard for it, either. I had confidence and just stepped up to the ball and hit it."

Watson was now in the lead, just as he had been 10 months earlier in the Hawaiian Open. He led by three strokes after three rounds in Hawaii, shot a 75 and finished third. "I choked and blew it," Watson remembered later in Pinehurst.

He'd still not learned to bring it home.

Watson exploded the next day with a 76—including an out-of-bounds tee shot on the fifth hole—and followed with another 76 and a 77. He finished in a tie for fourth with Al Geiberger at 576, six shots behind winner Miller Barber.

"I certainly didn't handle it very well," Watson says today. "The conditions turned very difficult. It was windy and cold and there was hardly anyone out there following the tournament. It's one thing to shoot good scores early in a tournament. It's another to win the golf tournament. I wasn't a winner when I

Most course maintenance 50 years ago was done by hand, on foot. Since the process was more difficult and took more manpower, less ground was actually maintained. The tees, landing areas and greens were well-manicured, but the rest of the course was left natural.

started. I had to learn to be a winner."

Watson would soon suffer another celebrated collapse—he led the 1974 U.S. Open at Winged Foot by one shot after three rounds but bombed to a 79 on Sunday and finished five behind Hale Irwin. Then he won the Western Open later that year, took first in the 1975 Byron Nelson Classic and won four times in 1977, including the Masters. Watson was the best golfer in the world when he teed off in the 1978 Colgate/Hall of Fame Classic. Make no mistake, he'd learned to win by now. And he was ready to win at Pinehurst—two years in a row, in fact.

"I love to win on great golf courses and Pinehurst is one of my favorites," he said that last week of August. "Just coming here gets me fired up."

The No. 2 course the players found in 1978 had been made more difficult by Pinehurst and tour officials after the assault it withstood a year earlier, when Hale Irwin shot 62 in the second round and won the tournament at 264, 20-under. That's the year Watson made the famous statement that haunted Pinehurst officials and had Donald Ross turning over in his grave: "The course is playing the easiest ever. The fairways are perfect and the greens are like dartboards."

The winning score in 1978 was 277—13 strokes higher. The rough was thick and high and the greens were firmer than a year before. Irwin led Watson by one shot after three rounds, but Irwin played badly early on Sunday and Watson led by five shots through the turn over Irwin, Howard Twitty and Tom Kite; the latter would have trailed by only four had he not called a penalty on himself when his ball moved a fraction of an inch on the fifth green. The leaders were bunched up when Watson bogeyed 12 and 15, but three straight closing pars held off the pursuers by one stroke each.

The 1979 Colgate/Hall of Fame Classic yielded two more 63s—one from Dana Quigley, another from Johnny Miller—and would be the last one played on No. 2 with the old bent greens. They were returned to bermuda following the tournament, which will be remembered not as much for Watson's victory but for the return to competitive stardom for Miller, who was mired in a lengthy slump. Miller led Watson and Keith Fergus by one stroke through three rounds, but bogeyed the 18th on Sunday to fall into a playoff with Watson. Miller missed the second green of the

playoff with his approach, couldn't get up and down and Watson won the $45,000 first prize with a three-footer for par. That gave him $447,636 winnings for the year and capped off a five-win season.

Watson would play one more tournament at Pinehurst, the following year when the event was the Hall of Fame Classic after Colgate dropped its sponsorship. He made the cut by one shot and fashioned a nondescript 283 as Phil Hancock won, eight shots ahead. Watson returned in 1988 to be inducted to the World Golf Hall of Fame but didn't have the chance to play No. 2. It's been 1987 since he finished among the Top 30 money winners on tour, but Watson hoped his game and putting stroke would be in order enough in 1991 to earn him a spot in the PGA Tour Championship, scheduled Oct. 31-Nov. 3.

"You bet I'm looking forward to coming

back," says Watson, knocking on wood. "I hope I'm lucky enough to get there. I understand the greens have been redesigned, or resurfaced, I should say. I hope they haven't been redesigned. I hear they're very close to the original greens. I'm looking forward to playing, even though they are bent. Hopefully, they'll get a break from the weather. If you have soft greens on No. 2 it takes the shot-making skill out of it.

"That's one of the problems they had in the '70s. I remember the greens were very soft. The comment 'throwing darts' came out and that was right. We played a little earlier in the season, and it was very hot. The bentgrass was not in very good shape. They watered it a lot. That's not the way Pinehurst was designed to be played.

"I remember how difficult a chipping golf course it was. All the greens were raised. That's very different from greens built today, particu-larly on TPC courses, that have sunken greens. The ball, when it hits, isn't rejected as much as it's collected. The ball hits around the edges and very likely will kick back toward the green. On Pinehurst No. 2 you can just miss the green a little bit, and under most playing conditions, if you hit it onto one of the slopes the ball might be 50 feet from the green."

Watson's most vivid memories of Pinehurst—besides his two victories, his eagle and the 62 in 1973—are of the resounding influence of golf that engulfs the community.

"I remember the smells and feels of the golf course, the pines of North Carolina," he says. "It was very special. I loved the gentility of Pinehurst. The area itself, it's such a very majestic area as far as golf's concerned. It reminds me of a quote I read not long ago. 'Golf is not a matter of life and death to these people. It's more important than that.'" ∎

BEN CRENSHAW

Ben Crenshaw won the first pro golf tournament he ever played in. His second was at Pinehurst, and he almost won that, too. Battling high winds, Crenshaw fashioned a 64 in the sixth round of the 1973 World Open that is among the best ever registered on No. 2. Donald Ross and his Sandhills masterpiece have been special to Crenshaw ever since.

Ben Crenshaw settles into a chair in the grill-room of Barton Creek Resort and Conference Center in the hills outside Austin, Texas, one bright December morning. Having breakfast at a nearby table is Darrell Royal, the former football coach at the University of Texas. Waiting in the wings is a photographer who later that morning will photograph Crenshaw on the site of a new golf course that he and partner Bill Coore have built.

Crenshaw takes a bite of banana nut bread, washes it down with a swig of coffee and nods out the window, past Tom Fazio's golf course to the distance, where his course is growing-in toward an April grand opening.

"There's no question, there's some of Donald Ross and Pinehurst No. 2 out there," he says. "Around the greens, we'll keep it really shaved close, top-dressed and aerated much like the green itself. The approach is the heart of a hole in most cases, and it's where you can deal with most classes of golfers. That's where the approach goes wrong in many courses today. There's no way in. You've got to fly the ball right to the pin. If you don't, you've had it. That's totally different from what the game is intended to be."

Crenshaw has been talking for some 30 minutes now about what's right with golf-course architecture and what's wrong—at least in his opinion.

For example: "Everyone knows that Pinehurst No. 2 is an extremely testing golf course, but it's there for the average player," Crenshaw says. "I'll say this, too. There are examples of architecture today that no question test the professional golfer and then they say they can be played by the average golfer, but that's not necessarily the case. While it's the aim and objective, and should be, the goal's not reached every time. Ross never once did not have the average player in mind. The easiest thing in the world to do is build a tough golf course. You go into another dimension when you do and truly make it playable and accommodating for the average player."

And this: "I think this instance of all or nothing on so many golf courses is totally wrong. First of all, golf was never meant to be a death or glory situation on every hole. It hasn't been that way for 100 years. A golfer cannot be continually punished if he's having an off-day. He cannot be battered into submission on every hole. That's why St. Andrews is so great. You can make a lot of bogeys, but it's hard to make a double. At the same time, you have to play excellent golf to make a birdie. That's what Pinehurst is all about."

In case you've not noticed, Ben Crenshaw is a devout fan of No. 2 and its architect, Donald Ross. He appreciates the course's quiet demeanor coupled with its ability to snap like a rattlesnake if you play mindless approach shots or chip with boxing gloves.

"Pinehurst could be, may be, the very best chipping course in the whole world," he says. "You have the ability and the opportunity to hit any club you wish, from a putter to a five-iron. You're allowed more choices. Because of the very small subtleties and the crowns on the greens and the little hollows and little-bitty swales that lie off of it, sometimes you get to a shot and it becomes a problem which shot to hit. That is the brilliance behind the making of those little undulations. The maintenance around he greens is important, because if the ground was not allowed to stay close, you lose the effect. The grass should be fairly well mowed around the greens to reveal those undulations. The great golf writer, Bernard Darwin, once said that long grass makes for bad golf courses. I think that's right.

"The idea of missing a green on so many courses today and hauling out a sand wedge is a mindless proposition. There's absolutely no choice involved. Therefore it is a dull pattern, quite frankly, very dull. At Pinehurst you've got a lot of choices. But it takes time to learn which shots to play. The more you play No. 2, the more you learn about it."

Crenshaw's first experiences on No. 2 vouch for that opinion. He came to Pinehurst in November, 1973, for the old World Open with shiny blond hair that covered his ears, a gaudy reputation as the "next, next Jack Nicklaus," three NCAA championship trophies and a bank account that bulged with more than $30,000

A 22-year-old Crenshaw watches a putt during the final round of the 1973 World Open. Two days earlier, a 64 had moved him into contention. He finished two strokes behind Miller Barber.

won just weeks before at the San Antonio-Texas Open. He'd visited Pinehurst before, to play in the Southern Amateur at the Country Club of North Carolina, but he'd never played No. 2. Already a student of the game and a strict traditionalist, the 21-year-old from Austin foamed at the mouth to learn more about this gem he'd read and heard so much about.

"I always wanted to play in the North and South, but we had final exams at the University of Texas every year when that was played," he says. "I played in the Southern Amateur in '71 but never got to play No. 2 until the World Open."

The World Open was Pinehurst's first foray into professional golf since Richard Tufts discontinued the North and South Open 21 years earlier. And what a return it was. The tournament was a 144-hole marathon that offered the largest purse ever for a golf tournament—$500,000, with $100,000 going to the winner—despite a modicum of controversy.

Jack Nicklaus didn't enter since he had previously planned to go elk hunting with Tom Weiskopf (known at the time as "the next Jack Nicklaus"), and Lee Trevino said he "couldn't stay anywhere two weeks in a row, not even home." Johnny Miller, the reigning U.S. Open champion, entered but withdrew because of illness. All of which left Arnold Palmer to remark, "It seems there's $100,000 just sitting there that nobody wants," and the wags in the press room to dub it the End of the World Open and the World Open and Shut.

The money was put up by Diamondhead Corp., which had owned Pinehurst for nearly three years, and it was seen in some quarters as an investment in additional real estate sales, a charge Diamondhead President Bill Maurer vigorously denied to the press. "We tried to do something different and worthwhile for golf, and nobody cared," he said. "I'll argue with anybody who says we did it strictly to sell land. We're selling all the land and condominiums that it's prudent to sell."

Bing Crosby, Fred MacMurray, James Garner and Stan Musial were among those who played in the Joe DiMaggio World Celebrity Pro-Am. Then Palmer, Gary Player, Miller Barber, Billy Casper, Bruce Crampton, Lanny Wadkins, Sam Snead and Gene Littler were among those who teed off on Thursday, Nov. 8. So did Tom Watson, who knew how to shoot good scores but hadn't learned how to win. And so did Crenshaw, who won his tour playing card in October at the Dunes Club at Myrtle Beach, won the first tournament he entered and moved on to Pinehurst. He and Allen Miller settled into the home of Peter Tufts just a wedge shot away on Cherokee Road from the second green at No. 2 for a memorable two weeks.

"I remember all the talk at the time about Ben being the next superstar," says Tufts. "But it hadn't gone to his head. He was very polite, just one of the nicest guys I've ever met. He wasn't too all-knowing or carried away with himself."

Crenshaw survived the Sunday cut after 72 holes but found himself 18 shots behind Watson after Wednesday's fifth round. Watson had just moved into the lead with a nine-under-par 62, tying the course record set in the opening round

---

"WOW! WOW! WOW!"

Once upon a time in Pinehurst there was a club called "The Wow! Wow! Wow! Rah! Rah! Rah! Club." Seriously. You can look it up.

Thankfully, the members voted on Feb. 15, 1904 to change the name to "The Tin Whistles." The following war cry was adopted:

"Yes we are, Yes, we are;
"Tin Whis'les! Tin Whis'les—Rah, Rah, Rah!
"Can we golf and can we sing;
"Can we make the echoes ring?
"Well, we rather think we can;
"For the rest just 'ASK THE MAN!'
"Yes we are; Yes, we are;
"Tin Whis'les! Tin Whis'les—Rah! Rah! Rah!"

The Tin Whistles have existed ever since as an exclusive club within a club at Pinehurst Country Club. Their counterparts for the fairer sex are called the Silver Foils.

A couple of stories have floated around about the origin of the Tin Whistles name. Many think it stands for the whistles that club members were known to blow upon reaching what is now the 12th tee of the No. 1 course. There was a spring house beside the tee in which members stored bootleg refreshments which they'd partake of after teeing off.

A story in the *Pinehurst Outlook*, however, traces the name all the way to a book being read by founding member Frederick W. Kenyon. A group of up to two dozen men would gather after dinner to talk about golf, the weather, politics and such and down a jigger or two. Some referred to this clique as "Kenyon's Golfers." Kenyon was reading a book at the time, *The Boss*, by Alfred Harris Lewis, in which there was a gang of rowdies called the Tin Whistles.

The group had 28 members in its first year, and its early by-laws included the following mandate:

"It shall be the duty of each member of the Tin Whistles to suppress the incipient conceit of any fellow member who thinks he is in line for the North and South Championship."

H.L. Milliken once said: "A large part of the club's charm will lie in our ability to be boys again. It would not do to take ourselves too seriously. So long as we continue to suppress the incipient conceit, so long as we continue to have some of the saving graces of nonsense, of boyhood, so long shall we remain sound and clean."

by Gibby Gilbert, and there were 24 players between Crenshaw and Watson. "I'm out of it," Crenshaw said.

But Crenshaw was learning more and more about No. 2's nuances each day—by sunlight on the course itself and during the evenings by listening to Tufts' fascinating tales of Donald Ross and how the Hogans and Demarets used to play No. 2. Thursday dawned bright and clear—and with a hard wind blowing from the north. The conditions took a toll on most of the field—Watson skied to a 76—but Crenshaw's approach shots were true all day, and he finished with a seven-under 64 (nine birdies and two bogeys). That vaulted him into second place with Barber and Jerry Heard. Given the conditions, that 64 might be best round competitive round ever played on No. 2.

"The 64 by Crenshaw today was better than the 62 I shot yesterday," Watson said. "The wind today was much worse. It made play much harder and it dried up the greens. Yesterday on some tough holes, like five, six and 11, you could drive right into the green without much worry."

Crenshaw, obviously, was pleased. "I think this is the best competitive round I've ever played," he said.

And he wasn't surprised. "No, I'm not stunned I'm doing this well," he responded in the interview room. "I've felt all along I could play with anybody if my game is together."

Watson shot another 76 in the seventh round on Friday, inching backward to the field, and Crenshaw shot a 73 to move within three of the lead. Entering Saturday's final 18, Watson was at 499, two-over-par, with Bobby Mitchell and Miller Barber at 501 and Crenshaw at 502. With a victory, Crenshaw would be two-for-two in pro tournaments and would have to make good on his promise to young Rick Tufts to buy the 14-year-old a motorcycle if he won.

Watson and Mitchell both faded early in the final round, leaving the baby-faced Crenshaw to battle the 42-year-old Barber, who remained up by one after the turn. Both birdied the par-five 10th with 15-foot putts and then followed soon with bogeys (Crenshaw on 11 and Barber on 12). Both birdied 14, leaving Crenshaw still one behind as they teed up on the par-five 16th, a hole Crenshaw felt he needed to birdie. He gave his drive a little extra moxie but wound up in jail when he yanked it 70 yards left of the fairway, in the woods between the base of the practice range and the 17th green. He bogeyed,

fell two behind and that ended it. Barber collected the $100,000 with a 69-570 total and Crenshaw won $44,175 for his 71-573.

"It wasn't inexperience," Crenshaw said. "I know how to win tournaments. And I wasn't feeling any pressure. I was just trying to hit the ball 500 yards."

Seventeen years later, Crenshaw has won 15 tournaments—including the 1984 Masters—and $4.5 million dollars. If he's played better than that 64, he's not sure when.

"To this day, that's one of the best rounds of golf I've ever played," he says. "It was really gusty wind, and I squeezed everything possible out of that round. The key was that I was pin-high with my approaches all day. I'll never forget that round."

His experiences on No. 2 and respect for the layout endure to the extent that he chose his business partner in part because both share Ross's classic design philosophy over the penal approach. Bill Coore is a native of Thomasville, N.C., and played Pinehurst often growing up. His work on Pete Dye's course-building crews took him to Texas in the 1970s. When Crenshaw saw Coore's design of Rockport Country Club, the match was made.

"I liked what I saw," Crenshaw says. "I could see the strategic design philosophy. We've talked about No. 2 so much. We've talked about every hole, over and over. And I've got to say, courses 1 and 3 are wonderful golf courses, too. They have some marvelous holes, little holes only 320 to 380 yards. I just don't think people understand how good those holes are. They're filled with interest. They're shorter, but there's plenty of character to them. But No. 2 is like the ideal." ■

A view of the village during the early 1900s. In the background is the Holly Inn. The building to the right exists today (housing the Villager Deli and several other shops).

CURTIS STRANGE

The Wake Forest sensation played "hit-it-go-chase-it" for two North and South Amateurs in the mid-1970s. He did both well enough to collect two Putter Boys and a load of memories.

Take one 19-year-old, put him in a town where he can play his favorite game in the world, send his college buddies with him, give him a truckload of trophies and a scrapbook of memories. The result is a fan for life.

"Pinehurst was just a place you fell in love with," says Curtis Strange, the two-time U.S. Open champion.

Strange is playing a practice round at Doral Country Club in Miami on this muggy February afternoon. Since last playing Pinehurst No. 2 in the Hall of Fame Classic in 1982—he finished tied for third and pocketed $17,000—Strange has won $4.4 million, 14 tournaments and earns extra lunch money by representing a sporting goods manufacturer and a company that lets you make phone calls from 747s.

Strange showed signs of greatness early by

Strange follows a drive during 1977 Tour School.

taking Pinehurst by storm in the mid-1970s. With legendary caddie Fletcher Gaines at his side, the Wake Forest University sophomore won the 1975 North and South Amateur by shaving defending champion George Burns, then followed with the 1976 crown by handily ousting Fred Ridley.

"He's a good man, Fletcher," Strange says as playing partner Bobby Wadkins hits an approach shot on the second hole of the Blue Monster course. The golf course he's playing, incidentally, was designed by Dick Wilson, then remodeled by Robert Von Hagge. Both Wilson and Von Hagge got their starts in the golf-course architecture field under the expertise of Pinehurst's own Donald J. Ross.

"We had a lot of fun," Strange says of the cherubic Gaines, who still dispenses good advice on the greens and sly humor around the 90 holes at Pinehurst Country Club. "He was a great help. I really got to know No. 2 with Fletcher. Playing those greens requires a lot of local knowledge. Back then, I was just kind of booming it. I didn't have much management or strategy on the golf course. I would hit it long and go chase it. Fletcher tried to condense that strength and manage me around. He did a great job. He read all my putts."

Pinehurst has always been a staple on the competitive rota of Wake Forest golfers. When the school was a college and located north of Raleigh, Arnold Palmer would visit for the North and South. Then it moved to Winston-Salem in 1956, became a university and Coach Jesse Haddock began turning out All-Americans nearly every year: Jay Sigel, Jack Lewis, Leonard Thompson, Lanny Wadkins, Joe Inman, Jim Simons, to mention a few. Sigel never turned pro and still is a regular in the North and South. And Thompson once said he'd like to have his ashes strewn across Pinehurst No. 2.

"Pinehurst has been a big part of the program," says Haddock. "If the weather's bad here we'd get on the road and go to Pinehurst. They say it's in some kind of thermal belt. I don't know, but it did always seem a little warmer there.

"The North and South was always played at

the break of spring. There's no place more beautiful than Pinehurst in the spring of the year. There's something about Pinehurst. You turn off Highway 5 and go into the village, there's an aura or something that gets to all five senses."

All of Haddock's senses were aroused late one particular night, a moment some late-1970s Deacons still giggle about. The team was staying in the Pinehurst Hotel during the old Pinehurst Intercollegiate and one Deacon, Gary Pinns, had missed 11 p.m. curfew. Haddock woke the whole team up, called a team meeting and waited on the eventual arrival of Pinns.

"To this day Pinns says it was innocent," says current touring pro Robert Wrenn, a 1981 Wake graduate. "He says he was playing the guitar with a girl that worked in the pro shop."

Haddock has been known for his imaginative methods for getting his points across, and on this night his fist made a modest dent in the hotel wall. Pinns, trying to circumvent his route to the dog house, attempted the next morning to mend the dent with toothpaste. That worked to an extent. A wall-hanging strategically moved finished the repair job.

"I don't know if you should tell that story," Haddock says. "We might get a bill."

Haddock had a juggernaut in 1974. Strange, Jay Haas, Bob Byman and David Thore—some say the best college golf team ever—won the NCAA title that year, and Strange, a freshman, was the medalist. He was still the defending champion when the 1975 North and South

A PINEHURST INSTITUTION

Besides Curtis Strange, the Pinehurst institution named Fletcher Gaines has helped legions of players to victory. Tom Robbins won nine senior championships at Pinehurst and 10 senior qualifying medals, and Gaines caddied every round. Robbins delighted in picking on Gaines, calling him, "Class B." Robbins often asked following a round: "Hey, what do you give a Class B caddie? Three bucks."

Gaines would glower back. "Yeah, you give me three bucks and I'll give you the wrong club."

Gaines has hauled the bags of noted golfers like Porky Oliver, Julius Boros and Tommy Armour. He even caddied for Donald Ross. "Ross used to hate it when someone broke par on No. 2," he says. "He always considered par to be an elusive animal and never wanted to see anybody shoot in the 60s." Gaines was also an excellent golfer in his prime, once in the 1960s playing four straight rounds from the back tees of No. 2 and shooting 71-71-72-71—285, three-under par.

"I only missed one fairway all week and I didn't three-putt once," he once told local newspaper columnist Bill Jones. "The secret to putting the greens on No. 2 is not to play as much break as you think and to remember that all putts under six feet will not break if hit firmly towards the cup."

"Fletcher instills a sense of confidence in a golfer that he can't get anywhere else," says Pinehurst pro Rich Wainwright. "He knows the greens. Lord o' mercy, he knows the greens."

rolled around, and all the Deacons were entered. Strange had added to his resume just weeks before, having won the Atlantic Coast Conference title at Foxfire Country Club, just outside Pinehurst. One match in the North and South provided insight into the tenacious attitude Strange would soon show the world and use to his advantage on the back nine Sundays of Open week.

The tournament started with a victory over a high school kid from Barrington, Ill. Strange won the match, 4-and-2, but was impressed enough with his opponent that he mentioned him to Haddock. "Coach, you got to see this kid," Strange said.

Haddock replied that he already knew of Gary Hallberg. "We're recruiting him," Haddock said.

Strange made quick work of his next three opponents—all his matches were over by the 16th hole—and ran up against teammate Thore, his roommate that week. By the time they reached the first tee, though, Thore may as well have been a perfect stranger.

"I probably didn't say two words all day," Strange said after the match. "I didn't want to put him at ease. When you step up on the first tee, you forget about friendship. Was it hard for me to have the killer instinct playing David? No. It was the same as it always is. During the match, he was just another player standing in my way of winning the championship."

Strange was three-up on the back nine, but the lead gradually slipped away, with the golfer getting irritated and the caddie trying to halt the skid. "Curtis would get a little upset over bad shots," Gaines says, "because he thought it was impossible for him to hit a bad shot. He's still that way today."

The match was even when they hit their tee shots to the par-three 17th, both about 10 feet away. "I'll never forget," Strange says today, "I think David's caddy was trying to play something on me. He said, 'Come on, David, we'll make this and go one-up.' I mumbled something nasty to him and made mine and that was all she wrote."

Strange then hit a nine-iron to within inches

on 18 and won, 2-up.

"We went after each other hard," Strange says. "That's match play. When you're playing pretty much a regional tournament and all your teammates are playing, that's bound to happen sometimes."

George Burns was the hot name in amateur golf that year. A former football player at the University of Maryland, Burns took his bum knee and four-handicap and joined the Terrapin golf team as 10th man. By his junior and senior years, he'd become No. 1 man on the team. He graduated in 1972 and had been on the amateur circuit for three years. He was also the defending North and South champion.

"He was the talk of the tournament," Strange remembers. "He was the best amateur and was winning everything."

Strange defeated Peter Green in his semifinal match, 3-and-2, and moved into the finals against Burns. The match was a classic—"the best I've ever been involved in," Gaines says. Burns had a three-hole lead after nine holes of the 36-hole match, but Strange cut that to a one-hole deficit after 18, and they were never more than a hole apart in the afternoon. The match was even when their tee shots came to rest on the 36th hole—Strange's on the short grass and Burns' just barely in the rough.

"We caddied by sight then, we didn't have any sprinkler heads," Fletcher says. "I saw Burns' caddy, Julius Richardson, pull out a five-iron. I looked at Curtis. 'We've got him now,' I told him. I knew that five-iron was gone."

Gaines was right, though newspaper reports said it was a six-iron. Burns caught a flier, hit his ball over the green and over the cart path. "Anything over that green is dead," Strange says. "I had an easy shot to the green, I think I hit an eight, and two-putted from about 30 feet to win. That was a big win for me."

In 1976, Strange became the first player to repeat as North and South champion since Billy Joe Patton 13 years earlier. Strange's trek to the final included an eagle on the par-five 16th in a 3-and-2 win over Buddy Alexander (Strange hit a one-iron 210 yards to two feet), and his championship opponent was Fred Ridley, the defending U.S. Amateur champion.

"Fred beat me the year before in the Amateur, so I kinda wanted a go at him," says Strange, who claimed an easy 6-and-5 victory.

Strange continued to play annually in the pro tournaments held each August or September, marveling more and more each year over

AN OLD-FASHIONED BIRDIE
Donald Ross would have been proud of the shot Gastonia's Charles Smith hit on the second hole of No. 2 during the 1960 North and South Amateur semifinals. Given the day's equipment, the shot was certainly one of the finest ever hit in Pinehurst in a pressure situation.

Smith, who would later play on the 1963 Walker Cup team captained by Richard Tufts, was in his second extra hole against Glenn Johnson. The second, a par-four that measures over 440 yards from the back tees, was built to be an animal requiring a large drive and a long-iron or even a fairway wood. Today, powerful young college golfers have hit eight and nine-irons into the green.

But Smith chose his four-wood, aimed left-center of the green and cut the ball into the back-right pin position. The ball stopped eight feet from the flag, Smith made his birdie for the win and went on to collect the championship the next day with a 5-and-3 win over Peter Green.

No. 2. He still lists it among his top five courses in the world and laments the tour doesn't stop regularly in Pinehurst.

"One thing I like about No. 2 is that it's not busy, and by busy meaning so many bunkers and so many grass bunkers and humps and mounds and water you've got to deal with," Strange says. "What you see is what you get. There's nothing fancy, and fancy isn't necessarily good, either. We, all of us architects today, ought to look at those types of courses instead of some of the newer ones we're building.

"You've got to hit good golf shots. When you miss greens you've got to use your imagination. You're not solely stuck on one shot out of the rough. You have options. That will bring out the good or bad in a player. I learned a lot playing there."

Not only did Strange win two North and Souths in Pinehurst. He won that ACC at Foxfire, won a Pinehurst Intercollegiate, teed it up as an amateur in several professional tournaments and even got his PGA Tour Card at qualifying school at Pinehurst in 1977. That came less than a year after Strange bogeyed three of the final five holes in the Tour School in Brownsville, Texas, to miss his card by one shot. Gaines buttered his bread that June with some side bets with the caddie of Lance Suzuki, who finished in the top five with Strange. "Curtis

didn't know that, though," Gaines says. "But I won 30 bucks."

It all adds up to a special place to Strange.

"Some of my proudest moments were some of the scores I shot there," he says. "Granted, it was match play. I won two in a row, which was lucky. But a lot of playing good has to do with where you are and you enjoy it so much and you get fired up. I shot some really good scores and hit a lot of good shots there. When you go to a place like Pinehurst and do well it means so much more than winning on a golf course no one's ever heard of. My name will be on that plaque in the clubhouse for a long time."

***

Fletcher Gaines looks like the cat who swallowed the canary one afternoon outside the caddie room at Pinehurst Country Club as he recalls working for Strange during the mid-1970s. He grips a make-believe golf club, takes his hands over his shoulder and says:

"Curtis would get it back to here and say, 'Is it square?' I didn't know what the hell he meant, 'Was it square?' But I'd say, 'Yeah, looks square to me.'"

Strange is told a few days later that his faithful Pinehurst caddie had been giving him bogus swing analysis. "Fletcher Gaines," he says. "That old son of a bitch."

Curtis Strange said that with a smile. ∎

An aerial view of the front nine of No. 2 and the village taken sometime between 1923 and 1935. Note the greens are still sand and that there are patches of unmowed fairway between tees, landing areas and greens. In the lower right-hand corner is a dogleg right hole that is currently the seventh hole. You can see where it was constructed out of two straight-away holes.

Everyone except the dog seems to be mesmerized by a golf exhibition from some 50 years ago.

BOOK TWO

PINEHURST JOURNAL

*Golf's library is the richest of any sport. Pinehurst is fortunate
to have caught the fancy of many of the game's finest writers,
and following is a smorgasbord from some of the best.*

PINEHURST REVISITED

BY CHARLES PRICE

Mr. Price has one great claim to golf fame: he was five-under-par after the first six holes of the 1948 North and South Open on Pinehurst No. 2. Then he took a nine on the seventh hole, making room for eventual champion Toney Penna. He retired from competitive golf in 1953 and later remarked: "I retired at 28, the same age at which Bobby Jones retired. The difference is Jones retired because he beat everybody and I retired because I couldn't beat anybody." What Price could do was write about golf, and he's done so eloquently in numerous magazines and a variety of books the last 45 years. He makes his home in Pinehurst, and following is an adaptation of several earlier columns on life around here.

I t's been more than forty years since I first played golf in Pinehurst and then, soon afterward, began working here. I became the star reporter for the *Pinehurst Outlook*, in part because I could spell, because I knew the difference between a backswing and a bogey, and because I owned a car, if you want to call a '46 Hudson that. But mainly it was because I was willing to work for fifty dollars a week.

As newspapering goes, Pinehurst then was not exactly Chicago. I covered flower shows, pony races, putting contests, lawn bowling, birdwatching, croquet tournaments, church sermons, road pavings, barn burnings and Alan Ladd movies. Because I owned a suit, I also wrote the society column. ("Mrs. Abigail Van Heusenduff, who winters on Piney Thorn Drive, recently returned from a trip to her home in Philadelphia, where she had her watch set.")

If I'm implying that Pinehurst at the height of the season was asleep, you should have seen it in the summer. It went into a coma then. Everything closed down: the shops, the theater, what passed for a drug store, and the barber shop, where I used to watch haircuts on rainy afternoons.

Two of the country club's courses were left to grow wild until September, although it might as well have been all three. The Carolina, the Holly Inn, and every other place of lodging were shuttered. Both restaurants stayed closed until October, even Henri's, where during the rest of the year I used to have *coq au vin* and Pouilly Fuisse while records of French opera popped and cracked and wheezed in the background and while Henri and Henriette told me about life on the Left Bank before the Nazis came. Life was never quite so mellow, if you could stay awake during the summer. And I made fifty dollars a week.

If that sounds like a complaint, the fact was you couldn't spend fifty dollars a week in Pinehurst then and, during the summer, you could hardly give it away. From October to May, what's more, I moonlighted at the Dunes Club, a high-class roadhouse with a floor show and a casino that stood halfway between Pinehurst and Southern Pines on Midland

Road. It was owned by a man named Carl Andrews, who got you coming and going. He also owned the nursing home on Route 5.

Mine was not altogether an honorable job, but it beat being a busboy. To be blunt, I was a shill. I'd march into the Dunes with a date on my arm, talk golf with the tourists at the bar, watch the show with a couple of steaks Diane at a ringside table, and then cavalierly sign the check—for which I never got a bill. I also never got paid.

After dinner, I'd saunter into the casino, where I'd purchase fifty dollars' worth of chips, making sure nobody but the cashier saw that I didn't pay for them. If there was an empty craps table, I'd start there. Sooner or later, customers would join in. Then I'd nonchalantly move to the roulette wheel, and then the blackjack table. If by some miracle I won, I'd cash in my chips and tell the cashier in a loud voice to credit my account.

All the girls in and around Pinehurst then thought I was rich and romantic, and a little bit naughty. When the Dunes Club was open, I had to beat them off with a brassie. But when it was closed, half of them couldn't remember my name.

With the passage of forty years, though, all that has changed. The Dunes Club burned down years ago, and Henri and Henriette went back to Paris even before that. (Their restaurant became the Red Door and is now The Coves.) A girl I used to take to both places was a grandmother three times over the last time I saw her, which was during the World Open some fifteen years ago. Her memory was not all it should have been. "Well, I de-*clay*-uh," she said, "if it isn't ol' Charley Pride! Whacha doing these days?"

"I'm a steamfitter."

"Oh," she said, and wandered off to watch Arnold Palmer. The last I heard, she had checked into Carl Andrews' nursing home.

I can't argue that things *haven't* changed in Pinehurst, given the past forty years. But so have things changed in New York, where I mainly lived afterward for twenty years, and on Hilton Head Island, where I lived for most of the next twenty.

V. Weller + ©

But in Pinehurst the changes have been gradual, almost too gradual to notice, the way trees are said to grow in Brooklyn. The country club has been open year round for some time now and has added four more courses to the original three. Other country clubs have sprung up all over the place, notably the Country Club of North Carolina, which may be the only golf development ever that lived up to what its brochures said it would be. I know. I moved to Hilton Head before it had a bridge and then watched 20,000 people somehow find it fashionable to move to a swamp.

The main thing, though, is that Pinehurst still maintains the ambiance of total golf. The aura of it is inside every shop, on every street corner, along every footpath. You cannot drink the cup of the game as fully anywhere else this side of St. Andrews, Scotland. The village doesn't just fabricate the game with ridiculous courses that look like moonscapes, with hot-shot amateurs and hot-dog pros dressed in polyester knickers and Corfam shoes, with

cutesy-cutesy street names like Niblick Road or Mashie Lane. To get to a point you only have to make to people who have never been here, Pinehurst *is* golf. The game's not just an amenity. Take golf out of Pinehurst—indeed, the Sandhills—and what have you got left? A bigger and better artillery range for Ft. Bragg.

Golf and Pinehurst have been inseparably one since the turn of the century, or not long after the game first took hold in America. People have always come here primarily to partake of its golf, not its social season, let's say, or its waters, even its weather. For all its lawns and courts, and for all the people frolicking on both, neither do they come here just for tennis, croquet or bowls, at least not any more than they'd go to Forest Hills for golf.

By and large, golfers visit Pinehurst, or settle here, for the seclusion it offered two world wars ago, for the *fin de siecle* atmosphere that makes it easier to hire a horse-and-buggy than hail a taxi, for gossip in the post office or the Pine Crest or the Deli that makes a daily paper a bother and

Southern Pines artist Vivien Weller used Ken Crow, Pinehurst's head teaching professional, as the model for this painting.

altogether superfluous, for an eerie quiet at night that has some newcomers waking up in the middle of it wondering what that noise was, only to discover it was a dog barking in the next county. But, preeminently, they come here to get away from all the things that golf elsewhere has unfortunately become heir to.

Pinehurst people don't try to outdo each other with homes that look like Concordes straining for airspeed. They don't drive golf carts with dry bars or Rolls-Royce grilles. They have no use for neon signs, bus tours, fat farms, night clubs, stretch limos, outsized swimming pools, art galleries that insult your taste, antique shops full of bric-a-brac made a week ago, restaurants

that award themselves three stars, or any of the rest of the confetti with which other golf resorts today carnivalize themselves.

For all its golf courses—nearly 40 within 14 miles—Pinehurst has not had an annual event on the PGA Tour's calendar since the late and not very lamented World Open. To accommodate it, the No. 2 Course was savaged by some California architects who thought they could improve on what Donald Ross had done, which was a little like installing an elevator in Monticello. Then, in 1978, architect Tom Fazio, with some over-the-shoulder advice from this writer, restored 26 bunkers and widened the

The village in the springtime. This corner used to house the General Store and Post Office.

fairways to meet the bunkers designed to guard them. Putting surfaces were returned to the original perimeters that made No. 2 a masterpiece in the fast-fading art of chipping and pitching.

Dozens of Ross's old pin positions then manifested themselves. Fairways presented three lines of attack to the greens, not just the one that the narrow fairways dictated. No. 2 became once again an adventure in golf, not a gymnasium for it, and one of the very rare courses without a single hole out of character with the rest. The result is what some people, golf people, think ought to somehow be declared a national treasure.

Whatever, No. 2 fits hand-in-glove with the button-down attitude and brown-shoe philosophy of a village dedicated to an old, old game, one that was already old, in fact, when the Mayflower landed. The next generation of golfers may shrug their shoulders at that, as I did when I made fifty dollars a week working for the *Outlook.*

But when the last yuppie throws the last cap in the air, when he shakes the last clenched fist at the heavens, when he gives the last high-five—after the last hurrah of youth, in other words—he'll begin to know what style is in golf as opposed to the merely fashionable, and why Pinehurst is here and has been for almost a century. ∎

THE MAN WHO WAS PINEHURST

By HERBERT WARREN WIND

Mr. Wind has enlightened golf enthusiasts for nearly five decades with his detailed and insightful accounts of the game, its venues and its people. Wind wrote golf for "The New Yorker" and "Sports Illustrated" from 1947 until retiring in 1990 and authored a dozen or so books on golf. He's best remembered for "The Story of American Golf" and titles he co-authored with Ben Hogan, Gene Sarazen and Jack Nicklaus. Wind, who lives in Weston, Mass., was a close friend of Richard Tufts, and following are some of his memories of the man he admired "probably more than any I met in golf."

I t is very difficult to know what there was about Richard S. "Dick" Tufts that made so many people so fond of him and devoted to him. In the final analysis, a good part of this was surely the sense of responsibility with which he approached golf, and everything else, along with his knowledge of every phase of the game from the logic of its rules and the true principles of the golf swing to the fundamentals of golf-course architecture and the value of international competition. Dick was a man with a strong Yankee conscience and high personal standards, and he would have laughed out loud if anyone had told him of his extraordinary personal charm. I think it was based on his generosity of spirit. He assumed that many of his friends in golf were at least as well-informed and discerning as he was. We learned a vast amount about golf and many other things from him, and we remembered him well because he enriched our lives.

I believe that the best way for me to explain what Dick Tufts did for those of us who were lucky enough to know him is to set down a number of glimpses of him with the hope that they will fit together like the pieces of a jigsaw puzzle and provide an insight into this remarkable man.

***

I had my first real conversation with Dick about a week after the one-sided American victory over the British and Irish team in the 1955 Walker Cup match at St. Andrews. There was a full week between the conclusion of the match and the start of the British Amateur Championship at Lytham St. Annes. Dick and his wife, Allie, spent the off-week at Turnberry, where the Firth of Clyde merges with the Atlantic. In those days, no other American I knew had ever been to Turnberry or to Dornoch, two superlative Scottish courses that the Tufts had known for years. On the Monday when the British Amateur got under way, I had

a chance to talk with Dick after breakfast in the Hotel Majestic in St. Annes-on-the-Sea. At my request, he told me which British and American players I would do well to watch that week and why he thought so. He mentioned the holes at Lytham that he felt might play a pivotal part in the matches. We chatted for a while. His kindness may have been based to some extent on my being from Brockton, Massachusetts, which is not far from Medford, the home of the Tufts family, and from Watertown, the site of the Oakley Country Club, the Tufts family's course, where, in 1899, they had installed Donald Ross, a young Scot from Dornoch, to serve as the professional and as the course superintendent. On second thought, I think my coming from Massachusetts had nothing to do with it at all. Dick was simply a very considerate man. This was one of the my first trips to Britain and I was just beginning to appreciate what a great deal there was to learn. Oh, yes. I ran out of American cigarettes at St. Annes—you couldn't buy them anyplace in Europe—but Allie, a good-looking woman with a bright, easy manner, gave me a carton of Lucky Strikes since she was flying home the next day. I mention this because I learned some time afterwards that many of the regular visitors to Pinehurst had regarded young Richard Tufts—he graduated from Harvard in 1917—as such a proper young man that they were taken off guard when he chose to marry Alice Vail, the daughter of Pinehurst regulars, for she was a modern girl who liked to smoke, drink and enjoy life.

***

As we all know, Pinehurst was founded in 1895 by James W. Tufts as a fairly modest winter health resort in the Sandhills region of North Carolina, where the longleaf pines give the air a salubrious quality. In 1900, Donald Ross became the golf professional at Pinehurst. Ross had no formal experience as a golf-course architect, but when he set about revising the

Richard Tufts wore his Tin Whistles blazer when he posed for this portrait with Southern Pines artist Beth Turner Bowers.

original nine holes that James Tufts had built, he reached back and tried to give them something of the look and character of the much-admired linksland course in Dornoch on which he had grown up. The next year, he added nine new holes to complete Pinehurst No. 1. Despite its sand greens, it was very pleasant to play, and it became exceedingly popular. The quality of Ross's work increased with experience. When the 18 holes of Pinehurst No. 2 were completed in 1907, the course, a lengthy one for that time, created a considerable stir. The 18 holes on Pinehurst No. 3 were open for play in 1910, and Pinehurst No. 4, another 18-hole course, was opened for play in 1919. Pinehurst then had the distinction of being the first golf resort in the world to offer its patrons 72 holes of first-class golf. Pinehurst No. 2, the most demanding of the four courses, became the venue of the annual North and South Open and the North and South Amateur, which were established just after the turn of the century. They grew into big events, surpassed in importance only by the national championships conducted by the United States Golf Association and possibly by the Western and the Metropolitan championships.

Along with the superior golf, Pinehurst presented its well-to-do clientele with the last word in equestrian sports, excellent facilities for tennis and the other popular games, and, most significant of all, the opportunity to meet the kind of people they enjoyed being with. Dozens of families returned year after year. Knowing his conscientious nature, I am certain that during his formative years Dick Tufts must have frequently reminded himself how lucky he was to be part of this bright and happy realm. (As a boy of eight, he took golf lessons from Donald Ross, the start of their close lifelong friendship.) In 1902, Dick's father, Leonard Tufts, had, upon the death of his father, James W. Tufts, taken over the operation of Pinehurst, and, in his quiet way, he had kept the facilities of the resort nicely up to date while preserving

a good deal of the charm of its early days. When Dick, the oldest of his three sons, returned home after serving in the Navy during the First World War, his father gradually turned the operation of Pinehurst over to him. He taught Dick all he knew and was always there to help out when an experienced hand was needed.

***

I first spent some time with Dick in Pinehurst in the summer of 1957 on my second visit to the resort. After we had chatted one morning, he invited me to lunch in the unfancy dining room of the Pinehurst Country Club. Nice old ladies waited on you. I ordered the tomato soup to start with, because the room had the definite feel of New England, and I knew that my mother, who liked simple food, would have ordered it. Dick also ordered the tomato soup. For my main course I had codfish cakes with pickled beets on the side—my mother would have done that. Dick smiled at me and told the waitress that he would have the same thing. For dessert, after studying the menu briefly, I ordered my mother's all-time favorite, canned halves of Bartlett pears. Dick ordered the same thing. Then he looked at me admiringly. "You certainly know how to eat," he said.

***

On my trips to Pinehurst the high spot invariably was a good, long talk with Dick in the offices of Pinehurst Inc., which looked out on the typical New England village green that Frederick Law Olmsted had designed. Until 1962, when a slight remodeling job was done without Dick's knowing it during the weeks he was away on summer vacation, his office on the ground floor had looked the same as it did when he had moved into it decades before. A dark-stained wood floor and varnished wood walls set off the flat-topped oak desks, with old New England illustrated calendars and dark green window shades supplying the only splashes of gaiety. When you visited Dick there, you felt that at any moment a local citizen might burst into the room shouting, "Rutherford B. Hayes is our new President!" I never saw Dick quite as excited as he was in the late spring of 1958 shortly after he had returned from a meeting in Washington, D.C., at which the representatives of the amateur golf associations of 35 countries had established the World Amateur Golf Council and arranged for the first World Amateur Team Championship to be played at St. Andrews that October. "I had no

---

CREED OF THE AMATEUR

The work that I have done has been done for amateur sport, and I hope that you won't mind if I leave you with my creed on amateurism. Amateurism, after all, must be the backbone of all sport, golf or otherwise. In my mind an amateur is one who competes in a sport for the joy of playing, for the companionship it affords, for health-giving exercise, and for relaxation from more serious matters. As a part of this light-hearted approach to the game, he accepts cheerfully all adverse breaks, is considerate of his opponent, plays the game fairly and squarely in accordance with its rules, maintains self-control, and strives to do his best, not in order to win, but rather as a test of his own skill and ability. These are his only interests, and, in them, material considerations have no part. The returns which amateur sport will bring to those who play it in this spirit are greater than those any money can possibly buy.

Richard S. Tufts

With a big trap here and a mound right there,

I laid it out with loving care;

And though I am not prone to boast,

It has no peer from coast to coast.

Richard Tufts and Pinehurst Country Club organized a testimonial dinner for architect Donald J. Ross in 1930—thus the verse and caricature Tufts prepared for the occasion. Tufts and Ross are caught in a rare unoccupied moment in the photograph below.

TUFTS ARCHIVES

idea that so many representatives of those nations would turn out to be such first-class fellows," he said. "They also know golf inside-out, and they care about it for the right reasons. I wasn't certain that establishing a World Amateur Golf Council would appeal to them, but they were so eager to get on with things that we're going right ahead." The first World Amateur Team Championship for the Eisenhower Cup was held that October in St. Andrews. With each team made up of four players, Australia defeated the United States in a closely fought playoff, and everyone looked forward eagerly to assembling again in 1960. When the second World Amateur Team Championship was held at the Merion Golf Club, outside Philadelphia, the United States team ran away from the field. Tufts had been called upon to set up the course. This was no easy job. The players from the countries where golf was a new sport would not have had the length or the accuracy to handle such a long,

tight and hazardous course as Merion. Tufts, I felt, did a superlative job. He widened the narrow fairways, used the front tees on some of the more forbidding holes, and kept the rough relatively short and playable. He saw to it that the firm, fast greens were much more receptive than they normally are and that they also putted a good deal slower. Last but not least, the pins were set in comparatively easy positions. These measures allowed the players from such new-to-golf countries as Finland, Peru and Ceylon to break 90 on their good rounds, and they also made it possible for the 20-year-old Jack Nicklaus, who was in terrific form, to bring in rounds of 66, 67, 68 and 68. Jack, the low scorer, has seldom hit the ball with such authority throughout his long career.

***

Following the First World War, Tufts had inevitably become active in the affairs of the USGA, the governing body of American golf. He served on more USGA committees than

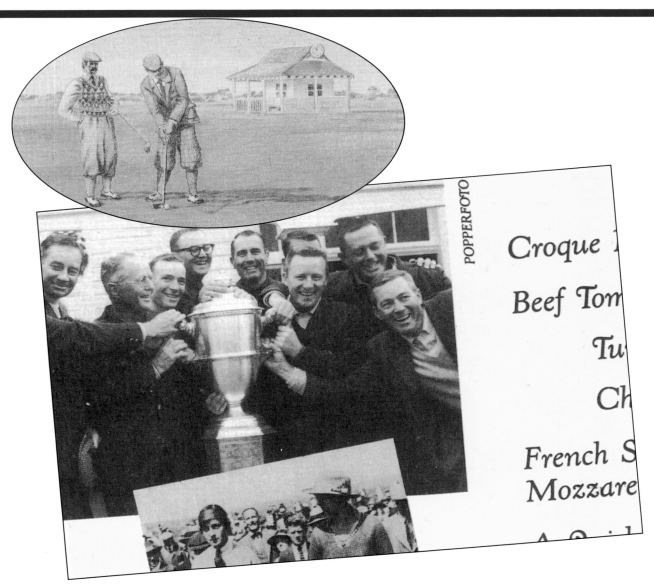

The menu of The Dormy House restaurant in the Turnberry Hotel in Scotland commemorates many of that old course's grandest moments: British Open wins by Jack Nicklaus, Tom Watson and Greg Norman and its hosting of the 1963 Walker Cup. The U.S. team that scored a stirring 12-8 triumph over Great Britain and Ireland is pictured alongside other vintage photos and listings such as "Steak and Kidney Pie, Baked Potato and Minted Garden Peas." Richard Tufts is second from left, Billy Joe Patton is far right, Deane Beman is on the front row, just to the left of Patton, and Gastonia, N.C., native Charles Smith is behind Beman and Patton. The patch that Tufts wore on his jacket (R) is on display in the Tufts Archives.

anyone before him. He never felt more fulfilled than he did as a member of the select USGA delegation which, in the years following the Second World War, met in St. Andrews with a delegation from the Royal and Ancient Golf Club and arrived at a universal code of rules. Tufts served as the Secretary of the USGA in 1950-51 and Vice-President in 1952-55 before beginning a very active and successful two-year term as President in 1956.

I would imagine that one of the golf experiences Dick especially prized was the chance to captain the U.S. Walker Cup team in 1963. The match was held on the Ailsa Course at Turnberry during the long stretch of years during which the British and Irish teams, which had last captured the cup in 1938, found it difficult to stay with American teams made more powerful by an ever-fresh supply of college stars en route to careers in professional golf. Tufts led a team that was composed of experienced Walker Cup players, such as Billy Joe Patton, Charlie Coe and Deane Beman, and by such capable young players as Richard Sikes, the 1961 Public Links champion, Labron Harris, the 1962 U.S. Amateur champion, and Richard Davies, the 1962 British Amateur champion. The home team had a brilliant veteran star in Joe Carr, of Ireland, and some promising young players who were improving with experience: Michael Bonallack, R.D.B.M (Right Down the Bloody Middle) Shade and Michael Lunt. The rest of the team, however, consisted of veterans past their prime and youngsters short of big-time experience. Tufts was taking nothing for granted. He worked hard during the practice rounds explaining to his players how each hole at Turnberry should be played in the various weather conditions one had to expect in Scotland. He devoted considerable attention to the 16th, a very difficult par-four, because it could alter the outcome of the individual matches. The ideal tee shot on the 16th is one that finishes on the high left side of a fairway

that falls down laterally from left to right toward the Firth of Clyde. Above all, it is a risky thing for a golfer to try to reach the high hilltop green on his approach shot if a stiff wind is blowing into his face, for the wind will knock the shot back and the ball will often end up in the stream at the foot of the hill which crosses the fairway on its way to sea. Tufts was an able teacher, and the players enjoyed learning how each hole at Turnberry should be approached. On the eve of the two-day competition they were quite confident, and Tufts was in good spirits when he handed in his lineups for the morning and afternoon matches on Friday, the first day of play.

After the four 18-hole foursomes matches on Friday morning—in foursomes, the two players on each side play alternate shots and drive from alternate tees—the American team led 2-1. Bonallack and Stuart Murray, a solid Scottish stylist, outplayed Patton and Sikes in the top foursomes, but Downing Gray and Harris, the second American pair, won their match, 2-up, and Beman and Coe, the third American pair, won theirs emphatically 5-and-4. Dr. Ed Updegraff and Bob Gardner, the fourth American pair, halved the fourth match. The score at lunch: United States 2, Great Britain and Ireland 1. (No half points were awarded then in a halved match.)

PINEHURST RESORT & COUNTRY CLUB

Tennis matches featuring the likes of Bill Tilden used to draw large crowds to the old tennis courts next to the clubhouse. The courts were moved to the other side of the clubhouse when that land was needed to build more golf courses. The first hole of the No. 3 course now sits in this area.

Tufts' offices and the general administration of Pinehurst Inc. were located in the Casino building in the lower right corner of this aerial view of the village.

TUFTS ARCHIVES

In the afternoon, a rainy, chilly and windy afternoon, the roof fell in on the American team in the singles matches. Beman, Sikes, Harris, Davies and Gray lost their matches, Coe and Charles Smith halved theirs, and Patton accounted for the only U.S. victory. In the sticky going, the home team had clearly outplayed and outputted the Americans. The score at the end of the first day of the match was Great Britain and Ireland 6, the United States 3.

That evening was a grim one for the United States team and its supporters. Patton was one of the few exceptions. He and his wife, Betsy, were among the first people to arrive at the room that had been set aside on the main floor of the Turnberry Hotel as a bar and lounge for the official American party. Billy Joe, to be sure, had won his singles, but he is a pleasantly up-beat fellow in all kinds of weather. He was worried, however, about how well Tufts, a close friend of his, would be able to handle such an unexpected blow. Tufts looked old and tired that evening. He had very little to say. He was patently trying to think through the changes he needed to make in the American lineup for the foursomes and singles on the second and last day of the match.

The weather on Saturday morning was somewhat better. It wasn't raining as hard, the skies were lighter, and the wind, for the most part, was less blustery. The key shot in the morning's foursomes was an error of judgment by Bonallack in the top match in which he and Murray were up against Patton and Sikes. It happened on the 16th, the dangerous par-four on which the fairway slides leisurely down to the deep stream and then climbs at a steep angle to the hilltop green. The Americans had been bunkered off the tee. I believe it was Sikes who had pulled the tee shot into a shallow trap and that it was Patton who, realizing that there was no chance to reach the green in two, elected to play the recovery well short of the brook. Anyway, it was Bonallack, that sterling competitor, who played the fatal stroke. The wind was dead in his face as he prepared to play the approach shot, but it wasn't blowing hard at that moment and he thought he could reach the green with a good, firm middle iron. He made sharp contact with the ball, but a split second earlier the wind had suddenly whipped up with startling force. It got hold of the ball as it neared the front edge of the green and knocked it back down the steep slope and into the brook. Patton and Sikes went on to win the hole with a bogey five to go 1-up, and they held on to take the match by that margin. The news of this sudden turn of events trickled back to the other Americans and undoubtedly stiffened their resolve. At any rate, Gray and Harris won their match 3-and-2, Updegraff and Gardner won theirs 3-and-1, and Beman and Coe completed a sweep of the morning foursomes by winning their match, 3-and-2. The United States was now in the lead, seven points to six, with eight singles coming up in the afternoon.

I don't remember seeing Tufts during the brief interim between the finish of the morning's golf and the start of the afternoon's. I must have grabbed a quick bite, for I wanted to watch the opening tee shots of the first singles match and was able to find a fairly good spot near the first tee shortly before Patton and Murray hit their opening drives. I wondered whether Patton, who could be wild, would concentrate on making sure he found the curving fairway on the first hole, a testing par-four that breaks to the right. He unloaded a fierce left-to-right tee shot that split the fairway, and he went on to quickly take control of his singles. Tufts had spoken to Patton just off the first tee shortly before he drove off. By then, Tufts was looking much better. The color had returned to his cheeks, the wrinkles were gone from his forehead, his eyes had regained some of their usual sparkle and his clothes seemed to fit him better. A hard afternoon lay ahead, but Tufts was calm and nicely in control of the situation. On that terrible Friday night, he had managed, despite his anxiety, to think out his problems clearly, and he had made the right changes. He had elected to place his confidence in Patton, a man who is at his best when the going is rough. Patton had played confident, attacking golf in Saturday morning's four-somes, and his teammates had picked up the spark. There was no assurance that the Americans would be able to maintain their momentum in the afternoon, but Patton was off winging again, and again it got them going. Davies and Gray lost close matches that afternoon, and Beman had to settle for a halve in his match, but after Patton had made it clear that he would almost surely defeat Murray—he ultimately did, 3-and-2—Updegraff, Harris, Gardner and Coe won their singles comfortably with sound, aggressive golf. On that second day, the American won a total of nine points, and the British and Irish only two points. The final score was United States 12, Great Britain and Ireland 8.

I have an idea that the 1963 Walker Cup match meant more to Dick Tufts than he ever dared to put into words. I think he felt that he had somehow mishandled his responsibilities and that his players had won him a reprieve.

***

Dick managed to get so many things done during his very active life that it is hard to touch all the bases. A protege of Donald Ross's, he was a sound, creative architect who built 40 new holes at Pinehurst and revised many more. (I admired the fresh approach he came up with when he rebuilt Pinehurst No. 4. That course had been closed during the 1930s and had fallen into utter disrepair. Nine holes were reopened in 1950, nine more in 1953.) He liked to write. He was a stickler for accuracy, as goes without saying. His best book without a doubt was "The Principles Behind the Rules of Golf," a slim volume published in 1960. It is not easy going. Tufts states at the beginning of the treatise, "If there is one principle more basic than any of the rest, it must be that *you play the course as you find it.*" He adds a few pages later, "The second great principle of golf is that you put your own ball in play at the start of the hole *and play only your own ball and do not touch it* before you lift it from the hole." He was a prolific letter writer. There were not enough hours in the day for him to do all the things he meant to get to and to learn all the things he felt he should know. His son, Peter, once told me that his father, that

---

U.S. AMATEUR RUNNER-UP PLEADS: "I DID NOT SNUB IKE"

It was bad enough that Downing Gray lost the 1962 U.S. Amateur final at Pinehurst to Labron Harris Jr. But the 24-year-old Floridian woke up the next day to newspaper headlines that screamed, "Gray Snubs Ike."

Former President Dwight Eisenhower, an avid golfer, was on a campaign swing through North Carolina with a local politician when their stumping brought them through Pinehurst. Stealing a free hour, Eisenhower was wheeled onto the No. 2 course in a golf cart to watch several holes on the back nine of the afternoon round of the 36-hole match.

As the golfers were hitting their tee shots on the par-three 15th hole, it was time for Eisenhower to leave. A member of the Eisenhower group suggested the players might want to meet the ex-President, but Ike waived that suggestion off. "Let's just send our best. Tell them I wish them both well," said Ike to an associate. "And congratulate them for making the finals."

Apparently, the exact message was lost in transition, and the golfers were told leaving the 15th tee that they could meet Eisenhower, if they wished.

"We didn't know he was there until one of his security people came up as we were leaving the tee," Gray remembered in the spring of 1991 upon returning to Pinehurst for the North and South Amateur. "They said the President's over there, if you'd like to go meet him and say hello. I said, 'Thank you, but I'd rather finish the hole.' He was in the 14th fairway, a par-three away. I remember Harris, standing right next to me, said, 'Well, I'll go on over and get it over with.' I was very nice and polite to them, and I said, 'He's a golfer, I'm sure he'll understand.' Harris said, 'I'll get it over with,' then they write me up, '*Gray Snubs Ike,*' and I say, 'Jeepers, creepers, you can't win.'"

Inside the program for the 1951 Ryder Cup Matches, Tufts mentions that the fourth, eighth and 16th holes of No. 2 were lengthened "to compensate for the increasing length to which modern players are capable of striking a ball." The fourth was lengthened from 508 to 528, the eighth from 473 to 488 and the 16th from 472 to 492, making the total yardage increase from 6,952 to 7,007.

hopeless perfectionist, liked to get away from it all by doing highly advanced woodwork and general repairs in his study. For example, he designed and installed new windows that provided the room with better light than the original ones, and he rebuilt his stereo system in order to gain a higher fidelity when he listened to his library of classical recordings.

Dick's happy, busy life came to a sudden halt in 1970 when his two brothers—between them, they owned the majority of the stock in Pinehurst Inc.—sold the resort despite Dick's opposition to Diamondhead Corp. for $9 million or thereabouts. Immediately after this, Dick's health started to decline, and it began to be said that the loss of Pinehurst had killed him. Very simply, Dick Tufts and Pinehurst had come into the world at about the same time. They had grown up together, and he had regarded himself as being personally responsible that, while Pinehurst had necessarily changed with the times, it preserved the general

atmosphere and the special qualities that had made it unique. I did not hear from him until late September, 1975, when he answered in characteristic detail a letter I sent to him that August asking him to explain how in the mid-1930s Ross had gone about building the delicate contours around and on the new grass greens that required such expert reading and touch from the golfer who wanted to stay close to par. "Your letter opens with the rather mild observation that it was 'something of a surprise' to receive my letter," he wrote. "What you should have said was: 'Where in hell have you been since November 11, 1971, when I wrote to ask you for some information on early course construction.'" He then went on to explain in characteristic detail how Ross worked with "drag pans" drawn by a single mule. We kept in fairly close touch after this happy reunion. In 1976, Dick started work on a fastidious account of the early years of his grandfather, James W. Tufts. The son of a blacksmith, James became an apothecary at a young age, and he had the vision to enter the infant ice cream industry. Thanks in part to the lively interest of his mother, Hepzibah, he went on to become the president of the booming American Soda Fountain Co. Dick's paperback booklet, "James Walker Tufts—The Founder of Pinehurst, North Carolina," was published locally. He then started writing and revising a detailed history of Pinehurst. Every now and then, one of us would telephone the other at night when the rates were cheap. Our conversations usually lasted about 45 minutes. When I put the receiver down, I invariably felt that all was right with the world. Chatting with Dick always had that effect on me.

In his last years, I got down several times in autumn to Southern Pines, a town close to Pinehurst, where I usually spent a week at Pine Needles Lodge and Country Club, the pleasant resort that Bullet and Peggy Kirk Bell had built around an excellent Donald Ross course. The day I arrived, I would telephone Dick around four in the afternoon to see how things were going. Invariably, I would jump in my car five minutes later and head for his home, Fairway Cottage, close by the opening holes of the No. 2 Course. In the center of the comfortable living room, two wing chairs were set at just the right angle for relaxed conversation. We always had a great deal to discuss over tea or a cocktail. When the lady who prepared Dick's meals arrived to get his dinner started, I headed back

The BOOK of GOLF

PUBLISHED BY **PGA**
THE PROFESSIONAL GOLFERS'
ASSOCIATION OF AMERICA

on the
occasion of

THE 9th BIENNIAL
BRITISH-AMERICAN

RYDER CUP
GOLF MATCHES

PINEHURST, N. C.
NOV. 2 and 4, 1951

Between teams representing the
Professional Golfers' Associations
of Great Britain and America

75¢

"...Then come the wild weather,
Come sleet or come snow,
We will hie us to Pinehurst,
Where the mild zephyrs blow."

BENTZ AMERICAN

This early color ad for Pinehurst beckons visitors during the resort's original high season: wintertime.

to Pine Needles, happy in the knowledge that I would be popping in for a few more chats with Dick before I went home.

***

No one I know wrote letters that were as long, detailed, and straight-from-the-shoulder as Dick Tufts. I kept a number of them, including one dated November 19, 1975, that ran to four large sheets of single-spaced typing. I know it was a personal letter, but I think it is all right to excerpt a paragraph, for it really reveals the kind of fellow Dick Tufts was. Earlier in 1975, I had sent him a copy of the revised edition of *The Story of American Golf* and told him I would welcome any comments he had to make. The first thing he mentioned was the 1950 U.S. Open at Merion, which marked Ben Hogan's return to our championship after his near-fatal highway accident in the winter of 1949. Hogan, as you will remember, won the 1950 Open after an 18-hole playoff with George Fazio and Lloyd Mangrum.

"In the story of Ben Hogan's 1950 win at Merion you mention one little incident that interests me: his slight pause before playing his second to the seventy-second hole on Saturday. I was assigned to that match and had naturally watched him closely for signs of fatigue, as many others had. He seemed to be experiencing no difficulty until he walked up the hill on the twelfth, and after that I could see that every shot was an effort. He missed his par three, but then seemed to recover until he missed the short putt on fifteen. To be sure, there was some break and the surface of the green seemed a bit scuffed up along his line, but the putt was not struck solidly and he clearly missed it. He seemed quite a bit upset, even more than when he took four on the seventeenth. Just before he reached his tee shot on the eighteenth he asked me whether it was true that Fazio was in with 286, and I told him I had been too busy refereeing to pick up any news. He seemed to be a bit uncertain, and to this day I do not know whether he played the rest of the hole for a three or four. He certainly played a beautiful second, but in view of the break back of the hole, he was very bold with his long putt, even for Hogan, and I remember being afraid it would go too far the moment he struck it. I would certainly have said that his return putt was longer than the yard you suggest, but, in any case, he made it and the rest is history." ∎

DONALD ROSS

BY DICK TAYLOR

Mr. Taylor has made his home since 1962 in Pinehurst, much of that period spent as editor-in-chief of "Golf World" magazine, which was published in Southern Pines until 1990. Taylor is now editor-at-large for "Southern Links/Western Links" and lives comfortably in a neighborhood named for a Donald Ross golf course in New Hampshire with his wife, Lynne, and a Golden Retriever named after good friend Harvie Ward. Perhaps no one else is as qualified as Taylor to recount the influence Donald Ross had on Pinehurst's emergence as "The St. Andrews Of America."

Diplomatic. Mean. Benign. A loner. Genius. Copycat. Helpful. Stubborn. Whatever such enigmatic recollections of one man's personality may add to, Donald Ross did it his way.

Ross would be a most surprised, but pleased, person to learn he had become a household name in his world of golf. The acknowledged patriarch and patron saint of American golf course architects refused biographical-type interviews and avoided the limelight, saying, "My work will tell my story."

It has and it hasn't. A hero among all golfers, but a mystery man.

That he has designed as many, or more, classic courses as anyone in his profession is accepted. That he believed that less was better, hated penal courses, and with a passion avoided water on his courses, is now being understood. And why.

That his design assistants now are his legacy is not as well known. There were and are some greats: Henson and Ellis Maples, Dick Wilson and Robert von Hagge can be counted. Content to toil in the Ross vineyard rather than seek fame and fortune on their own were "my right and left arms," as he would often call construction engineers Walter P. Hatch and J.B. McGovern; draftsman Walter Irving Johnson; his buddy and secretary, Eric Nelson; and perhaps his most important aide, Frank Maples, who was Ross's original greenkeeper and grew into his office manager when Ross's design interests took him across country. No monuments to them, but they were true disciples.

Happily, the beat goes on as Dan Maples (third generation) has picked up the family banner and has developed into a leading architect, with two fine courses in the Pinehurst area and an expanding worldwide representation. He served a term as president of the American Society of Golf Course Architects, of which Ross was a founder.

And Ross's disciples are myriad. Leading them is Paul (Pete) Dye, Jr., who has never gone a day in his adult life without referring to Ross or Pinehurst No. 2, which he considered the genesis of all courses. Pete will be remembered by two factions in golf: foes who played only his TPC courses, built to order; and fans who played TPCs but also his traditional Ross/Scottish-influenced courses (railroad ties are pure Scottish, not a Dye invention nor contrivance).

The Ross influence is as widespread as is his fame. In the Atlantic seaboard states you can't help but bump into a Ross course; there are originals in many other areas as well. But of the 600 he is credited with, even his most ardent admirers will have to admit some had to be remodels. And then there are his "mail-order" courses. Demand for Ross's work was so high that often he'd route a course from topographical maps, and construction would begin before he could get to the site. Ross expert E. Pete Jones of Golf Research Assoc., in Raleigh, N.C., attributes 385 to the man himself.

His courses all had a seamless, timeless quality as a signature as opposed to obvious trademarks our young practitioners feel compelled to insinuate on their work. A veteran player can stand on a tee of a course new to him, or her, and predict, "Great! This is a Ross course!"

JoAnne Carner made such an exclamation at Kahkwa Club in Erie, Pa., before embarking on her first U.S. Women's Open triumph in 1971.

How did she know? "From the first tee you could see exactly what you had to do. Then there was that nearly hidden swale in front of the green. It had to be a Ross. I love his courses."

That may be terribly brief and simplistic, but it just may explain Ross's work and his philosophy. No tricks, no surprises, no water if possible, bunkering showing you the route, framing greens, and generous fairways. The latter "trademark" offers an option off the tee: you may either choose to keep a drive in play, or carefully study the day's cup placement, which dictates a particular driving area if you need a birdie. He did not demand any one strength to play his courses, but buster, you had better be able to pitch and chip.

In the 1970s and into the '80s, Ross started to become something of a cult figure. The United States Golf Association, by this period, had placed 38 national championships on his

FABIAN BACHRACH

Donald Ross came to Pinehurst in 1900 to be a golf professional, but after the design bug bit, he designed some 385 courses.

Matchbooks are long-time advertising staples for businesses worldwide, but it's not often you see a company promoted on its own cigarettes. These Pinehurst smokes were introduced in 1940 by the R.W. Swain Tobacco Co. of Danville, Va., and heralded by company officials for their "milder and smoother" taste.

courses. During a U.S. Open week, pro tourists would endlessly praise the "old-fashioned" concept of design after having just come off an event at one of the "golden arches" TPC chain courses.

The practice of bringing today's breed of architect to "protect" these fine old courses from the encroachment of added distance has become prevalent. But when they began imposing their own philosophies—a la putting Whistler's Mother in a Barca-Lounger—purists become bellicose. During a U.S. Open held on a revamped Ross course that had suddenly sprouted water, Tom Weiskopf suggested to a large group at lunch the formation of a preservation society for Ross courses.

"The membership fee," said Tom, "would be $200 and half would go toward the purchase of a shotgun." There since has been formed such a society, but not of militant nature. These like-minded golfers, all of whom play on home-club Ross designs, once yearly pay homage to one of his courses with a friendly tournament. Naturally, No. 2 was the starting place.

A pleasant interlude during that week in Pinehurst in the spring of 1990 for Ross devotees was a party hosted by Mr. and Mrs. Wayne Ashby, who purchased the Ross home on Midland Road, which overlooks the third hole of No. 2. The Ashbys carefully and

lovingly restored the home, and they've also put up a brass plaque denoting its historical significance. Ross also owned the Pine Crest Inn, one of several small English-style hostelries in the village, now a local watering hole as well as tourist accommodation owned by the Bob Barrett family.

This, quite naturally, brings us to Dornoch, Scotland, as you shall see. Having lived in Ross Country, a/k/a Pinehurst, for more than a quarter-century (which makes me a newcomer), having played 90 percent of my golf on Ross courses, never seeing a Ross course I didn't like, I felt it behooved me to go to the roots.

It was during a period, unfortunately, when I was recovering from a severe broken ankle (suffered on a Ross course, oddly). But watching my companions the first three holes, I ditched my cane and played 16 holes the next day, to the later horror of my Pinehurst doctor, who scolded me over my reripped tendons.

Not one regret from this decision, as I found Royal Dornoch to be one of the most exciting golf courses I have ever played. One pleasant jolt after another as you reached the next tee. Sweeping sea vistas, little mesa greens, one par-three that whipped us all, subtly crowned greens and breaks and bounces. In springtime the vivid yellow gorse distracts you, even though giant hares had ravaged the course during this visit. In the distance the animals looked like airdales gone wrong.

That night I was assisted to—what else?—the Donald Ross Suite at the Royal Golf Hotel, where the staff brought to me a bucket of ice to reduce swelling and a seven-course supper. When you reach your 60s, I figured, you had to do things like that, sacrifice your body. What if I never got back to Dornoch?

(USGA Executive Director David Fay had those thoughts in July of 1990 en route to the British Open. He flew to Inverness first, rented a car, got to Dornoch around 11 a.m. and immediately was put in a game with members. After the round and a quick lunch, he joined a local couple for another 18. It was only 7 p.m. when he completed that round, so he went out by himself for yet another 18. Had he been *really*

A STROLL WITH MR. ROSS

John Derr was a reporter and photographer for the *Gastonia Gazette* in 1935 when he first visited Pinehurst. The occasion was a photographic seminar for the fledgling North Carolina Press Photographers Association. The meeting was arranged by John Hemmer, the celebrated *New York Daily News* photographer who spent much of the year in Pinehurst recording the golf and other activities for posterity.

That afternoon Derr had the opportunity to meet Donald Ross. Following are his memories of a trip around No. 2 with its designer:

"Mr. Ross learned I had seen Augusta National a few weeks before and still carried the aura of Augusta in my eyes. 'Very well. Come with me,' he said. 'I'd like to show you our course.'

"Out from the clubhouse we walked, to the first tee, and Mr. Ross explained that the first hole of a championship course should be moderately challenging but not overpowering.

"'Often a player's round is created by the first hole,' he said. I remember wondering why he had used the verb 'created' when I might have said 'determined.' Donald Ross himself was a creator, a creator of great golf holes, and he fancied how they should be played by a reasonably good player.

"It took us probably two hours to walk the course. We would stop and talk and Mr. Ross would explain why he added a mound here or created a swale there. Or whether a bunker should have grass or sand. The greens of the first three holes had just been converted from sand to grass. Mr. Ross seemed very pleased with these new greens.

"We didn't have golf carts in 1935, which was fine. But over the years I've regretted that little portable tape recorders were not yet available. Hearing Mr. Ross talk about each hole was a walking history of great golf architecture.

"I wasn't knowledgeable enough about any golf course to understand how great was his masterpiece. Had I known more about the game and its venues, perhaps I could have thought of some intelligent questions to ask as we walked along. I did ask questions but they were so meaningless that the answers escaped me. Only one I recall.

"Somewhere on the back nine, I noticed the flagsticks were of different heights. I asked why they were not all cut to the same length.

"'In Scotland,' Mr. Ross explained, his charming Scottish burr still evident but now with a little Carolina softness, 'in Scotland they used whatever stick was available to use as a flagstick.' And his answer didn't make my question sound stupid.

"What an experience that was. I just wish I had that tape recorder in 1935."

JOHN HEMMER

The Pine Crest was originally owned by Mrs. E.C. Bliss. A 1913 issue of the "Outlook" noted that the new hotel "provides for fully fifty guests, offering several suites with private bath; radiant with fresh air; sunshine, good cheer and 'hominess.'"

serious, he could have gone another nine before midnight gloaming—it never gets totally dark in Dornoch in July. Such is the magic of Scottish golf, and Royal Dornoch in particular.)

It is a sweet little village of no more than 1,200 or so residents, with most buildings made of sandstone. It may just seem so, but all lanes appear to cant toward the firth and the famed old course. This tranquility can't last. A bridge over a firth is being built that will cut almost one hour from a long drive from St. Andrews.

It was here that young Donald worked on the green crew, and club secretary John Sutherland took an interest in this bright youth. The secretary would also become a legend, holding the post for 50 years and being the last to make design changes on the course that had Old Tom Morris and James Braid as early designers. Ross left his imprint during a visit from America.

Ross was born on Nov. 23, 1872. His father was a stonemason, his mother a nurse. They lived in the middle dwelling of a three-flat building. Formal education was not as useful as a trade, so Sutherland recommended Donald learn the golf trade at St. Andrews. The youngster soaked up all facets of the business working for Forgan's Clubmakers and Morris, the club and ballmaker and architect. History was in the making. Ross had been an apprentice carpenter, played brass in the town band and was one of the better junior golfers in town.

Tom Morris became the first assistant golf pro, or apprentice to a pro, when the legendary

Alan Robertson took him on as a feathery ballmaker. Later his son, Young Tom, would learn the trade as well. Robertson has been acknowledged as the first club professional, serving the Royal and Ancient, and he was never beaten in the big-money exhibitions, the only competition in those days.

The advent of the gutta-percha ball led to Morris's split with his mentor. Robertson not only had a stock of featheries to sell, but he didn't feel the gutta was the wave of the future. So Tom began his own business in the store that still sits along the 18th green on the Old Course. And among his assistants was Donald Ross.

Young Donald was taught to repair and make clubs and balls. He learned whatever art there was to greenkeeping at the time and trailed around after Morris as he designed courses. At age 20, Ross was hired back by Sutherland to be his greenkeeper and head professional.

When I made my Dornoch pilgrimage, I sat in the upper lounge and chatted a full afternoon with members strolling in from the monthly medal. Few were aware of the full impact this homegrown hero had made in the United States and were interested in anything I could tell them. The Oldest Member shook his head and said, "And we don't even have a marker on his birthplace." When Rick Reilly of *Sports Illustrated* came to Dornoch later that year and wove a graceful paean to Ross and course, a brass marker was put on the Ross homestead, No. 3 St. Gilbert St., not unlike the one on his

Pinehurst home. "It won't bother the tenant," said the Oldest Member. "He's deaf."

Ross was 20 years old when he began his new role at Dornoch. At age 27 he made a huge decision for one so young. Opportuned by a regular visitor to Dornoch, Harvard professor Robert Wilson, Ross made his way to Oakley Country Club in Watertown, Mass., where he eventually built a home. It was here that, at the behest of the patriarch of the Tufts family, the direction of Ross's life changed once again.

Tufts' fortune came from the invention and manufacturing of the beautiful, marble soda fountain. He parlayed his wealth by establishing a health resort just off Highway 1 (and the Florida East Coast rail line) in North Carolina, five miles from the village of Southern Pines, and named it Pinehurst. It was to be a haven fall through spring for those ailing from chest complications. The Holly Inn was the first structure, built in 1895. A barn for a dairyherd was next.

But these walking wounded visitors were not ill enough to be inactive, and soon they were hitting golf balls amid the cows in the pasturelands, the only open property in his 5,000 acres of pine forest. So a rudimentary nine-hole course was built. When Tufts learned of Ross's background, he asked him to come to Pinehurst in the northern "off-season" and build a course. Quickly, Pinehurst became a golf resort. Visitors liked what they saw, and soon Ross was dedicating a lot of time to design.

That he worked with familiar land was plain luck. Known as the Sandhills of North Carolina, Ross carved four courses for Pinehurst Country Club and built wonderful layouts for Pine Needles, Mid Pines and Southern Pines Country Club, all within a six-mile radius. As at Dornoch, he had sandy soil with which to work (the Sandhills area is thought to have been a huge inland sea at one time). Developers continue to uncover golf holes scattered around the area, as parts of the original No. 4 course were abandoned as was a nine-hole course reserved for Pinehurst staff. "The help's course" began where the fourth hole on course No. 2 sits today and unfolded on property that now contains the No. 7 course, designed by traditionalist Rees Jones.

With very little earth-moving—Ross worked via mule and drag-pan—he subtly implanted his Scottish heritage in mounding, bunkering, breaking greens and fairness.

The latter trait is not found in all Scottish courses. Lee Trevino described Troon as playing golf on "an unmade bed" with little hope of controlling the finish of a driver. The true devotee who has played the Old Course at St. Andrews knows exactly what Trevino is talking about when an otherwise perfectly struck ball goes caroming off the fairway after striking hidden swales and knobs.

When Ross agreed to build courses in Pinehurst, they were used, at most, seven months of the year. As part of his arrangement he insisted they be maintained by a greenkeeper the year-round so they would be ready for the high seasons, which were George Washington's Birthday through mid-May, and mid-September up to Thanksgiving. All has changed now, of course, as all amenities are open 12 months.

(The area is becoming a designer's boutique. In addition to seven Ross courses, there are layouts at one stage of completion or another by the late George Fazio and nephew Tom, another by Tom himself, two by Dan Maples, one Ellis Maples/Willard Byrd collaboration, Arnold Palmer, Jack Nicklaus, Tom Jackson, Rees Jones, Trent Jones the elder, and now Gary Player. You could shop for a designer here.)

Ten years after his arrival in North Carolina, his design business had gotten so big that his former greenkeeper, Frank Maples, was now the autocratic manager of the company and its

---

AT PINEHURST

Oh, to be at Pinehurst when spring is in the air,
And all the mutts and all the nuts of golf are gathered there.
'Tis good to go to Boston; 'tis sweet to stop at Rye,
But I would go to Pinehurst where all the golf balls fly.

The governors and statesmen stand waiting on the tee,
The early ball has prior call though kings behind may be.
And yonder in the bunker with curses in his throat
Is presidential timber and a diplomat of note.

The air is sweet at Pinehurst, the sky's a lovely blue,
But where you walk, the people talk, or swing and follow through.
The preacher is a golfer, God's blessing he invokes,
But the richest men at Pinehurst are beggars wanting strokes.

And here I am at Pinehurst, for spring is in the air,
As Shakespeare said the addled head is little noticed there.
And though my game be faulty and erring is my pitch
I'm giving strokes to beggars and succoring the rich.

© 1928 by Edgar A. Guest

books, schedules and office. He had two fulltime engineer/construction men, and he began apprenticing young hopefuls.

By the 1930s he was the premier architect, with only the global-minded Alister Mackenzie and bright newcomer Robert Trent Jones as rivals. His credits by this time included The Broadmoor in Colorado; Wampanoag in Connecticut; Belleair, The Biltmore, Gulf Stream and renowned Seminole in Florida; Savannah GC, East Lake (redesign) and Augusta CC in Georgia; Beverly, Bob O'Link, Oak Park and Ravisloe in Illinois; French Lick in Indiana; Chevy Chase and Congressional (redesign) in Maryland; Cohasset, Oyster Harbor and Longmeadow in Massachusetts; Oakland Hills, Detroit GC and Dearborn in Michigan; Bretton Woods in New Hampshire; Echo Lake, Essex Falls, Montclair, Plainfield and remodeled plain Jane Seaview in New Jersey; Inverness (remodeled nine and added nine), Scioto and Brookside in Ohio; Aronimink, Gulph Mills, Kahkwa and Whitemarsh Valley in Pennsylvania; Agawam Hunt, Newport (remodel) and Wannamoisett in Rhode Island; Burlington CC in Vermont; The Homestead and CC of Virginia in Virginia; Essex, Elmhurst and Rosedale in Canada; and CC of Havana and Havana Biltmore in Cuba.

In addition to his Pinehurst area courses, he is responsible for other North Carolina designs such as Asheville CC, Biltmore Forest, Forsyth, Highlands, Linville, Mimosa Hills (Billy Joe Patton's teething ring) and Sedgefield. In 1922 he remodeled all 18 at Royal Dornoch and later put in two holes of his own. Whew! This but about one-eighth of his work.

He began as manager of golf at Pinehurst, became the all-powerful secretary, and when he surrendered much of his power at the club to devote time to architecture, he had been both corporation and club president.

That he was the boss of golf at the club during this period was a given, and he drew a staff around him, some from Dornoch, to whom he passed on clubmaking.

Rod Innes was one of his Dornoch boys. He is retired now after a career that survived Ross's

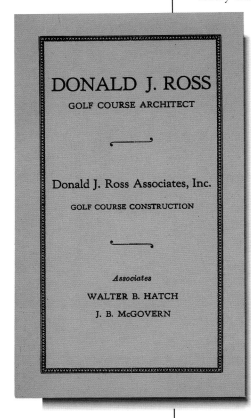

This 1930 listing of Ross golf courses includes 141 individual courses; ten sets of 36-hole designs and four of 27 holes; 14 remodeling jobs; and, of course, one club in Pinehurst with 72 holes.

fetish for perfection, then to managerial duties at a local bank, then Pine Needles, and finally, as treasurer for *Golf World* magazine, which has since been sold to *The New York Times* and moved north. Rod's father was a Ross friend and followed him to America.

Rod's memories of Ross are still vivid. "He was tough. He didn't miss a thing," Innes says. "He called all his clubmakers together one day and showed them a wood-working tool with a blunted edge. He had been a carpenter at one stage of his life and understood the importance of well-kept tools. While he berated us he put a fine edge to the tool on a sanding wheel. We did not forget the message.

"One time the caddies talked of a strike unless wages were raised. Ross heard of this, walked to the caddie pen, asked the leader what was going on. Hearing the grievance, he whacked the caddie on the head with his ever-present five-iron and informed him the strike was over."

"He could be mean," recalls Peter Tufts, great-grandson of Pinehurst founder James Tufts. "He was to my great-grandfather who hired him. He wanted his way. I was fascinated as a kid following around after him, watching him shape greens."

It got in Tufts' blood, too. He had input on the No. 5 course, the Seven Lakes course in this area is his from start-to-finish, and he has several other projects, mostly remodels. Pete has to be the least flamboyant member of a highly individualistic group of land-planning architects.

No. 2's history is baffling, until historian/*Golf Digest* columnist Charles Price explains. From 1901 to his death, Donald Ross fine-tuned this layout. He incorporated holes with other courses, abandoned others.

No. 2's evolution: 1901: nine holes. 1903: remodeled nine. 1907: added nine. 1923: remodeled two holes. 1933: remodeled entire course. 1934: remodeled three holes. 1935: remodeled all 18 for a reason important to him. And 1946: remodeled one hole.

The great Bob Jones had praised Ross's work at Augusta CC, according to Price, and Ross thought he had an agreement with this legend that he would build Jones's dream course in his native Georgia. But when Jones played Cypress Point in California, he nominated its architect, Mackenzie, for the co-design that is now Augusta National GC (this course has had a dozen architects since fine-tune it). An angered

Ross set aside all work to concentrate on his final plans for No. 2. He was going to bring in, first, the finest golf course in the South.

By now he had eight foremen in his company and could afford hands-on, daily attention to No. 2.

All the while, Ross kept his game honed. He won three North and South Opens and two Massachusetts Opens. But younger brother Alex topped him with victory in the 1907 U.S. Open and five North and South titles. His swing was compared to Bobby Jones's.

Ross became a loner, says Innes, when he lost his first wife. Ross had saved enough money to bring nurse Janet Conchie from Dornoch, where she had waited six years. She

died in 1922, leaving a daughter, Lillian. He remarried in 1924, to Mrs. Florence Blackinton, who died in 1954. Ross himself passed away in April, 1948, just after his No. 2 course enjoyed one its finest moments of amateur golf—the North and South triumph of popular collegian Harvie Ward over Frank Stranahan.

Ross was firm in his beliefs and capabilities, and that made him seem stubborn. Early demands made it seem he was building many courses from the same plans, mimicking Scottish holes, but he could not keep pace with demands and thus accepted his "mail-order" jobs.

His fame spread abroad via the North and South Amateur (now 91 years old), the North

The Pinehurst "Golf Boy" wins a trophy in this poster from the first half of the century. That's Ross directly behind him.

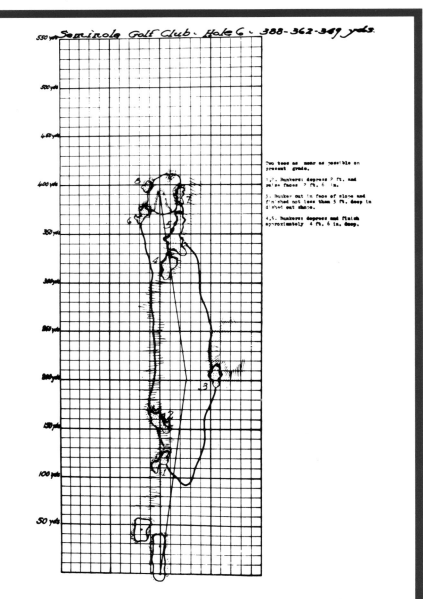

Seminole Golf Club in North Palm Beach, Fla., is another of Ross's most acclaimed courses. This is a diagram of the sixth hole.

"Mr. Golf" through his involvement with the United States Golf Association. Among his contributions was simplification of the Rules of Golf. He sat on every committee and rose to the association presidency. Tufts was the consummate volunteer amateur golfer. He and Ross were great friends.

When relatives sold their Pinehurst stock in 1970 to Diamondhead Corp., a land-development company, Tufts was so distraught he phoned me to say that anything written for *Golf World* should include the fact that he had nothing to do with the sale. His life had been shattered. The future of Pinehurst as the world had known it for 75 years was in doubt. "In writing this story," he requested, "please say that my son, Peter, and I had nothing to do with this sale. It was forced upon us." His strong hand at the helm, maintaining even (many called it snail's-paced) growth, had been overruled.

The change may have been unthinkable, but it was inevitable. There were swift additions to the resort by the new group: No. 6 course, the Members Clubhouse, a tennis complex. The PGA Tour came to town for a decade to compliment the new World Golf Hall of Fame. For those who loved the old Pinehurst, the bad news was waves of prospective buyers hustled in to inspect the lots, houses and condominiums that were now available. "Fore in the condos," was the dark joke that circulated. It was the only "go-go" time in Pinehurst history. In truth, this dowager queen had finally been discovered.

Many surprises followed the sale until Club Corporation of America bought out the floundering management that had turned assets over to a consortium of banks holding loans. The treasure was back in the hands of golf people. Pinehurst had survived because no one would think of altering the founders' New England village. And always there was the presence of Ross golf courses. The Untouchables.

There remains a strong sense of responsibility to the preservation of the history that is the fiber of Pinehurst. Richard Tufts' description of Ross's creations perhaps explains the solid continuity: "There was nothing vulgar about his work."

Thankfully, there is nothing vulgar about Pinehurst, as well. Harry Vardon could today roam the village and stand at the first tee, as he had done, and hardly know the 21st century was approaching. ∎

and South Open (held annually on No. 2 until 1952), the PGA Championship (1936) and the Ryder Cup (1951). He was compared, more than favorably, to Scottish designers. Every modern-day designer should be made to play No. 2 until he understands what subtle ways a green can be protected from a foozled chip or pitch. He was the premier strategic designer. Expert players delight in the examination they undergo on his courses; yet the less-talented can enjoy a round in what they perceive as a wide-open course with cantankerous greens.

Jack Nicklaus: "Other architects may lead a player to negative thinking on-course, but his courses led to positive thinking. His stamp as an architect was naturalness."

Richard S. Tufts was the third generation leader of Pinehurst. He also became America's

AN 1899 MATCH

Professional golf surely was different 92 years ago. Imagine Jack Nicklaus trying to "bulldoze" a referee after missing a putt. Or Curtis Strange taking a "brace" after losing two holes. Or Sam Snead passing around a hat after losing a purse. But that's what a professional named "Feelark" did in an 1899 match, as recorded by the "Pinehurst Outlook."

he only professional golf match held on the Pinehurst golf links this season took place last Monday morning between Sir Walter Scott and Willie Childs, alias "Feelark," two colored boys employed at the golf field.

Referee, stakeholder and scorer were chosen and articles of agreement drawn up and signed, and at 9 o'clock, the time appointed, fully 150 people had gathered to witness the match. It was a 12-hole game and the prizes were $1.50 for the winner and 50 cents for the loser.

Both the experts were on hand and Feelark won the toss. He started in with a grand swing of the club, but unfortunately just as he finished someone coughed and he topped the ball.

Twice more he tried and failed, but on the fourth stroke the ball went sailing not over but into the bunker, amid great applause.

Sir Walter then had his inning and sent the ball into the ploughed ground. Now an easy approach shot and both were on the green, which not being in good condition the putting was bad. Feelark rimmed the cup and tried to bulldoze the referee, but without success. The hole was won by Sir Walter, seven to nine. He also won the second hole 11 to 12.

Feelark then took a decided brace and won the next hole six to seven. The next two holes were won by Scott, Feelark being unfortunate in slicing his drives. Scott now had Feelark 3-up. The next two holes were halved, leaving the score 3-up and five to play. Had Feelark played his brassie on the next hole he surely would have won the hole. The next hole he played in very clever style and had Sir Walter stymied, but Scott was equal to the occasion and played one of Tucker's "English shots" to such perfection that he won the hole. The score then stood 4-up and four to play.

On the next hole both of the contestants made tremendous drives, balls carrying 200 yards. Sir Walter won this hole, which decided the match—5-up and three to play.

The purse was then handed to the winner, but Feelark, knowing the sympathy of the crowd was with him, passed around his hat while Sir Walter was making a speech of thanks, and collected $2. It was the unanimous opinion of all present that Feelark sold the match, so the referee decided all bets "off." ■

Francis Ouimet during early North and South play as Donald Ross (second from left) looks on.

THE SCOTTISH INVASION

BY RICHARD S. TUFTS

When the 1962 U.S. Amateur was held at Pinehurst, Mr. Tufts quickly nixed the idea of a tournament program. The thought of a magazine filled with advertising stuck in his anti-commercial craw. So he opted instead to publish a history of Pinehurst that quietly listed some three dozen "sponsors" in the back. The small green volume, "The Scottish Invasion," is now a local treasure and attests to Tufts' ability not only as a businessman and golf administrator, but also as a writer. This excerpt outlines the origins of Pinehurst.

The story of the early days of golf at Pinehurst must of course start with an account of how Pinehurst first came into existence. This is the story of James W. Tufts, the founder of the village.

Mr. Tufts was born in 1835 and started his business career 16 years later as an apprentice in the apothecary store of Samuel Kidder in Charlestown, Mass. At the age of 21, Mr. Tufts went into business for himself and was soon the proprietor of a chain of three pharmacies. He had always been interested in the concoction of syrups and the other products sold at the soda fountains of those days and soon gave up his apothecary stores for the manufacture of such products. His next step was to branch out into the manufacture of the soda water apparatus used in drug stores. The soda fountain of this time was a substantial, well-made piece of equipment in which Italian marble was used and many of the parts silver-plated. From the silver plating of fountain parts, Mr. Tufts also branched out into the manufacture of an extensive line of silver-plated items such as pitchers, dishes, and vases. The business, which had been carried on under Mr. Tufts' name, was consolidated in 1891 with other soda fountain companies and became the American Soda Fountain Company, the largest in its field, with branches in London and the principal cities of this country.

By 1895 Mr. Tufts had turned the active management of the business over to others. His health had never been robust and it had long been necessary for him to take frequent vacations. He had been associated with the well-known minister, Edward Everett Hale, in various philanthropic projects around Boston and through this work had become interested in the problem of people of modest means who, like himself, needed to seek a warmer climate during the cold New England winters. The idea of Pinehurst was born.

Mr. Tufts decided on a location in the mid-south and selected the Sandhills of North Carolina as recognized for its health-giving climate. In June of 1895 he investigated several possible locations and finally purchased some 5,000 acres of cut-over timberland from the Page family of Aberdeen, N.C. At this time the sandy land was considered to have little value except for the growth of timber. The soil was so poor that it was said to be necessary to bury a person with commercial fertilizer in order to afford some prospect of his rising on the day of judgment. The dollar an acre paid for the land by Mr. Tufts was an outrageous price for such property.

It took Mr. Tufts about half a year to plan, build and open his new resort. In this time he built a small hotel, a store, several boarding houses and about sixteen small cottages. Streets were built, a sewer and water system installed and a power plant and lighting system completed. The early town was a barren place. The few stunted and twisted pines that had been spared by the lumber man and had survived the frequent forest fires were so few and far between that they served only to add to the general air of bleakness. The new buildings stood naked of any garnishing since it was to be several years before the problem of growing grass and shrubbery in the sandy soil was solved.

The one thing Pinehurst had to offer in these early days was its climate. For amusement the early pioneers found entertainment principally among themselves. They were chiefly people of modest means, retired school teachers and army officers, ministers and a small sprinkling of Mr. Tufts' associates and business friends. They gave recitals, played cards, danced, walked, took carriage trips around the country and when they felt the need of strenuous exercise, played roque. There was no golf.

The game of golf began at Pinehurst much as it had with the other early golf clubs of America. Some hardy enthusiast brought a set of clubs to Pinehurst and by the fall of 1897 it was reported that people were disturbing the cows on the dairy field by chasing a little white ball around. Mr. Tufts was quick to follow this lead and by February, 1898, nine holes had been completed under the expert direction of Dr. D. LeRoy Culver of New York. These early holes probably consisted of no more than a built-up tee and a few feet of rolled ground around the hole but, like the others, at least it was a start.

An early Pinehurst golf exhibition (top); golfers and caddies cross the bridge on the 10th hole of course No. 1 around 1900. There remains water in the same vicinity today in the form of the pond fronting the tee to the par-three 11th hole on No. 1.

At first golf occupied a very secondary position in the Pinehurst picture. A small club house was built and John Dunn Tucker served as professional for two seasons starting in the fall of 1898. Thirteen entries was a large field in the few tournaments that were held and starting times were hardly necessary.

In the fall of 1903 the Pinehurst golf activities were formalized by the organization of the Pinehurst Golf Club. Leonard Tufts was president and Frank Presbrey was a member of the Board of Governors.

Three events gave Pinehurst golf the forward impetus which has made the village one of the world's great centers of golf. The first of these was the visit of the famous English golf professional, Harry Vardon, in March, 1900; the second the arrival of Donald J. Ross in December 1900; and the third the association with Frank Presbrey, which started with the 1901-02 season.

GOLFERS OF THE
VERY EARLY DAYS

This chapter on the first period in American golf would not be complete without a few words about some of the individuals who most largely influenced the game in the United States and Pinehurst during these times.

The four chosen for mention have been selected first because of their influence on

Strong men quail and braggarts stutter
When he strokes 'em with his putter.
With his knowledge of the game
Ain't it all a bleeding shame,
Due to Adolph and his flotsam,
As president he couldn't blossom.

Richard Tufts once published a small booklet entitled "An Eightsome of Golfing Badgers" that included sketches and rhymes he created in honor of eight close golfing friends. This sketch is of George Blossom, USGA president from 1942-43, when no competitions were held because of World War II.

Pinehurst golf and second because they represent four different sources of influence: foreign golfers, our own champions, club professionals and golf officials. Only lack of space makes it impossible to list the names of many others who had an active part in the formative years. It should also be noted that though Donald Ross has been chosen to represent the club professional, in which capacity he served during this period, his greatest influence on American golf came in the field of architecture during later years.

Harry Vardon

In 1900 Harry Vardon came to America to play a series of exhibition matches which he concluded by winning the National Open title. It was fortunate that a man of Vardon's ability and character should have made this visit. He was one of the earliest exponents of the modern swing and his smooth, graceful performance did much to influence the trend of golf style during these formative years.

He played four rounds at Pinehurst in March; the opportunity to watch such an expert in action stimulated interest in the game at Pinehurst, and Vardon's favorable comments about the course were repeated elsewhere. The visit was Pinehurst's first taste of big-time golf, the flavor was good and the new resort wanted more.

This was the day of sand greens at Pinehurst, but these greens always provided accurate putting surfaces; otherwise the condition and design of the Pinehurst course was, no doubt, on a par with the other championship courses of this period in American golf. Therefore, it is interesting to see how the play of one of the world's greatest golfers in 1900 would compare with that of a modern golfer on a modern championship course.

Vardon's best round was 71 on a course that measured 5,203 yards. Sixty-two years later, the qualifying round in the North and South Amateur Championship was won by Cobby Ware with a score of 70 on a course that measured 7,010 yards, a difference in length of over a mile. It is safe to assume that this score would be equaled by Harry Vardon were he playing today. The difference in results is of interest as a fair measure of the improvement that 62 years have brought in the condition of golf courses and the equipment of the game.

The 1900 account of Vardon's Pinehurst play credits him with tee shots up to 240 yards in length and mentions the fact that he used an iron on all holes of 200 yards and under. This would be a reasonable performance for any modern golfer if he were to use the guttie ball and wood shafts. Vardon's exceptional accuracy with the short game is emphasized and the account shows that he averaged 1.8 putts on those greens for which any record was given. The steadiness of his performance is attested by the fact that in four rounds his best and worst score for each hole varied by only one stroke on 15 holes and by two on the remaining three.

To play golf today as Vardon knew the game would be neither popular nor practicable, but there can be no question that golf required more

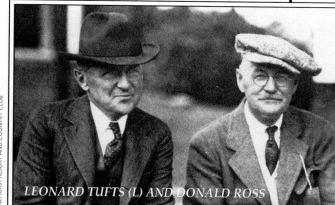

LEONARD TUFTS (L) AND DONALD ROSS

skill to play when the courses were shorter, the guttie ball was in use and the golfer's bag contained no more than seven or eight wood-shafted clubs. We can be proud of what has been accomplished, but progress does not always add to the fundamental enjoyment of living.

Walter J. Travis

The first player of prominence to develop his game in this country was Walter J. Travis. Born in Australia, he came to America as a youth and did not take up golf until 1896, when he was 35 years of age. In that year he returned a score of 110 in a competition held at Van Cortlandt Park but four years later won the Amateur Championship. In another four years he made history by winning the British Amateur, a feat not again accomplished by an American until Jess Sweetser won in 1926. The magnitude of Travis's accomplishment was well certified to when, at the presentation ceremony, Lord Northbourne piously expressed the hope that a similar disaster would never again take place in British sport.

AN INTERVIEW WITH DONALD ROSS

Following are some rough notes taken during one of the rare interviews that Donald Ross granted. The writer/interviewer is unknown, but the transcription was in the files of the late Bob Saunders, a former sports writer for *The Charlotte News*:

"Oldest child of large and poor family in Dornoch, Scotland. Worked at golf club there. One day (in 1899) one Professor Wilson of Harvard University came into the shop and made arrangements to take lessons from Mr. Ross. The prof proved to be a natural golfer and was delighted with the results. Was also very pleased with the tailor Mr. Ross recommended (named Moore and the first tailor ever to insist on taking measurements for BOTH sleeves). Prof. Wilson asked Ross why he didn't come to America some time, that golf was new here, that there was money to be made, and that if he ever did and came to Boston to be sure to call him up.

So he came. Knowing nobody in this country but the prof and the prof having no idea that he was coming. When he got off the boat he walked straight to the Grand Central. He had pored over timetables while still on the boat and knew that the fare to Boston was $5. The agent at the station sold him an extra-fare ticket (parlor car, I presume). Anyway, it cost our young hero $7.25—and to this day Mr. Ross dislikes railroad agents.

Once on the train, however, he was tremendously impressed with the comfort of his seat, and was so afraid that if he got up and left it for any reason that somebody might get it. And until seven o'clock that night he didn't budge. Not a bit of food—nor a trip down to the end of the car. Don't you know that was an unhappy day?

In Boston at the South Station he inquired about Mr. Wilson. He had never seen a telephone—didn't know how to get in touch with benefactor-to-be. An operator called the Wilson number for him and told him how to use the phone. (And to this day, Mr. Ross loves telephone operators.) On the phone, Prof Wilson told him how to come to his house, which was eight miles from South Station, which trolley to take, etc. Young hero had never seen a trolley—so he walked. And still with no food, thinking of course that a big dinner would be given him when he got there. He got there at eleven o'clock—and after talking for a while, Mr. Wilson offered him a sandwich and a glass of milk. He was delighted to accept.

In two years' time, he had saved $3,000, which he sent home for his mother to buy a home for her brood. He also wanted very much to send her an American stove, but this she did not want when she learned that you couldn't see the flames. At the end of six years he was able to go back to Scotland and marry the sweetheart he hadn't seen in that time.

He started the Oakley Club—built the course, taught golf, made clubs.

Mr. Ross met "many men with influence." Among them a Mr. Smith, lawyer for the fabulously wealthy Mr. Tufts, who had started Pinehurst. Mr. Smith told Mr. Ross that a client of his wanted a golf pro in Pinehurst. So. That's how that came about. Ross called at Mr. Tufts' home one Sunday afternoon. Young Dick, aged three, with beautiful blonde hair and a very shy manner, sat on his father's lap. Mr. Leonard Tufts was a firm believer in the future of golf in America, and at this time the general sentiment was that golf was a fad that would soon pass—and Mr. James Tufts, owner of Pinehurst and needer of a golf pro was not (a believer). He agreed with the general sentiment.

Mr. Ross's brother came to this country later. Mr. Ross says his brother was a more brilliant player than he, but that he was much steadier.

No grass at all on Pinehurst courses when Mr. Ross arrived. Fairways and greens were both rolled.

In 1909 gave up everything for architecture. No technical training.

Started grass in Pinehurst. Not a green lawn in village. Got first patch of Bermuda near Laurinburg.

This end of first and only interview with Mr. Ross.

His meteoric rise was made possible only by the "old man's" complete concentration and devotion to the game. He was a thorough student and a grim competitor, but always a fair opponent, a sportsman and a stickler for the Rules of Golf. Though his influence on American golf was considerable, he was not the sort of man to catch the public fancy and his followers were, therefore, principally his close friends.

Travis continued to be a threat in amateur tournaments until 1915, when he won his last big event, the Metropolitan Championship at Apawamis. But his influence on American golf was much broader than his playing record would suggest. In 1902 he published a book of instruction on golf that was widely read, and from 1909 to 1920 he edited *The American Golfer*, the leading golf magazine of its day. After his retirement from competition he became interested in golf architecture and was quite busy in this field during golf's growing years. Always a man of firm conviction who spoke his mind freely, he was for many years the stormy petrel of the game.

Travis spent a part of many winters at Pinehurst, winning the North and South there three times.

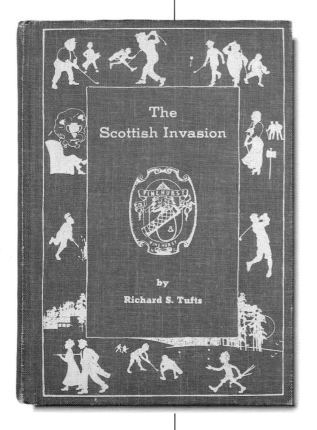

Tufts dedicated his book to "that most important person, the amateur golfer."

Donald J. Ross

The world is indebted to Scotland for giving us the game of golf, and America's debt to the Scots was further increased in the early days by the arrival of many of the Scottish professionals. These men not only knew how to play the game but were also steeped in the traditions of golf and knew how a golf course should be laid out and maintained. Had it not been for the guidance of these early arrivals from the old country it is more than probable that the inventive American would have developed his own ideas about the way golf should be played. Fortunately the availability of correct informa-

tion developed a desire to out-do the Scotch in the proper playing of the game. The equipment of the game was not the only imported product; the Scotch style of play was carefully studied, many early courses had holes patterned after famous holes across the water and even the Scotch practice of playing in red coats was generally followed.

Pinehurst also learned its early golf from Caledonian immigrants. The first professional was John Dunn Tucker, descended from the old Musselburgh Dunns of Scotland, who arrived in the fall of 1898 and served two seasons.

Shortly after golf had made its first start in America a young Scotsman named Donald Ross, wishing to become an expert in his chosen profession, left his home town of Dornoch in Sutherland and journeyed south to St. Andrews to take a position as apprentice under old Tom Morris, the acknowledged dean of Scotch professionals. Service under this wise old man gave to young Donald a knowledge of his profession and inspired in him a love for the game as a great sport ripe in the rich traditions of the past. Upon the completion of his apprenticeship in 1893, Donald returned to take the position of professional and greenkeeper at his home club, Royal Dornoch.

At Harvard University a certain professor named Robert Wilson had become infected with the germ of the new game and, as any good student would do, sought to learn more about golf by going to the source of all information and had spent several summers at Dornoch. Naturally he became acquainted with Donald and, recognizing his abilities, urged him to seek his fortune in America. In 1899 Donald reached the new country, having spent practically his entire fortune for the trip and without any idea whatever of where he might find a position. However, Professor Wilson did not fail the immigrant and quickly located him as the professional at the Oakley Country Club in Watertown, Mass.

In the summer of 1900 James W. Tufts, seeking a professional for his new golf course in Pinehurst, asked Donald to come to his home in Medford for an interview. At this meeting a verbal understanding was reached on the terms of employment. This agreement, covering Donald's arrangements at the club, was to be carried on for 48 years under the management of Pinehurst by three generations of the Tufts family.

At first Donald served only as professional

"THE SCOTTISH INVASION"

at Pinehurst during the winter and at Watertown and later Essex during the summers. As the demand for golf in Pinehurst grew, new holes were built by Donald and Frank Maples, the Pinehurst superintendent of courses. The architectural features developed by these two men proved to be popular, and as a result Donald was asked to build courses being developed by those who had visited Pinehurst and who had there developed their love for the game. Gradually Donald Ross's fame as an architect spread with the result that by 1910 he had terminated all his professional connections, except for Pinehurst, and was devoting a large part of his time to golf course architecture. Donald Ross not only designed golf courses, he also built courses and often had as many as six or eight construction projects in progress at the same time. During his life time he did work on a grand total of some 600-odd courses.

One of Donald's greatest services was the establishment of early golf at Pinehurst on the very highest standards. He never forgot his early training under Tom Morris and in all his work lived up to the traditions learned in the old gray town under the old master.

Donald Ross established his home in Pinehurst and in his later years became a director in the company which now operates the resort. He died there in 1948 after years of fruitful contribution to the game of golf in America.

Frank Presbrey

Though golf was derided in the early days as being an old man's game, by 1904 the younger players dominated play to such an extent that

After making his fortune in the soda-fountain business, James Tufts retired to North Carolina to build a village named Pinehurst. Golf wasn't his game—he preferred a game similar to croquet called "roque."

The Pinehurst Country Club clubhouse in the early 1960s.

wastes. We have just finished extracting the turpentine from a large number of pines on a big acreage and then cut them up for lumber. There are about ten thousand acres in all. I asked him to make me an offer and he suggested that it might be worth $1.00 an acre, but I closed the deal by selling it to him for $7,500. He gave me his check for $500 to bind the bargain, but I am afraid that I will never see him once he gets home and thinks it over."

When Mr. Presbrey, who was in the advertising business, learned that the deal had not fallen through he went to Boston to offer his services to James W. Tufts.

those who had attained middle age had little prospect of doing well in competition. Horace L. Hotchkiss of the Apawamis Club in Rye, New York, suggested that the club hold a special event for veterans. The first tournament was played at Apawamis on October 12, 1905 and was won by James D. Foot with a 36 hole score of 184. The tournament was a great success and was repeated each year. In 1917 it was suggested by Walter Brown of Montclair that the event be carried on by a national organization. Frank Presbrey, chairman of the tournament committee, wrote the by-laws for the new organization, the United States Seniors' Golf Association, and these were adopted at a meeting held in New York on January 29, 1917.

In 1917 Mr. Presbrey had been an active figure in New York golfing circles for many years, both as a player in tournaments and in his support of the game. In 1895 Mr. Presbrey had received a letter from his friend Walter Hines Page in North Carolina which read in part as follows:

"I have had an amusing experience. There is an old chap up in Boston who I fear has more money than good common sense, and he has a wild scheme in the back of his head that he can make a resort up here in these barren sand

From this contact developed an association that lasted the remainder of Frank Presbrey's life, first with the founder of Pinehurst and later with his son, Leonard Tufts. The association was an important one for the new resort as Frank Presbrey brought to Pinehurst expert advertising ability and, what is more important, he was of great help in the early development of golf there. Though Mr. Presbrey cannot be credited with starting golf at Pinehurst, it was his idea to promote the resort by the conduct of golf tournaments. Competition was very popular at the time and the many tournaments played at Pinehurst not only served to attract golfers but also gave the new place valuable publicity.

Among the first of the tournaments to be started was the North and South Amateur Golf Championship. The first event was played in April, 1901, and has been repeated without interruption every year since. As a result it has been played as many times as the National Amateur, which was not played during the years of the two World Wars.

Another early contribution of Mr. Presbrey's was the formation at Pinehurst in January, 1905, of the American Golf Association of Advertising Interests. Mr. Presbrey had brought to Pinehurst a group composed of advertising executives of both the agencies and the companies which they served. This golf outing was such a great success that the idea of a formal organization was the natural outcome. For many years this group met regularly in Pinehurst and brought the new golf resort to the attention of many men in the business world.

THE END OF THE VERY EARLY DAYS

The early formative years of golf in the United States may best be described as that period during which the game was endeavoring to find its place on the American scene. Golfers themselves were uncertain about the future of the sport; was it a fad which would fade with time and would the proud new clubhouses become skeleton reminders of the past, like the hoop skirt in the attic? Any derision of the game struck a tender spot; the jokes, the supercilious inspection of golf equipment when carried on public conveyances and the derogatory cry of "fore" by the passing urchin could not be shrugged off with the contempt of security.

But in the face of all this uncertainty the game continued to make healthy growth. New clubs were formed, many annual golfing fixtures were established, new adherents were attracted and a few old ones lost. Gradually golfers became less dependent on the old country; the background of American golf was forming and Americans were developing their own way of doing things. Walter Travis learned his golf here and what he learned was good enough to lick the British in 1904. Johnny McDermott became the first home-bred pro to win our own Open Championship in 1911. The total number of entries in the USGA's three championships had increased from 56 to 394. These and many other occurrences suggest that the pioneer years of golf had come to an end.

In Pinehurst, as well, there was every evidence that the game was coming of age. In 1910 the new resort had noted with pride that William C. Fownes, Jr.

had won the USGA Amateur Championship. At the time Mr. Fownes was a regular Pinehurst visitor and was later to establish his winter home there. The 1908 winner of the Women's Championship, Miss Kate Harley, who won her second championship in 1914 as Mrs. H. Arnold Jackson, in the course of time, likewise became a Pinehurst resident.

Pinehurst golf also began to develop a background through those occurrences that add life and interest to the history of any sport. In April of 1902, Mr. George A. Mosher made the resort's first hole-in-one on the 116-yard third hole of No. 1 course. In April, 1904, Mr. Walter J. Travis broke 70 for the first time when he played the 5,408-yard No. 1 course in 69. Also in 1904, Mr. James D. Foot, later the first champion of the U.S. Seniors' Golf Association, found his ball in a mole trap on the roof of a cabin to the left of the green of the 153-yard 11th hole. Nothing daunted, Mr. Foot climbed to the roof, played ball and mole trap to the ground and finally holed out with a six. The next year Mr. Foot improved his aim by putting his ball down the chimney of this same cabin but was unable to continue play of the hole with the ball driven from the tee, since it had been badly burned in the fireplace. An indication of what the golfer of those days hoped to receive as a reward for his prowess on the links is suggested by the list of prizes awarded during the 1904-05 season: 76 cups, 33 medals, two steins, two cream pitchers and one plate. ■

Growing up around Pinehurst means unlimited golf challenges—like the par-three 13th hole on Pinehurst No. 4.

BORN AND RAISED

BY BILL FIELDS

Mr. Fields was born in Pinehurst in the spring of 1959 and grew up in Southern Pines. When he realized he wasn't fast enough for basketball or tough enough to face an inside fastball, he took up golf in earnest. He is still waiting to make his mark as a player, but happily he has been able to write about and photograph the game for most of his adult life, most recently as senior editor/photographer for "Golf Illustrated" magazine in New York City. A piece of him is always in the Sandhills, however, and he comes back every chance he gets.

I came home last fall for a vacation. It had been a while since I'd been back, and I wanted to make sure the Pinehurst-Southern Pines that I knew was still there. It was, of course, although there were a few more stores, stoplights and condos than the last time.

To people who live there now, like my Mom, my mother-in-law and some good friends, the area's growth has turned it into some kind of metropolis waiting to happen. Then they come to visit me in New York and are reminded to think again.

Once I convince people that I was born in Pinehurst—and many think it's strictly a place to spend the *other* end of your life—I try to tell them what makes the place special. I can do a pretty good job of this now, but I'm glad I didn't have to give any testimonials while I was growing up. You don't think much about where you're growing up while you're growing up— at least I didn't. I was too busy playing ball, pitting my good-guy plastic soldiers against the bad guys or getting a haircut. Since I kept my hair cropped to major-championship speed, it seemed like I was forever at the barbershop. Other kids got lunch money; I got haircut money.

In time, I let my hair grow out a little, and, nearing 32, I have most of it left. But the gray hairs are starting to pop up in irritating numbers, like so many three-putt greens. Alas, that is what the big city does to a man.

I went north about five years ago to further my career as a golf journalist. It is a culture shock to move to New York from anywhere— the city is like no other—but perhaps especially unsettling to come straight from the peaceful Sandhills. I had been lucky enough after graduating from the University of North Carolina to return home to work for the World Golf Hall of Fame. That was indeed a kick, especially since I had been a school kid in the crowd when the hall opened in 1974, with President Gerald Ford on hand. There's nothing like having one of the best par fours in the world (the fifth at Pinehurst No. 2) just 40 paces from your office.

I was only at the Hall for a year, but I came back to the area two years later to work for *Golf World* magazine. Talk about a perfect fit: a golf publication in a golf capital. But what a change in lifestyles I endured when I left *Golf World's* clubby confines for The Big Apple. For my daily athletic diversion, I went from hitting balls at lunch on a beautifully grassed practice range to watching a bunch of screaming, cursing teens playing a version of baseball on an asphalt field as I made my way home from my subway stop in Brooklyn. The nearest grass was being smoked down the street, and as for golf, I ventured out to a couple of driving ranges in distant New Jersey. I had nothing personal against those ranges, but I do have a thing about rubber mats. The only one I knew growing up was the one that kept me from slipping in the shower.

There isn't a golf writer worth his ID card who isn't familiar with Pinehurst, of course, but I don't know another one who was actually born and raised there. If it's not the American equivalent of growing up in St. Andrews, Scotland, I don't know what is. My high school, for instance, had a practice green (thanks to horticulture class) and putting intramurals.

But some things may surprise you. If you have the good fortune of being born in Pinehurst, you don't necessarily come out of the crib carrying a five-iron. And your birthplace, however golf-rich, doesn't guarantee that you'll hit the ball long and straight. Long, maybe, but not long and straight. For that you have to drink lots of magic spring water over in Jackson Springs, and I obviously didn't drink enough of it, despite visiting my grandmother there every Sunday afternoon.

My family didn't have a rich golf heritage. My uncle, a furniture salesman who traveled a lot, enjoyed playing now and then. But my father didn't know Ben Hogan from Ben Hur, and he wasn't interested in golf until I urged him to bury a couple of potato-chip dip cans in the back yard so we could chip and putt. While he eventually caught the fever—and had some of his happiest times playing golf—Mom and my two older sisters were a different story. During our annual summer vacations to North Myrtle Beach, I would cajole them into playing

MR. SMITH AND MRS. JONES VISIT PINEHURST

Before sophisticated computers with mail-merge and other bells and whistles were developed to help a large business like Pinehurst with its correspondence, office staffers were left with balky typewriters that would print out letters from a roller like that from a player piano.

As Richard Tufts' long-time secretary and right-hand lady, Mildred McIntosh was in charge each fall of churning out hundreds of letters to past guests, updating them on improvements to the property and plans for the coming year.

"We had a form letter and there were places to put in the person's name, to personalize it," she says. "You'd put in Mr. Jones' name in the proper place and then say, 'We're looking forward to seeing you and Mrs. Jones this season,' that kind of thing.

"Well, sometimes we'd get busy and forget to change all the names. It was so easy to send out a letter to Mr. Smith saying, 'We look forward to seeing you and Mrs. Jones this season.'

"I'm telling you, there were some pretty rough times. We had a lot of explaining to do on several occasions."

miniature golf. They usually weren't much of a threat, but they did keep a neat scorecard.

Their reluctance, however, did nothing to dim my enthusiasm for the game. By junior high, I was into golf full throttle, convinced that, like Julius Boros, I could swing easy and hit hard all the way to the pro tour. I even had an Amana cap, just like Julius did. But the cap didn't help my game. As things turned out, I mostly swung hard and hit crooked, breaking my heart much more often than I broke par. But I had fun trying.

First there was Knollwood, a nine-hole course with size-four fairways and a driving range that remains my favorite, even if the range balls were sometimes kept in circulation for a year or two too long. During the 1970s, when the tour came to town every year, some of the fringe pros would come over to Knollwood to practice. One year, Chuck Thorpe, Jim's brother, played the course. Thorpe had one of those early model graphite-shafted drivers, and he could move it. He played through us on the fifth hole one day, and it was the first time that I had seen anyone launch a drive that started like a Roberto Clemente liner and then climbed as if it were in an elevator. Once I also saw Tommy Burleson, the 7-foot-4 N.C. State basketball player. Let's just say he didn't look comfortable over the ball.

Thanks to Jesse Nelson, a kind-hearted man who tended the shop, I could hit all the balls I could handle, as long as I picked up the empty buckets and helped him heat Stewart Sandwiches if he got tied up. And I went around those nine holes so often I could diagram them in my sleep—even now.

The same holds for Mid Pines, where I began working part-time in high school so I could play the classy Donald Ross layout. Mid Pines wasn't long—only about 6,600 from the back tees—but if you didn't drive the ball accurately, you'd find trouble. I've played lots of courses since I was making a buck there parking golf carts and carrying suitcases, and it still ranks among my favorites. Nearly every summer evening I would go out to test my mettle with the assistant pros—Barry, Lloyd or Gary—and I had a running duel on the putting clock with the head pro, Jim Boros, Julius's nephew, another man who gave me every chance to improve my golf.

Then there was Pinehurst itself. When I was real young, Pinehurst held a certain mystique. Even though our home in Southern Pines was only five miles away, Pinehurst seemed like another world—a place where the monied came to play golf in the spring and fall. It was that, of course, but it was also a real town where people worked—many at the resort—lived and raised families.

Later on, Pinehurst was where I carried a scoring standard during the World Open. One year, I happened to get Tom Watson's group on Saturday and Sunday. I remember waiting in the caddie area on the morning of the final round. Caddie Bruce Edwards was ridding Watson's bag of some surplus balls and I couldn't believe it when he handed over a dozen balls to another kid who was hanging around, not me. As for Watson, he hit the ball higher than the pines, but not always straight. But I remember reaching for red numbers more often than not, because it seemed as if he holed everything. We would-be Watsons got to play our high-school golf at Pinehurst, and that was as much of a treat for the other conference teams as for us. We never played any matches on the No. 2 course, but courses 1 and 4, where we usually got to play, sure weren't bad compared to some of the other conference layouts, where a power line could be one of the prominent design features.

Of course, at the time, I took it for granted that we had access to some of the grandest golf in the land. And that we lived in a place where the air was clean and the streets were safe. Kids do that. Grownups, however, can reflect. I do that often, usually when I look on my desk and spot the enormous pine cone that my father put in a Mason jar so many years ago. It has held its shape nicely, and still looks good.

THE BRAVE SCOTTY

BY O.B. KEELER

Long-time "Atlanta Journal" sports editor O.B. Keeler was a regular visitor in Pinehurst, either as a professional observer of the North and South competitions or an eager player on the resort's golf courses. In this story written for the tournament program of the 1936 PGA Championship, played on No. 2, Keeler recounts one of the more amusing sights from his days in the village.

In the long generation of golf at Pinehurst—two generations, one might well rate it, in this rapid era—I've seen a lot of the game, in its better competitive phases, as the North and South Open; and an increasing number of the happier interludes of my life have been in the famous Pinehurst setting. And now that the PGA Championship at last and most worthily has been awarded to Pinehurst—the National Professional Championship, I always term it—the great No. 2 course achieves its rightful place in the front rank of competitive golfing arenas of North America and the world.

I've seen many wonderful things in golf at Pinehurst. I've watched George Dunlap, Pinehurst's own bright particular star, in some of his amazing victories. Once I stepped off the tremendous driving of Phil Finlay, in a match with Dunlap, when the tall Californian averaged 290 yards in 14 wallops. That's the most consistent display of long-range walloping I have yet observed—and I've watched Ted Ray in his prime, and Charlie Hall, and Freddie Brand; and in later years Jimmy Thomson and Lawson Little and most of the other long boys.

But the most whimsical thing I ever saw on a golf course was at Pinehurst, some years ago, in the Women's North and South Amateur, in a match between Mrs. Opal Hill and Miss Margaret Maddox. The sixth green was the stage. The match was level. Mrs. Hill was left with a putt of a dozen feet for the halve.

Mrs. Hill was on one knee, back of her ball, lining up the putt when out of the gallery trotted a bright-eyed little Scotty, one of those born canine actors and comedians. Bristling with interest, he sized up the situation—as he saw it.

"Now, there's that little round hole," you could follow the Scotty's mental processes. "That lady—she's worried, because she thinks there's something in that hole. She's backed clear away from it. She's frightened. But I, the brave Scotty—I will investigate!"

And he did. He trotted fearlessly to the hole, peered in, and then, a front foot on either side, stuck his long nose down into the hole, clear up to the ears. Then he raised his head, looked straight at Mrs. Hill, sneezed slightly, winked, and actually nodded reassuringly. And then, with both players and the gallery convulsed, the brave Scotty lay down and rolled on the hole! Then he got up, shook himself, nodded again at Mrs. Hill, and trotted back to his place in the gallery.

"There, now," he seemed to say. "Everything's under control. There's nothing in that hole!"

When Mrs. Hill stopped laughing, she sank the putt, and went on to win the match. Pinehurst, with all its memories of championships, is clustered with pleasant recollections beside. ∎

CINDY FUQUAY

THE '51 RYDER CUP

By HENRY LONGHURST

Many Americans know the late Henry Longhurst best for the pungent commentary he delivered annually from the 16th hole at Augusta National during CBS' telecasts of the Masters. But Longhurst's greatest talent was writing. For 45 years he penned a weekly golf column in "The Sunday Times" of London and authored more than a dozen books on golf. This essay on the 1951 Ryder Cup Matches in Pinehurst, won handily by the United States, 9 1/2 to 2 1/2, is reprinted from "Round in Sixty-Eight." Note the controversy golf-course architecture and livelier golf balls created even 40 years ago.

U nlike the orthodox oasis, which consists of a few trees in a sea of sand, Pinehurst is an oasis of sixty-three rectangular grass strips, plus a certain amount of sand, in a sea of trees. The grass strips are, of course, the fairways of the three and a half golf courses which its protagonists like to call the St. Andrews of America—a fair enough claim, no doubt, though challengeable I thought from later experience, by the Monterey Peninsula in California.

Other more elongated strips indicate the roads by which nonaviators can wriggle their way into and out of Pinehurst by car. In clearings off these roads, each protected from the prying eye of the populace by a fringe of pines, are specimens of those lovely, white, Colonial-style American homes familiar to the British film-goer. General Marshall rents one. Dick Chapman, the 1951 British Amateur champion, and his conversational wife, Eloise, have another, and so has the hospitable Earl of Carrick.

As to the others, what with Singer Sewing Machines, Heinz's 57 Varieties (surely more by now?), Somebody's Ball Bearings and Somebody Else's Motors, the guide on my privately conducted tour might have been reciting from a handbook of the industrial nobility.

With all this, and bearing in mind its resounding reputation, it was a surprise to find Pinehurst a village of some 998 inhabitants. They are, of course, outnumbered all the year round by visitors and it must be many a long day since less than 1,000 souls were in Pinehurst at any one moment. In the summer they come up to escape the sweltering heat of the south; in the winter they descend from freezing New York, Detroit, and Chicago. Pinehurst, in fact, has it all ways.

Nevertheless it remains, curiously yet completely, a village, and a model village at that, law-abiding, of good behavior, and, as Pepys put it, "all things civil, no rudeness anywhere." I cannot imagine there to exist a Pinehurst policeman.

And now it really is time to make our way down to the club, either by a pleasant stroll through the pine trees or by the ancient bus which long since came of age and lingers on as a symbol of an unhurried way of life that lures people back to Pinehurst year by year as an antidote to city life. The bus has been driven since birth by an elderly bespectacled character called "Happy," and you feel that the two of them, despite their savage arguments over the gears, are now part and parcel of each other. "Happy" drives back and forth, waving at all and sundry, stopping dead at each little crossing to peer right and left over his spectacles, and, in contrast with others of his kind, cheerfully stopping to encourage those on foot to jump in and join the party. His lounge and locker room cry of "Bus to the Ho-tale. . . Bus to

the Ho-tale" must be an almost universal Pinehurst memory.

The clubhouse, by comparison with the little converted farmhouse at Mildenhall or the tin-shed architecture of Rye or Westward Ho! so beloved of all who know them, might seem positively Ritzian, but by American country club standards it is by no means ostentatious and reflects the fact that the Pinehurst visitor, while liking to do himself well, has come mainly to play golf. I had not been there long when the Ryder Cup team arrived, fresh—or, rather, far from fresh and for the most part, alas, unshaven—from a night on the train, little suspecting that they were to be driven straight to the club and lined up for pictorial purposes for a ceremonial unfurling of the flag.

"They have come," I recorded, "to a land of soft accents, smiling faces, and unfailing courtesy. Dozens of times daily someone seems to be saying, 'You're welcome!' and all appear to mean it. And if this does not remind them of home, there are in the clubhouse those universal pictures of golf—the foursome on Leith Links in 1682 and the rest, and Harry Vardon playing here in 1900—to say nothing of the Quorn in full cry over the reception desk.

Golf is the Esperanto of sport. All over the world golfers talk the same language—much of it nonsense and much unprintable—endure the same frustrations, discover the same infallible secrets of putting, share the same illusory joys. And nothing, it has seemed to me in my travels, so symbolizes this common language as the pictures they hang on their walls. I have seen the same pictures in St. Andrews, Shanghai, Singapore, Ceylon, Rochester, N. Y., Pinehurst, Atlanta, California, Christchurch, Melbourne, and Sydney. Perhaps the most familiar, after the long-faced gentleman in the red coat and three-cornered hat carrying over his shoulder an equally long-faced wooden putter, with an

TUFTS ARCHIVES

Nine members of the victorious American team gather around their trophy (L-R): Jack Burke, Lloyd Mangrum, Henry Ransom, Clayton Heafner, Sam Snead, Skip Alexander, Ben Hogan, Jimmy Demaret and Porky Oliver.

Nov. 29, 1921

Mr. Frank Maples
Pinehurst

Dear Frank:

Miss Gray has just handed me the figures on the cost of building the golf courses here, which are as follows:

No. 2 — $ 13,703.09 from Jan. 7, 1906 to May 31, 1921.
Changes on No. 1 and No. 2 — $5,939.93 (mostly to No. 1).
No. 3 — $8,242,75.
No. 4 — $12,138.20.

Yours very truly,
Isham C. Sledge
Pinehurst Inc.

uncouth caddie and the Blackheath windmill in the background, is the St. Andrews scene entitled simply "The Golfers." This is the one showing a distinguished body of spectators clustered around four players in the foreground, the latter peering down in great animation at what might have been a stymie. Irreverent Americans, not appreciating the hallowed nature of the scene, have been heard, I fear, to call it "The Crap Game."

As for Harry Vardon, what a fantastic ball he set rolling in those tours of his at the beginning of the century! All over the States he set the golfing flame alight. North, south, and on the Pacific coast you see the same fading, sepia-toned photographs of "Vardon here in nineteen-o-something"—the elementary, barren-looking terrain, the thin line of bewhiskered, bowler-hatted onlookers with here and there, greatly daring, one or two lady spectators attired as though for motoring, and in the foreground the familiar figure in his tight knickerbockers, with coat tails flying as he swings. What a flawless swing, too, for all your present-day bashers!

The Pinehurst courses—Nos. 1, 2, and 3, they call them, in a manner strangely prosaic in a country given to romantic nomenclature—radiate fanwise from the clubhouse. The left edge of the fan is the first hole on the No. 2, or championship course. Beside it is the eighteenth, then a practice ground, then the eighteenth and first holes of No. 1, and finally, away on the right, the first and last holes of No. 3. In front of the club are two enormous practice greens, of which my last memory is of Hogan lining up six balls from perhaps 15 feet. "You watch!" said a man beside me. "He'll hole the lot." I watched, and he did.

All three courses, and the odd nine holes which is squeezed in somewhere between No. 2 and No.1—I never did quite discover its whereabouts—were designed by a Scot, Donald Ross, who left his mark all over the American golfing scene at the turn of the century. Whether his architectural ideas seemed

advanced then, I do not know, but his Pinehurst courses, little altered, I believe, from the day of conception, stand up to the most modern ideas of strategic and "intelligent" golf architecture, in distinction to those of his contemporaries in England and Scotland, notably Willie Park, whose formula in those days was the pure frontal attack, a kind of Grand National Steeplechase, with a great cross bunker to carry with your drive and another to jump with your second. As I played the No. 3 course with N.C. Selway—the Cambridge golfer of the twenties, whose accounts of this Ryder Cup match appear in the *Times*, his first venture in this sphere, proved that all you require, in order to write first-class descriptions of golf, is to know the game and then write home and tell your friends what happened—we found ourselves constantly brought up short with the feeling, "Surely, somewhere, we have played this hole before?" There was indeed, on this course and on the No. 1, a remarkable similarity with others we both knew well. At home, Swinley Forest, Woking, the Blue course at the Berkshire, and New Zealand, that little frequented but delightful course near Byfleet, all came to mind, but none was the one we were searching for. I do not know who thought of it in the end but the answer was Morfontaine, the delightful heather, fir, and silver birch course outside Paris—where incidentally, and damn it to this day, I once lost the French Amateur Championship final by a putt on the last green.

The No. 2 course, the scene of the Ryder Cup match, is Pinehurst's pride and joy. When we were there, it had been closed for some three months, specially nursed for the occasion, and by a kindly dispensation, to enable to me to comment for the *Sunday Times*, I believe I had the honor of playing the first round on it. I asked them if they could manage to fix me up with a partner.

In 1930, when, as I have mentioned, 10 of us set forth from Cambridge to tour the United States, we had played a match against Harvard. Of our opponents, I remembered through the years the name only of Jim Baldwin, whose mighty slugging of the ball was then notorious in undergraduate golfing circles. Walking back to christen the No. 2 course at Pinehurst, I found waiting to partner me none other than Baldwin, now a prosperous New York businessman. Baldwin is one of those golfers, like P.B. Lucas at home, who in practice or out, seem unable to hit the ball at all without hitting it a long way, a secret which those of us who become more and more puny as the years go by may envy but no longer hope to fathom. If ever there was a course on which length was everything, it was Pinehurst at this time. Hogan, they said, had once done it in 65 and had had 271 for 72 holes, or 17-under fours, and Tommy Armour claimed to have done 18 consecutive rounds of 68 or better. With the grass about three inches thick on the fairways and the ground untrodden for three months, they could hardly have done such things to it then. For minor fry, at 7,007 yards on the card and playing more like 9,000, it was murder— brassies, brassies all the way, as the poet might have said—and it was not long before my partner and I agreed upon it as an admirable battlefield for the Sneads and Mangrums of this world but no fit stamping ground for aging investment brokers and golf correspondents.

Still, we established one record which, unless some radical change comes over American golf, is likely to stand for years. We did it in two hours and 25 minutes.

Even after the fairways had been "played in" by the practice rounds and later had been mowed, the course was still gigantic. And it was good in these days, when so many people will go to absurd lengths to prevent low scores, thus ruining the designs of the architect, to see that for the match itself many of the farthest tees were not used.

What a farce is this business of length! Golf is surely the only game, either in the United States or Britain, whose whole character has been changed solely by so-called "improvements" in the instruments with which it is played. None of these changes have been solicited by, or had the approval of, the ruling body. Year by year we have altered 36,000 tees, and the Americans, I suppose, have altered 90,000, to accommodate Messrs. ——'s confounded new ball. Year by year we walk farther and farther

and year by year get fewer shots in the process. No one, so far as I can see, benefits and many lose. X drives farther than Harry Vardon did, but only the dumbest of clucks would derive much satisfaction from that, since Y and Z and even your humble servant do the same. What with all this and the creeping paralysis that has come over the game in that country, innumerable Americans now play nine holes in two hours in the morning and another nine in another two hours in the afternoon—and then call it a day's golf. Vardon's golf comes by no means within the category of "ancient." The problems he faced were the same in principle as today; his style and methods were recognizable in Bobby Jones and are certainly recognizable in the classical style of Jackie Burke, perhaps the most promising young player in the world at the moment of writing. Yet when Vardon

Tommy Armour once said that Pinehurst's practice tee, dubbed "Maniac Hill," is to golf "what Kitty Hawk is to flying." The early North and South Opens provided the best time (and about the only time) for pros to study their own games with expert advisors present.

JOHN HEMMER

played Pinehurst at the turn of the century he had only to walk 5,400 yards. He averaged 73 and his best score was 71. In the Ryder Cup, Dai Rees, who was twice round in 71, had in each case to walk almost a mile further. I cannot believe that the parties concerned would alter the stands at Wimbledon, Forest Hills, Wembley and the Yankee Stadium simply to accommodate a new ball, which when struck in the same manner, happened to go further. I rather fancy they would tell the manufacturers what to do with their new ball.

The Americans, however, as befits the now senior partner, have taken some sort of lead in this matter. They have an apparatus consisting of a 15-foot trough, behind which is a rotating wheel with "club" attached. You insert the ball; it flies up the trough; an "electric eye" measures its speed; and if this exceeds 255 feet per second, the ball is illegal. They take balls at random from professionals' shops and even from players on the course in tournaments.

The above impressive technicalities were described to me by Mr. Richard S. Tufts, a slight, earnestly genial figure whose name is as synonymous with that of Pinehurst as the late C.B. Macdonald's was with the National. His grandfather founded it and he has now ascended the throne as uncrowned king of "Pinehurst Inc." This benevolent and, I believe, non-profit making institution is the complete Lord of the Manor. It owns all the ground, the club, the golf courses, and the stately homes. As a member of the U.S. Golf Association, Mr. Tufts has done much not only for the game over there but indirectly for us all, since he was a member of the "negotiating body" who came to consult with St. Andrews over the rules. Their deliberations, which resulted in the present universal code, were conducted in a spirit calculated to give poor Molotov a heart attack. Opening in the cloistered calm of a committee room in the House of Lords, as guests of Lord Brabazon, they settled down not to be two negotiating bodies from rival establishments but a single body of grown-up people with a common affection for golf and a common desire that we should all play to the same rules. As presiding genius of Pinehurst Inc., Mr. Tufts was organizer-in-chief for the Ryder Cup matches. He did the job so well that, even with a blank first day, they took in this remote hamlet, some 23,000 dollars. What it cost them over and above this is anybody's guess.

I had not intended to go into golfing

technicalities but, in view of Hogan's eminence, will risk one exception. After watching my puny efforts on the practice ground he asked why it was that British players brought the club up so abruptly after impact. When I demurred that, fat and forty, I was "hardly representative . . . etc.," he said, "No, no. All your team do it. I have often noticed. Why? We reckon," he went on, "to keep the left arm straight on the way back and the right arm straight on the way through, right to the end—like this." It was here that he seized me and performed the armed combat demonstration.

To the original question I replied with some confidence that it was because we habitually wore more clothes for our all-the-year-round golf. Hogan and those who follow the tournament trail also "follow the sun," as the title of his film confirmed. They play in shirtsleeves. For much of the year we play with a pullover, surmounted by a thick sweater or jacket, in which this right-arm elongation is impossible save to the ultra-lissom. Dai Rees, on the other hand, thought the British method of following through resulted from "trying to get the ball up off hard ground"—but this, with due respect, is simply not true for at least half the year, and I must prefer my own explanation.

At any rate, unimpeded by spectators, I watched Hogan closely in a practice round with Burke, Demaret and Claude Harmon. Each of these three was driving a colossal sort of ball which, when it should have been descending, would bore onwards towards the hole, and it seemed impossible that a man the size of Hogan, who happened to be driving last, could reach them. Time and again, however, he lashed the ball along 30 feet from the ground, or "quail high" as they say in Texas. It ran perhaps

JOHN HEMMER

30 yards where theirs had stopped almost dead on the soft fairways, and finished five yards past the lot.

Since then I have been consulting his book, *Power Golf*, to see whether, unlike so many golfers who write books, he practices what he preaches. The answer is "Yes, he does." I never saw anything quite like it. By taking his club far away from him on the backswing, and then almost as far back round his neck as our own James Adams, and then thrusting it even farther away in front after impact (by which time he is already on the outside of his left foot, with the right heel high in the air) he attains, in fact, the swing of at least a six-footer. His right arm never bends after impact and it finishes in a position with which the reader may care at his own risk to experiment, namely dead straight and pointing, almost horizontally, behind his head. "The speed and momentum," says the caption, "have carried me to a full finish." They would carry most of us to the infirmary.

The Ryder Cup match itself is ancient history, though I will later append the results, but the play, as Sherlock Holmes would have said, "presented certain points of interest."

Wise before the event, for once—and prepared to produce written testimony to this effect in the shape of newspaper cuttings—I reckoned the British team's "Par" to be one foursome and two singles (out of four foursomes and eight singles). In fact they won one foursome and one and a half singles.

Perhaps the most extraordinary feature of the proceedings was the weather on the first morning. With the impression still fresh in the mind I find that I cabled back that evening:

"This really has been one of the most extraordinary days of golf I can remember. We have been sweltering for days, sometimes in almost tropical heat, and now we wake up to what might be a December morning at Gleneagles or the Berkshire, with an authentic Scotch mist limiting visibility to a drive and a brassie, shivering spectators, and players blowing on their fingers to keep them warm.

"Among the gallery in the fourth match, bearing no outward and visible sign connecting him with the proceedings, is a small dark man with gray raincoat, gray cap, gray trousers and inscrutable expression, looking somewhat like a Pinkerton detective on unobtrusive watch for pickpockets. This is the world's greatest golfer, Ben Hogan, participating in the Ryder Cup match. His partner, the normally flamboyant Jimmy Demaret, is concealed in a flowing check ulster with a distinctly Sherlock Holmes air. From time to time they step forward, undress, give the ball a resounding slam, and return to anonymity.

"As if this is not enough, the afternoon turns to rain, pouring relentlessly down on the avenues of silent pines. Sodden spectators, strangely woebegone in their bizarre headgear, trickle back to the clubhouse, the refreshment tent runs out of 'hot dogs,' and what has so long been a sunny, colorful scene turns to something approaching a wet Sunday afternoon in Wigan."

One cannot see everything in these matches, but one part of the encounter between Hogan and Charles Ward still lingers in memory. After seven holes in the afternoon Ward was still only 2-down. The eighth is a hole of some 488 yards, with a narrow opening to the green, and the only man I saw reach it in two was the equally diminutive Hogan. Ward pitched his third gallantly up within holing distance, whereupon Hogan, in the silent, steely-eyed, remorseless way that hypnotizes his opponents, rolled in his 10-yarder for a three.

The ninth is a short one, with the pin on a plateau to the left. Ward's ball did its best but eventually slithered down to the right, leaving a putt long enough and awkward enough to arouse suspicions of three more to come. He struck it beautifully. It breasted the slope, pushed along towards the hole, and fell in for a two. This brought them to the longest hole on the course, declared by the card to be 593 yards but only, I rather suspect, because Pinehurst Inc. is a little shy of admitting it to be more than 600. Some estimates put it as high as 630. At any rate after two shots as hard as they could hit them, the longest hitters on either side were still debating between a four-iron and a five-iron for their third. Here Ward, only two-down again now, played three good orthodox shots and his ball lay safely on the green, some distance from the hole. The great man on the other hand had driven into the forest.

Here he manufactured some sort of shot which moved him along down the fairway but still far enough away to need one of his biggest to reach the edge of the green. This he duly delivered, but it left him still every bit of 25 yards from the flag. He surveyed it from end to end, tight-lipped and inscrutable, and you could have heard a pin drop as at last he hit the ball. Up and up it came towards the hole. As it dropped in, the whole population must have heard the roar. Golf may be the slowest game in the world but, my word, there are times when it can be exciting!

Before closing the Ryder Cup episode let me lift my hat to Hogan, that mighty minnow. Hogan is a fascinating study, almost as fascinating, in an opposite way, as Hagen, with whose name his own used so often to be confused. Hagen was colorful, eccentric, theatrical, gregarious. He loved wine and women and his fellow man, from caddies to Princes of Wales, and saw no reason why life should not permanently be standing him a bottle of champagne. Hogan is the reverse of the coin—steel-hard, wiry, self-disciplined, austere. Hagen was a gift to golf writers. Of Hogan, till his motor smash and subsequent recovery made him an idol of sporting America, they could find little to say except that he had again gone round in 68.

Nowadays, after physical and mental suffering on the grand scale, the genuine adoration of a whole nation, and the comforting feeling that he has no more golfing or financial worlds to conquer, Hogan has mellowed a good deal—on the surface, that is. Perhaps, underneath, he was mellow all the time. At any rate I must record that I find his company highly stimulating. I am not by nature a celebrity hunter—if anything the reverse—but, if you have seen so much of golf and golfers, you can hardly fail to be intrigued by a man who plays it better than does anyone else in the world. ■

MATCH-PLAY EVENT WINS NO MEDAL

The PGA Tour has experimented with various forms of match-play events over the years in an effort to relieve the week-to-week tedium of 72-hole, stroke-play tournaments. One such experiment was held at the Country Club of North Carolina in Pinehurst in September, 1971. Its official name was the Liggett & Myers Inc. Tournament Players' Division U.S. Professional Match Play Championship. Unfortunately, some of the biggest names didn't play in it long enough to pronounce it.

Jack Nicklaus played in the pro-am on Tuesday, then lost to Raymond Floyd the following day. "I didn't make one bogey in two days, but I'm going home," Nicklaus said. Gary Player lost his first match on the third extra hole to Homero Blancas and said: "I've just flown 20,000 miles to make a bogey." Arnold Palmer lost in the quarterfinals.

The 64-man field actually played "match-medal" competition. The winner of a match was the player with the lowest medal score for 18 holes. The semifinals featured DeWitt Weaver, Phil Rodgers, Bruce Crampton and Ken Still. By the time ABC-TV's broadcast began Sunday afternoon, Weaver was seven shots up on Rodgers in the final, prompting Dan Jenkins of *Sports Illustrated* to surmise that Chris Schenkel was up in the booth saying: "We've got plenty of action for you today, folks. We'll be going out to Latrobe to watch Arnold Palmer file down an eight-iron and then we'll take you to Palm Beach to watch Jack Nicklaus scrape his boat."

The presentation ceremony capped the week off appropriately enough. Weaver collected his $35,000 prize from the giant tobacco manufacturer and announced: "I finally won a golf tournament. I promised my wife if I ever won one, I'd quit smoking."

A VISIT FROM YOGI

BY GERALD HOLLAND

The peace and quiet. The camaraderie. The distance from the real world of phone messages and budgets and schedules. There's nothing like a visit to Pinehurst to rejuvenate the spirit. That goes for doctors, lawyers, Indian chiefs and even managers of the New York Yankees—as Mr. Holland so adroitly explains in this November, 1963 piece from "Sports Illustrated."

They sat in a circle on the lawn of the old and comfortably elegant Carolina Hotel in Pinehurst, N.C., 12 business and professional men on their annual golf holiday. All were members of the White Beeches Golf and Country Club of Haworth, N.J. They were pleasantly dog-tired after 18 holes on one of the five courses that fan out from the clubhouse of the Pinehurst Country Club. All had slept fitfully on the rocky train ride from New York the night before, although one of their number, Dr. Edward N. Bookrajian of Tenafly, N.J., had prescribed sleeping pills all around.

They were silent, drinking in the beauty of the starlit night and the soft breeze that now and again sent a leaf fluttering down from the aged trees. It was one of those moments that is savored best when a man is weary from a day well spent.

There was a celebrity in the group, but he was not being treated as a celebrity here. Perhaps that was why his homely handsome face was creased by a faint smile of contentment. For here, on the lawn in Pinehurst, he was with friends and neighbors and golfing pals. He was Larry, one of the gang, and only incidentally Yogi Berra, the new manager of the New York Yankees.

He needed this respite, this company. That is not to say that he had not taken pleasure and pride in the way things had gone a few days before when he faced the largest press conference in Yankee history. He had been frankly apprehensive about this occasion, but once he had mounted the podium (he stood on a box to clear the cluster of microphones) he had responded good-naturedly to the cries of the cameramen, fielding the questions of the reporters with poise and grace and enough uncalculated Berraisms to brighten the uniformly enthusiastic press notices that followed. Take away Harvard, and President Kennedy himself could not have done much better.

Yogi broke the silence of the circle on the lawn.

"Eight years," he said. "Eight years I've been coming down here. This place gets better all the time. And my golf gets worse."

"Larry," said John Mahmarian of Oradell, N.J., a six-handicapper (Berra's handicap is 13), "you're not getting the distance on your drives that you used to get. You used to hit a very long ball."

Yogi nodded. "I'm not getting the distance."

"You know what you're doing? You're turning your head on your backswing. You're swinging that club like it was a baseball bat."

"I'm hooking and I'm slicing," said Yogi. "I'm in the woods all the time. I'm liable to get bit by a snake."

"You're looking up on your iron shots. You're looking up even before you hit the ball."

Yogi scowled and smacked the arm of his chair. "I got to stop looking up. I just got to do that. Why can't I remember?"

"And you were pretty heavy-handed on the greens, Larry."

"I know, I know," said Yogi. "Putting. I got a touch like a blacksmith." (Yogi is a rarity in golf: a switch-hitter. He swings right-handed with his woods and irons, putts left-handed.)

Francis D. Murphy, a New York attorney who lives in Fort Lee, N.J., suddenly jumped to his feet. "Objection!" he cried. "Let the boy up. Naturally he was off his game today. He was tired. He's been through a lot." He tapped his head. "He's got a lot on his mind."

The group fell silent again. Somebody yawned. Then there were yawns all around. But the group seemed reluctant to call it a day and head for the suite, which included six connecting double bedrooms and a spacious sitting room. For the first time the subject of Yogi's new job as manager of the Yankees came up.

"Who are your coaches going to be, Larry?"

Yogi shook his head. "I don't know. Actually, I don't know. If I knew, I'd tell you fellows."

"Well, now, Larry," said another voice from the darkness, "do they pick your coaches for you? Houk, will he tell you who your coaches are?"

"I pick the coaches," said Yogi, raising his voice ever so slightly. "If I couldn't pick my coaches, I wouldn't take the job."

They talked for a while, then slowly drifted off to bed. Next day they were like new men.

He might be Yogi in New York, but in Pinehurst he's just a golfer named Larry trying to keep his ball in the fairway.

Bright-eyed and rested, Yogi Berra was at the eight o'clock Mass at Sacred Heart Church. The service was brief as services usually are at resorts and, instead of a sermon, the pastor limited himself to an announcement that two collections would be taken up to help along the campaign for a new roof.

Yogi was better at golf that afternoon, his drives truer, his putting improved. He dubbed some iron shots, and once he hurled his club with all the fury of a Tommy Bolt. Once he sliced deep into the rough and yelled, "Timber!" Once, asked for his score on another hole, he growled, "The number on my back." The number on the back of his Yankee uniform is eight. But for all of that, he was in the high 80s for the round.

Now that everyone was rested, the nights were given over to gin rummy and some moderate drinking. Baseball talk kept creeping into the conversation despite all the protestations that this was to be a non-baseball holiday for Larry.

"I'm at the stadium one day," someone said. "A man walks, Mantle's up, hits the first pitch and grounds out. Should Mickey have waited the pitcher out if he was getting a little wild? Shouldn't the take sign have been on?"

"Not with a power hitter like Mantle," said Yogi. "Mantle hits on his own. Maris too."

"Will you be calling pitches, Larry? You know the hitters better than anybody on the club."

"I wouldn't second-guess my catcher," said Yogi.

"Will you miss talking to the umps?"

"I kind of think I'll be talking to them once in a while."

"You going to bring the lineup cards out to home plate or send them out with a coach?"

"I'll take them out," said Yogi.

"Man, the first day you do, the fans are going to tear the roof off the Stadium. Everybody's pulling for you, Larry."

Yogi frowned and, half to himself, he muttered, "I think I can manage. But I got to find out. Handling the players, I'm not worried.

Band leader John Philip Sousa (standing with dark coat) was among famous folks from other walks of life who were regulars in Pinehurst.

Like Joe Garagiola says, 'You got their respect, you don't have to win it, you can only lose it.' I don't blow my top often, but I can get mad. I can be firm, I can put my foot down if anybody gets out of line. I don't know. Eighteen years with the Yanks, a catcher's got to learn something."

The third day of golf was the best yet. Everyone was relaxed and playing better, including 13-handicap Yogi Berra. But, as it happened, he and Eddie Marck were matched with two of the best golfers in the group, John Mahmarian and John Ravaschio. Yogi and his partner were soundly beaten. Ravaschio was the star of the match with a 76 that included some shots that would have done credit to Nicklaus or Palmer. He came off the 18th green enormously pleased with himself, although he tried hard to dwell modestly on a couple of bad shots. A sudden inspiration came to Yogi Berra and his friends. They decided that Ravaschio was ripe for "a tank job," a frame-up in which

his own partner would do everything he could to throw the match and the gallery would cooperate by every evil means possible. Yogi and Mickey Cullere challenged Ravaschio and Mahmarian (who was, of course, in on the joke) to a nine-hole match for an $800 side bet. Ravaschio, flushed with success, didn't hesitate an instant. They teed off immediately.

With everyone conspiring against Ravaschio, it seemed reasonably certain that Yogi and Mickey would win. But despite everything, Ravaschio was hotter than ever. Golf carts raced ahead of him, and his ball was kicked into the rough or a sand trap. They beat him to the green and moved his ball away from the cup. His partner putted atrociously. When Ravaschio putted, half the gallery was seized with coughing fits and the other half jammed the brakes on their golf carts. On the ninth tee it was getting dark and, by the time the foursome reached the green, Ravaschio had only the moonlight as he holed out for a 37.

The gag was revealed back in the suite at the Carolina after everyone had a drink in hand. Attorney Frank Murphy paid eloquent tribute to Ravaschio's golfing prowess, described him glowingly as a sportsman and a gentleman. Murphy concluded by saying, "Finally, my dear John, I must tell you that you have been had, that you have been in the tank—we were all in on it—and, dear friend, you do not get $800. You do not get a dime. Gentlemen, let us drink to John Ravaschio!" The victim, who knows all about tank jobs, shook his head and said, "I only got suspicious once. Remember when I said, 'Who am I playing with, the Marx Brothers?'"

"Ah, yes," said attorney Murphy. "That worried us for a moment. We thought you were wise." Murphy raised his glass and drank deeply. He was obviously pleased with his little speech. Immediately, there was a huddle at the far end of the room. It was agreed: Attorney Murphy would be cut down to size—he would be framed at gin rummy that very night. ∎

A Run Of Threes

BY WILLIAM C. CAMPBELL

Mr. Campbell won four North and South Amateur titles from 1950 to 1967, but one of his most enduring memories of his annual April visit was watching Billy Joe Patton and Hobart Manley battle for the 1951 championship. He remembers the sportsmanship and an incredible run of golf in this piece he contributed to "Famous Golf Stories," edited by LPGA Hall of Famer Carol Mann. The story, says Campbell, is a tribute to "The Ultimate in Amateur Golf."

One of my most vivid memories of some two decades of traveling to Pinehurst for the North and South Amateur was watching the 1951 championship match between the charismatic Billy Joe Patton of Morganton, N.C., and his attractive, fun-loving young friend, Hobart Manley, of Savannah, Ga. Both long-hitters, they had attracted a crowd which grew as their match progressed, and it turned into an intense and memorable golfing experience for all of us onlookers—not to mention the finalists themselves.

On the par-five eighth hole of the afternoon round—the 26th of the match—Manley drove far left into some scrub pine trees. After advancing his ball, he emerged from the pines and shouted to Patton that he had incurred a penalty stroke and thus lay three. Rather than going for the green, Patton then played a conservative second shot short of the green.

When Manley returned to the fairway, the referee, native Scot "Willie" Wilson, asked him about the penalty. Hobart replied that his ball had been moved slightly by something he had stepped on in the underbrush while entering the area with his hands held high. Mr. Wilson ruled that no violation had occurred, and so advised Patton. When the result was a halve in fives, Hobart told Billy Joe how badly he felt about the rules incident. Billy Joe's quick response was, "Get me a Coke (at the halfway house behind the green) and we'll call it even."

But Hobart still felt badly and brooded until the long 10th hole, which he obviously contrived to butcher by aiming his drive into the right woods, then left and right, before conceding the hole. On the 11th tee the match resumed its high level of play, stroke for stroke, as tension mounted.

Patton stood 2-up on the 14th tee and proceeded to play those five great finishing holes in one stroke *under* par—scoring par-four, par-three, birdie-four, bogey-four and birdie-three—only to lose, 1-down to Manley's *five straight threes*, which were *four strokes under par*: birdie, par, eagle, par, birdie. That both players were under such intense pressure, and at the end of a long, competitive week, made both their performances no less than remarkable.

Just watching the drama unfold made my heart pound and left me limp. And I wasn't alone, for it was apparent at the presentation ceremony that both winner and runner-up were emotionally spent. Indeed, there were few dry eyes in the audience, for we all seemed to realize that we had been privileged to experience amateur golf at its very best in both performance and sportsmanship. Now, 40 years later, I still regard the '51 North and South final as one of golf's greatest days.

In later years Patton would become a folk hero to play-for-fun golfers, as he burst on the world scene in the '54 Masters and went on to confirm his talents in several subsequent Masters and U.S. Opens and on several Walker Cup teams. He would also win three North and South Amateurs—one of them, in 1962, he won after beating Manley in a rematch, 7-and-6.

Manley had the greatest natural ability I have seen in a half-century of amateur golf. The game probably came too easily to him, for he missed the discipline needed for even gifted athletes to reach and sustain their full potential. But on that fine April Saturday in Pinehurst, he achieved such heights that anything else could well have been anti-climatic.

Of course, Patton was the other half of that story. Together, they were beautiful. ∎

Hobart Manley (L), Billy Joe Patton.

A RETURN TO THE SHRINE

BY JOHN M. ROSS

Mr. Ross was chairman of the original Golf Writers Association Committee that established the guidelines for election to the PGA/World Golf Hall of Fame in Pinehurst. He remains the Association link with the Hall. Ross is the former editor-in-chief of "Golf" magazine and one-time executive director of the World Cup of Golf. The following piece is adapted from "American Golf Magazine."

Going back to the PGA/World Golf Hall of Fame is always a memorable journey. It's a bit like a class reunion or a return to the old neighborhood. Familiar faces are everywhere and priceless memories, too. For the golfer who has that special place in his heart for the game, it is a visit he will likely carry with him for years to come.

I've been making the trek to the handsome shrine in North Carolina since President Gerald Ford dedicated it in September, 1974. Imagine that—the President of the United States, and a weekend hacker to boot, taking the time to officially launch golf's hallowed hall. And that's hardly an overstatement. He had been in office barely a month following Richard Nixon's resignation, and the Oval Office was a hectic thoroughfare, but when he heard that Arnold Palmer, Jack Nicklaus, Gene Sarazen, Sam Snead, Byron Nelson and Ben Hogan, among others, were going to be on hand, he responded like any other dedicated golfer. He simply made time for it.

When the final confirmation came that the President would be attending, the Carolina Sandhills vibrated with excitement. But just hours before his departure from Washington, there was a report of an assassination plot, supposedly because he had given Nixon the presidential pardon the day before. Some of the Pinehurst natives feared the visit might be canceled. But they didn't know Gerry Ford.

"He was so anxious to meet Ben Hogan," a confidante revealed, "he would have gone even it meant riding in an Army tank."

There were jittery Secret Service agents everywhere, but the ceremonies went ahead as scheduled, installing the "original 13"—the aforementioned six as well as Patty Berg and Gary Player; inducted posthumously were Bobby Jones, Walter Hagen, Harry Vardon, Francis Ouimet and Babe Didrikson Zaharias. Ford insisted afterward on going ahead with plans to play nine holes with some of the inductees. He was in pretty fast company when he checked in at the first tee of Pinehurst No. 2—one of the world's toughest courses. The fivesome consisted of Palmer, Nicklaus, Player

and Deane Beman, the commissioner of the PGA Tour, as well as the President. You and I would have been trembling under those circumstances and probably would have struggled just to set our golf ball on a tee. But Ford simply beamed and chatted amiably as he waited to hit.

Ford, an 18-handicapper at the time, went off like he was playing on the Ryder Cup team. Whistling the ball straight down the middle of the fairway, the President uncorked a 270-yard drive that drew an enormous roar from the gallery and sent his companions jestfully turning and heading for home. When all the tee balls had been played, only Nicklaus had outdriven Ford—and by only eight or 10 yards.

That evening at a black-tie banquet at the Pinehurst Hotel, the President puffed happily on his pipe and listened to his golf heroes tell tales of their days on the fairway that ultimately brought them to canonization. Some of Ford's friends said that the President talked about the night for weeks afterward, indicating that he would cherish it for years to come.

To my mind, it was one of the game's finest hours. We had this handsome, gleaming white edifice sitting there behind the fourth green of famous No. 2. It was chock-full of memorabilia, artifacts and collections pinpointing the game's enormous growth. And we had the President of the United States giving it official status as an American landmark. Baseball had gotten its hall in Cooperstown years earlier. And basketball's hall had been in place in Springfield, Mass., tennis at Newport, R.I., and pro football in Canton, Ohio, before we got ours at Pinehurst. But we seemed to have caught up in a spectacular splash.

The golf shrine, highlighted by stately columns and an abundance of glass in its design, almost bulges with displays, memorabilia and exhibits that pinpoint the game's enormous growth. But more than anything, it is the nostalgia—the priceless memories—that provides the Hall with its greatest riches and attracts over 45,000 visitors a year.

Enshrined within the walls of the spacious buildings—either as the legends of the fairway or as unique contributors to the game's growth—are 60 of the golf world's greatest names. Each has his or her face and golf deeds cast in bronze, often accompanied by some memento of their careers. This represents the very heart of the Hall.

Golf was one of the last major sports to create a shrine for its great heroes and achievers. And for years there had been an ongoing debate as to where it should be located. When the Diamondhead Corp., a real-estate and development firm, purchased the Pinehurst Hotel and Country Club in the early 1970s, it proposed building the Hall here. What's more, it also put up $2.5 million—a huge outlay in 1974—to get the job done.

The Diamondhead proposal was well-received, since storied Pinehurst was always on any list of potential sites for a golf shrine. To put the project on solid footing, Diamondhead asked the Golf Writers Association of America to establish and oversee the selection process for those to be memorialized. The system has worked without hitch or squabble since the beginning.

There are three categories into which honorees are grouped: Modern Era Players (covering the last 20 years), Pre-Modern Players and Distinguished Service. Nominees in the first category must receive 75 percent of the votes cast annually by the writers to gain entry. Candidates in the two other groups are elected directly by a select committee of writers, golf officials and leaders.

The Hall's auspicious beginning did not really put it on a trouble-free course for the future. Most sports shrines and museums must be subsidized in order to survive, and when Diamondhead began to run into financial difficulties with its widespread real-estate operations, the Hall—and Pinehurst, too—was at risk. Ultimately, a consortium of Northeast banks acquired the property and at one point toyed with the idea of converting the shrine's buildings into a conference center. Happily, kinder hearts prevailed.

Several other interim reorganizations failed to guarantee the Hall's future before the Professional Golfers Association of America (the group that represents the club pros) took over the operation in 1985. In recent years, the PGA has invested more than $600,000 in improvements and renovations and has put new collections in place. For instance, the formidable Otto Probst Library, containing more than 7,000 volumes, has been positioned

in the former theatre area and now functions as the world's largest golf reference library.

A mainstay of the museum is the renowned Auchterlonie Collection, which consists of 101 antique and historic clubs. Two of them date back to 1690 and are among the oldest and most valuable in existence. The old clubmaker's shop, showing how the old clubs once were created by hand, is an extremely popular exhibit, and the Eisenhower Memorabilia Case also attracts great attention. There is a display of vintage golf cars; an exhibit of the evolution of the golf grip; the four trophies awarded in the Grand Slam of Golf; historic scorecards and prized photos of golfers of yesterday and today—and so much more.

To be sure, the most time and interest of visitors is focused on the honorees—their bronze plaques and original paintings. It is a trip down memory lane that most golfers cherish for a lifetime. ∎

Gerald Ford (above left) would have made the trip to Pinehurst to meet Ben Hogan and speak at the Hall of Fame induction if "he had to ride in an Amry tank." Today the shrine sits majestically behind the fourth green of Pinehurst No. 2.

OUT OF BOUNDS

BY FURMAN BISHER

Mr. Bisher grew up in Denton, N.C., some 50 miles from Pinehurst, graduated from the University of North Carolina in 1938 and was writing for "The Charlotte News" when he wrote the following column from the North and South Open in Pinehurst for the Nov. 1, 1949 edition. Bisher would go on to carve his niche in sports journalism with impeccable style as sports editor of "The Atlanta Journal," where he works today.

D ear Dad:

I'm weathered in in the section of Pinehurst Country Club known as Out of Bounds, a sort of informal infirmary where several other individuals and I are fighting off desperate cases of pneumonia. Nice young men in white coats keep bringing us brown medicine (with soda or branch water). We've got the germs on the run, I understand, but we can't do a thing about the weather, which is what put me where I am today. If it were raining grits, there'd be enough in Pinehurst to serve the whole South until General Sherman rides through again.

The unpleasantness doesn't stop at the excessive showers. The North assumed complete control of the North and South Open today for the first time in 47 years. We also have the wind to go with the rain in our hair. The temperature dropped 20 degrees in 24 hours, and the golfers went out on the course this morning dressed as if preparing to go over Niagara Falls in a barrel. I watched Skip Alexander dress (with his permission), and I timed his sweater course. It took him 12 minutes, 35 seconds to put on his sweaters, approximately seven in number.

When I got out to the first tee I heard Frankie (Muscles) Stranahan, who was roughing it in only two sweaters and three pairs of pants, say: "Now's the time I wish I had scrawny little arms so I could put on four or five sweaters and not feel like I was in a strait jacket." There are those who wish he could feel like he was in a strait jacket, and Frankie might have been among them after he finished the first six holes six over.

The score, however, was no reflection on Stranahan's game, rather on the weather, which has constantly refused these last three days to recognize Pinehurst's grand reputation as a health spot and its lovely, lovely climate. I've gotten so I can't put a mite of faith in George Shearwood, the ever-so-neighborly retired British Army officer who's publicity director here. George had told me that Sunday was the worst day he'd seen in his five years here. Today he's got a new story. This is worse yet.

I decided to go out and see for myself, which leads up to my case of pneumonia. Once I hit the course I began to wonder why they ever sent the poor pawns of the gallery out. It was the kind of a day on which you wouldn't even send your wife to the corner alehouse to fetch a brew. The wind was so fierce that the pros must have felt the same futility swinging against it that the average 90-and-above swinger feels on any day. Clayton Heafner was still short after hitting a driver and three-wood on No. 1. He's usually there with a driver and six. Stranahan fired four times before he got to the green on No. 3, 340 yards long.

It was the sort of day that would have been perfect for Boatwright and Rainwater, the two amateurs who were named for such conditions. Johnny Bulla and a fellow named Freddie Bolton from St. Louis were the only ducks in the field. Bulla just naturally goes for foul-weather golf and has shot some of his best tournament scores in the muck and wind. Bolton was the only par-marker among those who finished the first nine. When the end finally came I was huddled on the leeward side of a shelterhouse somewhere out in the pines with George Case. We had been caught in a snarling sou'easter while we tried to follow Dick Chapman, Dave Douglas and Lou Barbaro. This Chapman won't quit, sorta like Lineberry Hill used to be about checkers. The rain was pouring and he was playing bareheaded, with no rain jacket. When Eric Nelson, the man who runs the country club, drove up and waved the red flag that meant he could get in out of the rain, Chapman didn't and hit his next shot anyway.

The weather wasn't so much a damper, though. This isn't like most golf tournaments. It's not the money, for heaven knows the $7,500 purse went out with turtleneck sweaters. Paperhangers, furnace salesmen, undertakers, peanut growers, they all have conventions. Well, this is sort of the golfers' convention. This old tournament has been rocking along for 47 years now, since Donald Ross won the first one in 1903, oldest in the country. There's more tradition and prestige around the North and South than in a Masonic goat-riding. The old guard always make it a point to get back, and they're here this year, Gene Sarazen, Tommy

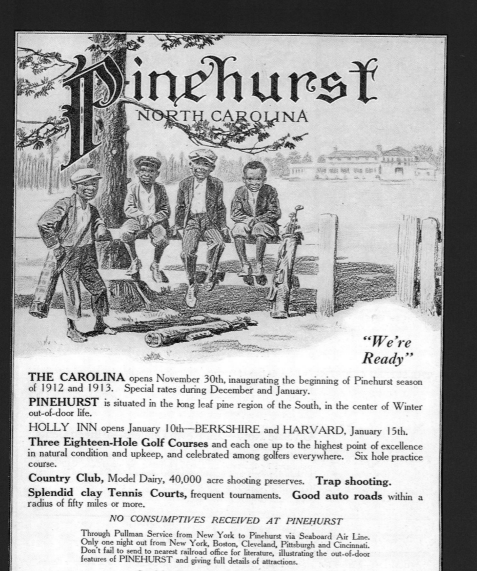

Although Pinehurst was planned from the beginning as a health resort, it guarded vigorously against being known as a sanitarium or a hospital for the treatment of communicable diseases. All early ads stressed that "No consumptives received at Pinehurst." This one from 1912 uses caddies to beckon visitors to play golf on the resort's three courses, and it mentions a "six-hole practice course." Those holes would eventually become part of the first nine of the No. 4 course.

Armour, Bobby Cruikshank, Denny Shute and Johnny Farrell.

The young fellers like to start off here, like Cary Middlecoff in '45. Art Wall, the kid from Duke whose latest hole-in-one box score was 28, tried his best to become a pro today. He'll have to wait, officially. He's got a nice job at Pocono Manor up in Pennsylvania. This Ray Hill, who disturbed the bigshots a lot in the PGA last summer, is celebrating a new job, about the strangest I ever heard. He'll be Babe Didrikson Zaharias' assistant at some club up Nawth. Next thing you know women'll be wanting to vote.

Oh yes, your son. He's in purty high cotton right now, staying at the Carolina Hotel. I'm afraid there ain't nothin' like it around Denton. Sounds sorta plain, you know—Carolina Hotel. Must be one to every county in the state, most of 'em the $2.50 and up per night type. This is the grandpappy of 'em all. It's so big that there are parts of it even Bill Fitzgibbons, the manager, hasn't seen yet. The customers bring a purty big sockful to pay for it all, but one of the meals is enough for a Rotary Club luncheon. And the culinary qualities are boundless. Needless to say, I've been playing their nine-course meal in par.

Your loving son,
Curly

THE VILLAGE, 1903

By GILMAN CROCKETT

Montgomery A. Crockett was hired in 1902 by Pinehurst Inc. to serve as resident physician at the Carolina Hotel and, according to his contract, to "assume entire charge of a certain tract of about 15 acres of blackberry plants which have been planted by the party of the second part at said Pinehurst." A cousin of Pinehurst President Leonard Tufts, Crockett moved wife Helen and two sons to Pinehurst. One of the sons, Gilman, collected the following thoughts in the mid-1970s for the unpublished history which Richard Tufts was preparing.

 y earliest recollection of Pinehurst was the arrival of the four of us— me, brother Albert and my mother and father. It was about 1903 that we all arrived at the hotel Berkshire and my mother remarked how soft the air was. After we had become more or less permanent residents, there was a sort of gathering of the guests in a game or something called "books"—everybody had to put on some sort of rig that represented a current book. I believe at the time that the power house was occasionally failing in putting out the necessary power to produce light and once or twice there were "blackouts." Hence the candles in each room which mystified us. My father was persuaded to wear two electric light bulbs strung around his neck and was, of course, Kipling's *The Light That Failed*. This did not set so well with my uncle Leonard.

The General Store was a real institution to me. Next to the school house, I spent much of my time there. It always smelled of kerosene, stale tobacco smoke and just plain sweat. It seemed always crowded with men in bib overalls and black hats. Goods were not only piled on counters but hung from the rafters. There was an iron hitching rack outside, but I'm not sure whether it was used for horses or support for the bulging rear end of several colored inhabitants. The light was always dim—due to the kerosene lanterns, no doubt.

The Village Green at that time was a large oval with a little sparse grass growing on it. The Holly Inn was at the head end and the Little Red School House was at the other end. It was very sandy and soft and only the boldest of boys dared to run across, leaving telltale steps to be seen and explained. Mr. T.B. Cotter, who was the manager and the nemesis of us youngsters, seemed to be everywhere and woe betide us if anyone was caught crossing the Green or breaking off the top of a young pine tree. I best remember him always with the black moustache and straw hat and perpetual fast walk.

The electric street car ran on the weed-grown tracks which ran around to the various spots in town. The conductor and general handy man was Owen Farrey. He was very popular with us kids because sometimes we could wangle a ride, and he would occasionally let us run the car when out in the sticks. His regular motor-man was Elmer Isaacson—a Norwegian or Dane, I believe. It was a great day when we could bum a ride to Southern Pines. At full speed the car rocked like a row boat in a head sea. Of course, one of us would clank the bell loudly when passing one of our friends.

The Seaboard Airline, or SAL as it was sometimes referred to, ran to Pinehurst and connected us with the north. Some unkind person said the letters SAL stood for "She's Always Late." This was not an exaggerated statement. The Aberdeen-and-Asheboro was the local line which serviced the locality and stopped at the stations that the Seaboard turned up its nose at. The freight trains on this line were pulled by wood-burning locomotives which had big, V-shaped stacks, complete with spark arresters. I used to watch the black fireman open the fire door and throw a four-foot log of pine all the way into the fire box. Most of the steam whistles were of the wailing type, and when an expert fireman got hold of the cord he could almost play a tune with it, especially when passing Smokey Hollow. The passenger trains on this line were made up with about five freight cars and two passenger coaches—one for colored and the other for the whites.

There was the famous time when some rich moguls from up north visited Pinehurst in their private car, which was parked over at the siding near the depot. It was a very ornate affair—lots of bright work on the observation platform, which had an awning over it. We used to sneak over for a quick look but it was soon forbidden ground when it was learned that the party consisted of booze and a few ladies of the evening. It caused considerable whispering among the matrons of the community, so suddenly the private car and all its inhabitants, both good and bad, disappeared one night. I never found out who the owners were and never got so much as a peek at the ladies. So the morals of Pinehurst were saved.

As far as the Little Red School House was concerned, at that time it was just that, com-

plete with a two-holer in rear which was divided into stalls. The school was heated by a wood-burning stove and a lot of pine cones were consumed there. As to teachers—there were a succession of them. The first headmaster was known as Papa Warren, and he had many strange ideas. He kept us boys busy stoking his stove. There was a Mr. Wallace, who was in charge of our room and was first subjected to having a half-dead garter snake wrapped around the door handle of the entrance. This seemed to have little or no effect on him, so some fiend planted two well-formed pine cones in his drawer, base to the rear and pointy ends toward the front. When the drawer was closed it compressed the pines, but when the drawer was opened a little way, the cone spread out and made further manipulation of the drawer impossible. I believe Wallace got so mad he yanked on the desk drawer so much that the knob flew off. My brother and I were the main

troublemakers and it ended by my brother being permanently expelled and I was suspended for two weeks.

Just before the era of Papa Warren ended, there was another couple of brothers that were a part of the devils of doom—Levi D. Jones and his younger brother Russell. At that time it was thought to be very daring if you smoked a Quebeb cigarette. That was a stinking compound sold under the excuse that it cured a cold. Of course, the leader of levity used them but only if you were able to sneak out and not be seen by the high brass. I remember one morning when I went to the two-holer in back of the school and, while engaged in the calls of nature in one of the cubicles, someone came into the other. I was sure that it was Russell Jones, so I popped over my head at the same time shouting, "Hi, Russell, how about a Quebeb?" Imagine my horror when I saw, instead of a black unruly mop, the partially bald

The Holly Inn was Pinehurst's first hotel, opening Dec. 31, 1895. The Inn's first brochure boasted of electric lights, steam heat, telephones, a solarium, billiard room, an orchestra and "an abundance of choice food, daintily served by girls from the North."

A ZONE OF ITS OWN

The 1962 U.S. Amateur was played in P.D.T.—Pinehurst Daylight Time.

The tournament was moved back to late September that year to accommodate the Southern heat and to allow Pinehurst officials to get the course and hotel ready in time after closing for the summer.

In order to get 72 first-round matches finished by dark, USGA Executive Director Joe Dey noted that it would require the first matches to go off at 6:30 a.m. "I'll be darned if I'll make anyone play golf at that hour," Dey told Richard Tufts. "Let's institute Pinehurst daylight savings time." The first twosome teed off at 7:30 a.m., Pinehurst time, and the town was in its own time zone the entire week.

head of Papa Warren! That was one time that I never heard anything further about the subject.

Then came the strict reign of Philip D. Lightbourne. He took no nonsense from anyone, and the discipline of the classroom was felt in every corner. I ran afoul of him early in the game and spent many unhappy hours after school.

While my father was resident physician at the Carolina, the leader of the orchestra was Trev Sharpe, and it was considered a great joke by the younger set to shout after him, "Press the black notes down," which some of the more musically minded young hellions said were the sharp notes on a piano. I believe all we ever got from him was a dirty look. Of course, after each Sunday concert the hymn *Nearer My God To Thee* was played, which I thought was the most doleful song I ever heard, even if it was done in accordance with the wishes of the first Mr. James Tufts. Nothing could induce me to sing along with my mother, who sang it lustily.

Then there were the bull fights. These were staged in the ballroom as most of the chairs there were a sort of canned bottom variety and could be easily busted through by the leg of another chair. When the call went out, "rough

house Fatty Felix in the ballroom," that meant the signal for five or six vandals to assemble and one would be the bull and run his chair along the floor on one leg, tilting it back so that the other three legs assumed the position of the bull's horns. The others, with the few remaining whole chairs, would slide around and try to avoid being gored or speared by the bull. It was a high point of the evening when the bull speared a cow and pushed it and the unlucky manipulator off to the side before being disengaged. The damaged chairs were always lifted up and placed well in the rear, up against the stage. I never knew who Fatty Felix was other than he was a guest at the hotel.

On Saturday—or was it Sunday?—afternoons the hotel held a tea, which was served in the lobby. One of the side dishes was very tasty vanilla wafers made by the Nabisco Co. If the waitress that had your regular table in the dining room was on duty, it was possible to sidle up and grab half a dozen, but if there was a stranger guarding the tray all you got was a dirty look and a low hiss—"Get away from here boys." Then there were nail-driving contests. A big two-by-six inch plank would be set up with some suitable nails started in it. Each contestant was given a hammer and tried to drive the nail flush with the surface with the fewest blows. Much girlish laughter was forthcoming when a big strong man missed the nail a couple of times and dug great gouges from the plank.

The original John D. Rockefeller was at the hotel at this time, and I remember seeing him hand out dimes, but I never got one from him. Another highlight in my life was over at the trap shooting range and seeing Annie Oakley

A hardy group of young golfers poses prior to an early 1900s junior tournament in Pinehurst.

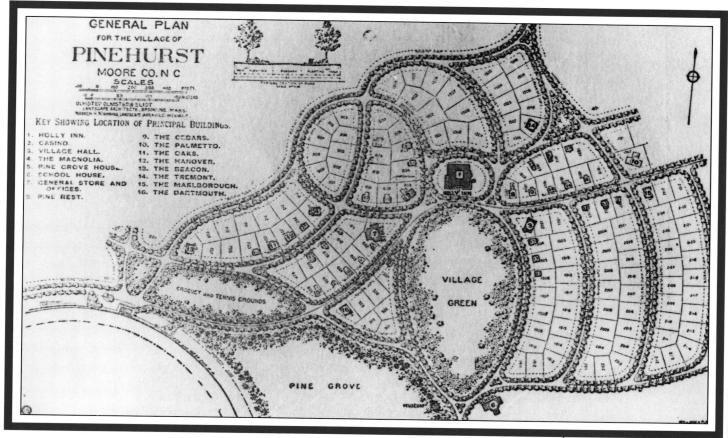

break numerous clay pigeons.

The main golf course at Pinehurst was the 18-hole front one, complete with sand greens which were smoothed over by means of a rug tied on a broom handle. The tees themselves were made of hardpacked clay and the tees on which the ball was placed were made of sand gotten from a box alongside. There was also a bucket of water handy in case you wanted to wash your ball. We never got to play on the big 18 unless there was nobody on or we had a "junior tournament." We were relegated to the "back nine"—a rough narrow course that ran along the car tracks almost to the little red school house. I had three clubs—a brassie, a mid-iron and putter. I took several lessons from Donald Ross, who was a very patient instructor and really tried to instill some ideas of golf in my thick skull. I never remember any of my scores. His brother Alex Ross used to play in the pro tournaments and at the time, golf pros were not allowed in the main clubhouse.

One of the main attractions of Pinehurst was the quail-shooting, and I used to watch the two-horse drawn hunting wagons take off from the hotel. They carried two dog crates in the rear, each containing two dogs—one for the morning hunt and one for the afternoon. A driver and

dog handler and guide went with each party. The kennels where all the hunting dogs were kept were down past the Power House, and I used to be down there so much that the bossman, Dan Morgan, put me to work. I fed the dogs and occasionally, when Morgan wasn't there, would show visitors around and was able to name the leading dogs and their pedigrees. I believe down in this section was a portion of the domain called Smokey Hollow. I was under the impression that it had a bad reputation and only the "poor white trash" lived there.

When my father took over the blackberry patch we became permanent inhabitants and for one summer lived in my uncle Leonard's house. I recall my father remarking during a rainstorm that he had never seen a rainstorm like that and likened it to a tropical downpour.

So that was about the end of my intimate touches around Pinehurst, and I often wonder where all my friends went and what became of them—Dan Morgan the dog-handler, Donald Ross the golf instructor, Trev Sharpe the orchestra leader, Owen Farrey the car motor-man and Fred, the gold-toothed head bellman at the Carolina, and the numerous inhabitants of our Little Red School House. ∎

The original plan for the village of Pinehurst. James Tufts drove a stake near the present site of the Given Library (across the street from the Holly Inn), and the town's new boundaries were extended one mile in all directions. Tufts commissioned Frederick Law Olmsted, the landscape architect who designed New York's Central Park, to "draw a set of plans for a village with open park spaces and winding streets that attain their usefulness by following lines of beauty."

BEYOND GOLF

BY CHARLES NEAVE

Golf was not on the activities list of the resort James Tufts founded in 1895. In fact, it was more than two years after the resort opened before it had a nine-hole course. Activities such as tennis, croquet, lawn bowling and shooting have rich heritages in Pinehurst as well. Mr. Neave, a writer visiting from Maine, finds challenge and fascination in these sports in this piece originally published in "Private Clubs" magazine.

he world of sports is wreathed in its own glossary of special terms: downs, innings, strikes, laterals, chukkers, sets and scrums. And, up to a point, I am comfortable with a wide assortment of them. But now, surrounded by the tall trees and manicured lawns of the Pinehurst Resort & Country Club, I am at a loss.

A retired Air Force colonel, battle-seasoned pilot and "Bear" Bryant's first quarterback to boot has graciously allowed me to humiliate myself at croquet. And an amiable and obviously very successful retired businessman from Pennsylvania has just shown me that, while lawn bowls might be fun to play from the outset, the game is simple in the same way that quantum physics is simple. So what is this? Croquet with a combat pilot? Lawn bowls with a man that could hold his own in any boardroom in America? Perhaps I need to digress.

I came to Pinehurst to shoot trap and skeet and to talk about shooting sporting clays, a sport I shall get to in a minute. But first, a brief reminiscence: In summer camp many, many years ago, having just tossed an opponent somewhat handily (I thought) to the mat, I swaggered up to my judo instructor. He was an older, more experienced man (about 16 years old). "Pretty good, don't you think?" I said, full of spunk. "Kid," he said, "you're about to learn something: A little knowledge is a dangerous thing." Whereupon I went and challenged a boy a couple of pounds heavier. Half an hour later I woke up in the infirmary—with an ice pack on my forehead.

I tell that story for a reason. A few months ago I decided to take up shooting, to the extent that it dealt with inanimate clay targets. I called friends who shoot regularly—and well—and the Orvis Shooting School in Manchester, Vermont, was given a unanimous endorsement. I went. While there I acquired a wonderful shotgun, some Barbour shooting outfits, and untold number of accessories. And I became a semiproficient beginner. Then one day I received in the mail some information on the Pinehurst Gun Club. Could any gun club that once had Annie Oakley as an instructor be anything but the best? I made reservations.

Pinehurst is nothing if not a gracious host. And, as gracious hosts are wont to do, the resort encourages all kinds of activities. Thus, during a game of tennis, the resident pro, Larry Wolf, suggests I try a game of croquet. Because the Gun Club is open only in the afternoon, we set up a croquet lesson for the following morning. Which is how and why I find myself dressed all in white, trying to hit a red wooden ball through a wicket two feet away, and failing. And that is also why I am remembering that judo story, because I am about to learn just enough about a new sport to humble myself all over again. I am lucky this time that none of the activities involves aggressive bodily contact.

Croquet, played under the auspices of the United States Croquet Association (as it is at Pinehurst and at better clubs and resorts throughout the country), bears little resemblance to the game most of us played in our grandmothers' backyards when we were children. Back then the game was something to keep the kids busy on the Fourth of July while the hamburgers and hot dogs cooked on the grill. The set probably came from the local five-and-dime, and the wickets, bent this way and that from years of haphazard use, would have allowed a small truck to pass through their portals.

Serious players today can spend $3,500 on a top-of-the-line croquet set. The wickets are just large enough to allow the ball to pass through. In fact, there is a space of less thickness than half a dime on either side. The strategy in USCA play is akin to the billiards played by professionals, and the strokes are as varied. There is the drive, the stop shot, the roll, the pass roll, the takeoff and a pair of roquet shots. Played well by people like George and Joan Barnes, the Air Force veteran and his wife, it is an amazing thing to behold. Balls literally jump over one another on certain shots; on others, angles are figured out by way of a sort of croquet trigonometry.

The Barneses moved to Pinehurst for golf—or at least that was the plan. Then, four years ago, George discovered croquet. And his wife says, "That's when he put down his golf clubs, picked up a croquet mallet, and for two years,

Seeing players dressed in white on the manicured croquet lawns of the Country Club is to step back into another era.

© PAUL BARTON

"MISTER B"

Charles Barrett is an institution in the kitchen of the Pinehurst Hotel. For 45 years, he's been dishing up some of the many dishes that make the Pinehurst experience not only a treat for the golf game but the palate as well.

He started in 1945 working at the Holly Inn, then moved to the big hotel and later worked at the Country Club. He opened the kitchen of the new clubhouse at Pinehurst No. 7 in 1987, then returned to the hotel a couple of years later. Today he works breakfast and lunch and often can be seen in his red chef's hat at the omlette station of the Carolina Dining Room.

His ability and resolve under pressure have been tested many times, but perhaps never as much as the evening in the late 1970s when a power outage hit in the midst of preparing a gourmet dinner for 200 people.

"There was a wreck somewhere that knocked down some power lines," he says. "The power went off about 7:30, and dinner was to begin at 8. We just lit a bunch of candles and put candles on every table, and it went off without a hitch.

"The funniest thing about that night was at about midnight, everyone had gathered in the lobby, and the lights finally came back on. Then a man streaked down the hall, coming from the west side and went into the East Wing."

Golfers have been known to streak to the clubhouse at No. 7 following a round for a bowl of Mr. B's Chicken Chili.

MISTER B'S CHICKEN CHILI

8 large onions, diced
12 cloves garlic, diced
4 jalapeno peppers, diced
4 tablespoons oil
4 teaspoons cumin
6 ounces chili powder
6 tablespoons oregano
1 gallon water
1 No. 10 can diced tomatoes
6 fryers
4 ounces chicken base
Roux to thicken

Saute onions in oil in heavy skillet; add garlic and jalapenos and spices. Add tomatoes, water and chickens. Bring to boil and simmer for 90 minutes. Remove chickens and cool. Thicken chili lightly with roux and season with chicken base. Bone and shred chicken, add to chili.

---

back to his New England roots for the look and design of the town, which is why many visitors from the Northeast walk around wearing a perplexed look. For here, in the midst of North Carolina pine, sits a small Connecticut village, as interpreted by Frederick Law Olmsted, the designer of Central Park in Manhattan. And it's only a short stroll from the front porch of the hotel.

But for the moment what Pinehurst is to me is lawn bowls. Not satisfied with being confounded by croquet, I have placed myself

with the exception of Christmas, he played every single day."

Seeing players on the three perfectly manicured courts at Pinehurst is to step back into another era. But then, that is Pinehurst. The main hotel, a sprawling white building with front porch that seems to go on forever, populated with plants and rocking chairs, golfers in bright clothes and croquet players and lawn bowlers in white, has deservedly been called "the Queen of the South." With seven championship golf courses it has also been nicknamed "the White House of Golf." But the more regal title seems to fit better—especially in the early morning mist, when the stately house has a ghostlike quality, and the expanses of the copper roof shimmer in the refracted sunlight. Pinehurst is almost magical when the grounds are still and only the family of skittish cats under the side porch are stirring.

There are two Pinehursts. There is the town of Pinehurst, population 3,000 or so, and there is the Pinehurst Resort & Country Club. They are inseparable if for no other reason than that they have the same founder, Boston philanthropist James Walker Tufts. In 1895 Tufts purchased 5,000 acres here, for one dollar apiece. Most locals felt that he had been had. Originally called Tuftstown, the name was changed after six months to Pinehurst, meaning a wooded plot of rising ground with pine trees. Tufts went

and my partner at risk once again. It is later in the morning and, still dressed in white, although now lightly fortified by a stop at the 91st Hole, we take to lawn bowls. Larry, taking a break from the tennis court, has come to lend friendly encouragement. It is much appreciated.

The object of lawn bowls, I am told, is to place your bowl, or ball, as close to a much smaller white ball as possible. Your opponent's wish is to discourage this, either by knocking your bowls away, or by obstructing the small ball, or "jack," with his own bowls. Already this looks a bit simpler than croquet, if for no other reason than the stance is easier to learn.

Our lawn bowls instructor is another retired Pinehurst resident, a true lawn bowls aficionado by the name of Don Duckworth. His style of teaching is simple. "Have fun," he says. "You can learn to play in 15 minutes, I promise you. From then on it is just a matter of improvement." Eying each other warily, we take him at his word. And, to the delight of all involved, we find he is right.

Strategy aside, there are three basic elements to lawn bowling. The first is the release, which must be smooth and consistent. Then there is the amount of power used. As in croquet, a little effort will take the ball a long way across grass that's as smooth as a putting green. Then there is the placement of the ballast side of the bowl. This determines which way the bowl will

Twenty-eight meticulously groomed hard-surface and Har-Tru courts provide a haven for tennis players amidst all the golf.

curve. That is where reading the greens is so important, just as it is in golf. It all comes together quickly, although any form of expertise is a long way off. But, as promised, it is fun.

In the days that follow, usually at twilight, we come back and play some more. New sports are a wonderful leveling factor for everyone, and none more so than those genteel pursuits, played against a backdrop that is part Old South, part New England.

Away from the whites and greens of the country club, set on a hill above a forest that stretches as far as the eye can see, is the Pinehurst Gun Club. Just as the lawn sports are as they should be, all pastels, whites and greens, the Gun Club is as it should be, a kind of Teddy Roosevelt-style refuge (the same style that Ralph Lauren has been known to appropriate at will). The clubhouse is full of comfortable chairs, a card table, a gun vault, old photographs of past champions and a big stone fireplace.

Outside is where the serious business starts, with nine trap and six skeet fields. It was here that Annie Oakley, accompanied by her husband, Frank Butler, gave lessons and

shooting exhibitions. Between 1916 and 1922 she taught almost 15,000 students. Today Doug Sheffield is in charge. A native of the area, he not only knows how to shoot and how to teach, he also knows all of the best shooters, the best spots to hunt, and bits of trivia, historical facts and downright tall tales that only a native would know.

As a teacher he is exceedingly patient. Given my short history of shooting sporting clays, where clay pigeons are released in a multitude of speeds, numbers and varieties, Sheffield decides that I should begin by shooting skeet. In skeet shooting the clay birds come from either a tower on the left, the high tower, or a tower on the right, the low tower. Or they are released simultaneously. Moving from station to station through a 180-degree arc, your angle on the target is constantly changing. The relative speed of the clay is also a variable, depending on whether it is crossing, coming toward you or going away.

Using the over-and-under 20-gauge from Orvis, a pretty little Beretta with a delicate but precise feel to it, I do, if not well, at least acceptably. Acceptable to me is better than 50

Carriage rides through the village with Frank Riggs and Currier are a staple in the Pinehurst experience. And when Currier has the day off, Holly and Magnolia take over. The carriage shown is an 1899 Victoria that's been restored and is on display in the lobby of the Pinehurst Hotel.

percent. To a real pro, missing one out of 25 is acceptable, but just barely, and then only in a hurricane. We move on to trap, where the clays all come from one low station in the center of the field. All shots go away from you, but you never know in which direction they are headed. The machine from which they are shot is constantly oscillating. Here I do better, at least on the first round, scoring about 80 percent. Then I begin to think about the process instead of shooting by instinct, and it is downhill from there until Sheffield tells me to set my mind on hold and just shoot. I improve immediately.

Later we talk about the new sporting clays course that is being constructed at Pinehurst. He describes it for me, and without thinking I promise to visit in the fall to try it out. Sporting clays has often been called "golf with a shotgun," so what better place to put such a thing than at the golf capital of the country.

Shuttles run constantly to all spots in the resort, but that evening we opt for a slower form of transportation. Intrigued by a treatise in the room entitled "Etiquette of Carriage Riding" (one example: "the lady will enter upon the left side, the gentleman assisting her by the hand"), we schedule a carriage ride into the village before dinner in the Carolina Dining Room. As it turns out, they complement each other perfectly: the twilight ride into New

England and dinner in the Old South, with fresh Carolina seafood; executive chef Art Elvins' superb hickory-smoked tenderloin of beef; greens, vegetables and herbs from the kitchen greenhouse; desserts that are far too sinful to eat; and excellent wines from a fine cellar.

Afterwards, over a dram of 25-year-old MacAllen's scotch, amid the muted tartans, burnished wood and polished brass of the Ryder Cup Lounge, there comes not just a sense of place, but one of contentment, accomplishment and a deep appreciation for the late James Walker Tufts. We sincerely hope he enjoyed his creation as much as his many guests have. ■

Annie Oakley made a name for herself from 1885-1901 shooting in Buffalo Bill's Wild West Show. In later years, she spent the winters of 1916-22 in Pinehurst with her husband, Frank Butler, and their setter, Dave. The Annie Oakley Trapshoot is a revered annual event.

BOOK THREE

PINEHURST TODAY

Pinehurst's 126 holes of golf offer unequaled variety and challenge. Most prominent, of course, are the 18 of No. 2. They represent where golf architecture has been—and very likely, where it is going.

No lake, no railroad ties, no multi-tiered green: the beauty of holes like the third on Pinehurst No. 2 is its simplicity.

THE GOLF STORY

It's just you, your caddie and the golf course. It's golf in its purest form and it's what has made Pinehurst one-of-a-kind for almost a century.

n the first tee of the 91st North and South Amateur Championship on a bright Monday afternoon are three generations of American golf.

"From Chicago, Illinois, please welcome Mr. Joel Hirsch." Hirsch is three days shy of his 50th birthday on this day in May, 1991. He's a successful businessman in insurance and commercial real estate. Hirsch has been coming to Pinehurst for the North and South since 1964, ever since Charles "Chick" Evans phoned Pinehurst's Richard Tufts on his behalf and got him an invitation to the tournament. Hirsch was just a year out of college and didn't have a lot of money, so he was pleased to learn he could stay at the Pine Crest Inn for $6 a night—breakfast and dinner included.

"They gave me the college rate, even though I was a year out of school," he says. "I remember Bob Barrett, the owner, saying if you won a match you got a free steak dinner. That's my first memory of Pinehurst. It couldn't have gotten any better, and it's stayed just as good."

"From Greer, South Carolina, please welcome Mr. Julian Taylor." The 31-year-old Taylor first played in the North and South as a teenager in the mid-1970s. As a college golfer at Clemson University from 1979-1983, all he dreamed about was playing the professional golf tour.

"That's what all of us growing up planned on," he says. "But when the time came, I just didn't feel I had progressed enough. I felt you needed to be beating a bunch of amateurs on a regular basis to have a shot on the tour. I guess if there had been a real burning desire, I would have found a way."

Instead, Taylor decided on a career in the golf business. He's a sales representative for Titleist, covering the western half of the Carolinas, and has some promotional responsibilities as well. After joining the golf equipment manufacturer in 1984, Taylor deferred golf to business, but after his territory and finances developed a foundation, he's set aside time the last three years to get back into amateur golf.

"The challenge I set to myself was, my work was going to come first," he says. "If I was just having an average year or behind what I did the previous year, I would not come play. I challenged myself to get my numbers up, and then I can come play. And then when I get back to work, I can't wait to go back to work. And when I go play, I can't wait to play."

"And from Southern Pines, North Carolina, please welcome Mr. Kelly Mitchum." Talk about bright eyes and bushy tails. This 20-year-old's never met a five-footer he didn't like. Mitchum is a rising junior on N.C. State University's golf team. He won three college events as a sophomore and is the best junior player that Pinehurst teaching pro Ken Crow has seen among the 500 or so he's watched over the last decade. College golf, the North and South and the amateur circuit are the preliminaries. The Big Dance is a couple of years down the road.

"Sure, I'd like to play the tour. I think everyone would," Mitchum says modestly.

Among those who stood where Mitchum stands today have been Arnold Palmer, Jack Nicklaus and Curtis Strange, to name three.

***

Pinehurst Resort & Country Club today operates 126 holes of golf that cover 600 acres and stretch for over 27 miles. More than 200,000 rounds of golf are played a year and more than 5,000 golf balls will be bought at the pro shop.

And to think: it all began in 1899 with 18 coarse holes that featured square sand greens, cross-bunkers in every fairway, only one tee on every hole, played to a length of 5,203 yards

---

PINEHURST LOVELY TRAINING GROUND

Twilight in Pinehurst was a wonderful time for young Davis Love III. The 27-year-old PGA Tour regular, who had won nearly $500,000 through mid-August in 1991, honed many of his skills as a teenager at Pinehurst during the summers when his father was an instructor in schools operated by *Golf Digest*.

"My brother and I would wait until late in the day, when everyone was off the golf course, and sneak out and play a few holes," says Love. "We'd play 16, 17 and 18 on No. 2 as many times as we could before it got dark or someone ran us off."

Love would later win the North and South Amateur in 1984, using many of the shots taught him in Pinehurst by his father, the late Davis Love Jr., and Jack Lumpkin. Love can't remember which hole it was, "But I remember Jack Lumpkin setting me up on one of the courses and making me learn to cut the ball. It was a par-five, it seemed like it was near the horse stables. He put me to the right of a cart path and had me cut the ball into the green. If it didn't cut, the ball would go into the road.

"I have a lot of memories of him teaching me little wedge and chip shots around those greens, things I still work on today. We'd go out by the 14th green; it was near where the teaching center is. I didn't have a very good short game at the time. He taught me a little flop wedge shot to get the ball close on those crowned greens of No. 2. I was like a kid with a brand new toy."

Only tees, landing areas and greens were maintained years ago, as these 1948 views from the second (top) and ninth tees of No. 2 attest.

and had splotchy bermuda grass on the fairways that was covered once a year by a ton of fish scrap per acre of fairway. "My, how Pinehurst smelled!" Richard Tufts of the founding family once remarked.

None of those early holes exist today exactly as they once did, of course, but piecing together early maps indicates a number of similarities in the first course and the land over which No. 1 sits today. The 1899 course opened with four holes occupying what is now the practice range, then took off in a southern direction and crossed "County Road" (now Morganton Road), as it does now, and ran in the same counter-clockwise direction back to the clubhouse it does today. The 10th hole crossed a pond in the same location as the pond fronting the tee to the long, par-three 11th hole on No. 1.

By the turn of the century, a young Scotsman named Donald Ross had arrived and began retooling the Pinehurst golf operation in the image of his linksland home. He built four courses at Pinehurst Country Club and even a nine-holer used primarily by employees.

Rees Jones was in the preliminary stages of designing the No. 7 course in 1984 when he found three ancient relics of Ross's old work. Amid the pine trees near the PGA/World Golf Hall of Fame, where the tee of the par-four fourth hole would be, was one large bunker and two smaller ones that had been part of the old, long-abandoned No. 5 course.

"It was pretty exciting to find a little piece of history like that," says Jones. "I said, 'Clear this by hand, don't bring any machinery around this bunker.'"

Jones left the bunkers right where they were. The large bunker is just to the right of the championship tee, and there's a pine tree growing through one side of it. Down the fairway about 100 yards are the two smaller bunkers. None have anything to do with

playing the current hole. They survive merely as testaments to the storied history of Ross and the ancient golf holes he built.

According to *The Scottish Invasion*, the entertaining history of Pinehurst that Tufts wrote for the occasion of the 1962 U.S. Amateur being played at Pinehurst, the golf courses evolved this way:

Nine holes opened in 1898, then 18 holes of No. 1 were completed in 1899. They were redone by Ross after his arrival at Pinehurst in 1900. Five new holes were built in 1913 when Ross built a huge practice range, the first of its kind in America.

Nine holes of No. 2 opened in 1901 and were lengthened in 1903. Then nine more were added to No. 2 in 1907. All indications are that the routing of the first two holes and 11 through 18 have remained the same since that time. In addition, the current eighth, ninth and 10th holes have always existed—but at various times at different places in the routing.

Nine holes of No. 3 were competed in 1907, and nine more were completed in 1910.

Six holes of No. 4 opened in 1912 as "practice holes." Three more were completed in 1912, and No. 4 became a full 18 holes in 1919.

Nine holes of No. 5 were built in 1928, then abandoned in 1935 when the first and ninth holes became the fourth and fifth holes of No. 2.

So from 1928 to 1935, Pinehurst Country Club had 81 holes of golf. Ross had also designed courses at Pine Needles, Mid Pines and Southern Pines Country Club. No wonder the area was already acclaimed "the golf capital of the world."

"The man who doesn't feel emotionally stirred when he golfs at Pinehurst beneath those clear blue skies and with the pine fragrance in his nostrils is one who should be ruled out of golf for life," said Tommy Armour.

The *Pinehurst Outlook* captured the game's early appeal in 1898 by concluding a piece on the nine-hole course with the following:

"Is it not evident, then, that in two brief sentences one may condense all necessary advice to those to seek rest and health? 'Go to Pinehurst. After you get there, play golf.'"

Today No. 2 gets most of the acclaim. But there are six other options that offer a challenge to players of all skill levels.

"When we came in to do No. 6, I was amazed at the contrast in the land compared with No. 2," says Tom Fazio, who began work on the course with his uncle, George, in 1976.

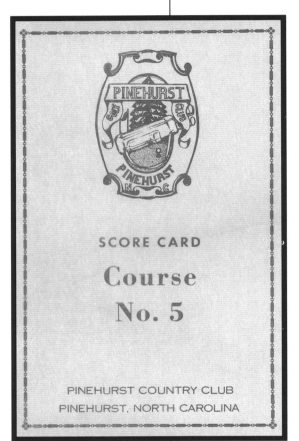

SCORE CARD

Course No. 5

PINEHURST COUNTRY CLUB
PINEHURST, NORTH CAROLINA

Pinehurst has used a variety of logos and crests over the years on its letterheads, scorecards and brochures. This scorecard for the newly opened No. 5 course is from the early 1960s.

"It was a very dramatic site with lots of elevation change. You didn't have the subtleties and the soft flow of No. 2. I welcomed the change. No. 2 is so special I didn't want to do a course and have anyone compare it to No. 2.

"What I saw was the ability to create a dramatic golf course on a strong piece of land, a different style golf course. No. 4 also had a reputation as being a strong, hard golf course. I wanted a different style than that, too. I think it's important in a club like Pinehurst that you vary the golf courses, have different styles so people have options and don't get bored."

The options at Pinehurst today range from the short No. 1 and 3 courses that are favorites with seniors and beginners; to the sterner challenges of the No. 4 and 5 courses, which have hosted professional golf at various times over the years; to the No. 6 and 7 courses, which are removed from the central clubhouse complex, feature significant elevation changes and, from the tips, are all anyone wants.

"The variety we have is unbelievable," says Crow, a member of the Pinehurst golf staff for more than a decade. "You go from No. 2, which has virtually no out-of-bounds and no water and where it's almost impossible to lose a golf ball, to No. 6, which is heavily wooded with water on several holes. They tell the story at No. 6 about a guy buying a dozen balls one time and having to buy a dozen more at the turn."

The No. 1 course today plays 5,780 yards for men and 5,329 for ladies, to a par of 70. The course features small greens and lots of 340-yard par-4s. One highlight is a plaque beside the tee of the 12th hole that commemorates The Tin Whistles Club—the exclusive club-within-a-club. In the early days, members would arrive at that hole, blow a whistle and a man would emerge from a spring house bearing spirits to mix with the cool spring water. The hardest hole on the course is the 11th, which is a 216-yard par-three; perhaps the easiest is the 16th, a mite of 313 yards that is so short because the green was once 45 yards farther back, on the

JUNIOR CHAMP RETURNS AS PRO, THEN AMATEUR CHAMP

The first chapter of David Eger's Pinehurst experience was the stuff of boyhood dreams. Pinehurst is like Disneyland to a young golfer growing up in the Carolinas. Eger, a 17-year-old from Charlotte, won the Donald Ross Memorial in 1969 on Pinehurst No. 2, then teamed with his father to win the Carolinas Father-Son. That win was accomplished in the alternate shot format when young Eger bombed a drive to within wedge distance on the 18th hole, Pop foozled the approach into the bunker and a steaming youngster holed-out from the trap for a three.

"I was so mad I wouldn't speak to him," Eger remembers. "Then I holed out and he said, 'See, my bad shot allowed you the opportunity to hit a great shot.'"

The second chapter of Eger in Pinehurst wasn't as memorable. As a rank-and-file member of the PGA Tour, Eger toured No. 2 in the early 1980s when the Hall of Fame Classic was held each September. He never accomplished much. Eger won $1,387.50 in the 1979 event, then missed the cut the next two years, shooting 79-72 in 1980 and 75-76 in 1981. He earned only $4,521 total in 1981, leading to his decision to look for another line of work.

"I probably should never have turned pro," Eger says. "Everybody has illusions of grandeur. You need to have a lot of ability and a killer-instinct personality to be successful out there. I couldn't even get to middle range. But I had my opportunity, my shot. I don't regret it."

That led Eger into his current job and his next opportunity to play

THOMAS TOOHEY BROWN

golf in Pinehurst. Eger joined the PGA Tour staff at the end of 1981 as an administrator, regained his amateur status in 1986 and has chalked up such heady milestones as winning the 1988 U.S. Mid-Amateur and being named to the 1989 and 1991 Walker Cup teams. And on the first day of June, 1991, Eger trimmed University of North Carolina star Tee Burton, 2-and-1, to win the 91st Men's North and South Amateur on Pinehurst No. 2.

"Obviously, this is very special to me," says Eger. "I've always loved this golf course. You grow up in the Carolinas and you're around golf, Pinehurst is *it*. It means a lot to come back here and win."

other side of Morganton Road.

The original No. 3 course is separated from the clubhouse and courses 1, 2 and 4 by N.C. Hwy. 5. It's difficult to talk about No. 3 unless the No. 5 course is included; when Pinehurst decided in the late 1950s that it needed a fifth golf course, it chose acreage surrounding No. 3 and, in effect, married some No. 3 holes into the new No. 5 course and built new ones for each course.

No. 3 is another short course—it measures 5,593 from the men's tees and 5,198 from the ladies. The seventh hole, a short par-three over a pond that plays 145 yards from the back, was one of Ross's first and infrequent water holes. It used to be the 14th hole.

Close at Donald Ross's side throughout his career was Frank Maples, his construction chief and greenkeeper. Perhaps it was fitting then, that Maples' son, Ellis, was hired to take Ross's work on No. 3 and add another 18 holes on the west side of the highway. No. 5 opened in 1961 and provided a course that could stretch as far back as 6,827 yards. The course features one of the hardest holes in Pinehurst and one of the prettiest. The ninth is a 453-yard par-four,

dogleg right that requires a long drive and an exacting approach to a plateaued green. The upslope is so steep it's difficult to bounce a ball on the green. The 15th is a 175-yard, downhill par-three over a pond that once was the sixth hole on No. 3. The green sits in a forest of tall pines that resemble the pipes of an organ—thus the "Cathedral Hole" moniker.

No. 4 has had the most tinkering of all the Pinehurst courses, primarily because Ross's original course was abandoned in the 1930s and not revived by Tufts until the early 1950s, after Ross's death in 1948, though some of the holes exist today as they did under Ross. Today's course, from the back tees, provides probably the second-stiffest challenge (behind No. 2) of the five courses that fan out from the main clubhouse. Diamondhead Corp., which bought Pinehurst from the Tufts family in December, 1970 and created the marathon World Open of 1973 (144 holes over two weeks), needed a second course worthy of professional talent and

hired Robert Trent Jones to soup up No. 4.

Jones lengthened the course from around 6,000 yards to 6,905, added the par-three 11th and turned what had been a par-four 11th into a par-five 12th. The latter move caused quite a stir among the pros, who claimed that the green to the new 485-yard hole wouldn't hold a second shot if they went for it in two.

Then Rees, his son, was hired in 1982 to soften the course.

"There was a huge outcry among the pros after my father redid No. 4," says Rees. "He lengthened it, bunkered it tightly. He left the greens the same size, and they had been designed to accept shorter shots. Now with longer approaches, in some minds the targets had become too small. So I went in and rebuilt all the greens and enlarged them. The longer course just needed some bigger targets. I took out bunkers that created forced carries and opened up the entrances to greens."

No. 6 opened in early 1979 on a hilly site about a mile removed from the village. Because George was spending most of his time in Florida, Tom actually was the hands-on designer. His finished product included more water, more elevation changes and more doglegs than any Pinehurst course. Combined with its woodsy setting, the 7,098-yard course from the back tees became known as Pinehurst's sternest test. The greens were rebuilt recently and reopened in early 1991.

"Over a period of time the grass had mutated into several different strains," says Fazio. "Some of the greens, we widened a little and created a few more pin placements. We took out a few real hard pin placements on several others and softened them a little."

Rees's work on No. 4 led to his being asked to design the No. 7 course, which couldn't have pleased Jones more. He remembers childhood trips to Pinehurst when Trent and family would be en route from their New Jersey home to golf courses in Florida, and they'd stop overnight in Pinehurst. Landing the No. 7 job excited him so "that I was up until 2 in the morning that night working on plans."

The resulting course, opened in 1986, has

Joel Hirsch (center, top) and Julian Taylor wait with a caddie before teeing off on the sixth hole in the 1991 North and South Amateur; moments later, Kelly Mitchum watches a chip that will find the bottom of the hole for a birdie, the first of three chip-ins.

more mountain feel than any of Pinehurst's courses and includes two backside par-threes that require carries over a natural berm and waste area (the 13th) and a series of sandy fingers that stretch from tee to green on the 16th.

"I think it's one heck of a golf course," Jones says. "It's a rugged site. The golf course fits very naturally, hitting from elevated tees, down into the valleys and back up. There's not much fairway bunkering. The natural lay of the land created a lot of bowls, and there are so many trees I didn't think it needed a lot of bunkering."

***

The heat is scorching as the afternoon wears on and Hirsch, Taylor and Mitchum make their away around No. 2. Everyone's walking. Hirsch and Taylor, both wearing gray slacks and white shirts, have caddies; Mitchum, in white shorts and a red shirt, carries his bag on his shoulder.

Hirsch and Taylor are grinding; both are several shots over par through nine holes. Mitchum is gliding; the slender youngster with strawberry blond hair and a graceful swing is three-under through eight holes. He birdied the second hole with a six-foot putt, chipped in from the fringe on six and chipped in from 75 feet on eight. He hits it longer and straighter than his companions. He also seems to have the demeanor and maturity reserved for older players. On the 14th hole, he comes over the top of his approach shot, and the ball bounces down the slope to the left of green. But there is no cursing, no

iron banged into the ground, no gyrating. Mitchum simply watches the shot, then addresses a make-believe golf ball and makes another swing, presumably one with a corrective adjustment.

Then he walks to the green and chips in for a birdie.

"I don't enjoy seeing people throw clubs, things like that," he says. "I figure I better not do it. It doesn't do any good. You've just got to go on to the next shot. If one doesn't go off good, you just have to work harder on the next one. That's how I look at it."

***

Donald Ross did not chisel Pinehurst No. 2 out of the pine trees and sand and wire grass in six days and then rest on the seventh. Eighteen holes of No. 2 were open for play by 1907. But the routing didn't reach its present configuration until 1935, and the greens weren't contoured, crowned, planted with grass and surrounded by mounds and dips and swales until then. The fairways are wide, the green entrances are mostly open, but it's those green settings and their hidden challenges that help make No. 2 the ultimate examination in golf. "It may be the best chipping golf course in the world," says Ben Crenshaw.

"This mounding makes possible an infinite variety of nasty short shots that no other form of hazard can call for," Ross wrote before the 1936 PGA Championship, played on No. 2. "Competitors whose second shots have wandered a bit will be disturbed by these innocent appearing slopes and by the shot they will have to invent to recover."

Ross fine-tuned the layout until his death in 1948, and his successors lengthened it some and tinkered with bunker configurations. Charles Price remembers playing the 1948 North and South Amateur with there being no fairway bunker on the left of the 10th fairway, a hundred yards or so short of the green. But Ross had already drawn the bunker, and following his death that April, the bunker was built. It was there when Price returned for the North and South Open in November.

"Great golf courses become what they are through the process of evolution, not revolution," Price wrote in a 1979 piece for *Golf Magazine*. "Nobody—no architect who ever lived—can go out and build a golf course, no matter how few the restraints placed upon him by realtors or members, and then declare the finished product, however original, 'great.' The proof of his pudding lies in the playing of it."

And the playing of Pinehurst No. 2 is an

education in golf. It is where the game has been and where it is going. It's quite appropriate that the pro golf tour is returning to Pinehurst in the fall of 1991 for the Tour Championship. For after a decade of sometimes harsh and extreme golf-course design, the pendulum is swinging back to the traditional. Greens jutting into water are, for example, giving way to greens surrounded by the subtle slopes like those on No. 2. Everyone in golf has an opinion on the subject, on what makes No. 2 the standard of the past and the model for the future. Here is a random selection from an architect, an administrator and a player:

From Bill Coore, a Thomasville, N.C., native, former Wake Forest golfer and the golf-course architecture partner of touring pro Crenshaw:

"The golf course takes strokes away in almost half shots, very gently. It lulls you into mistakes as opposed to bludgeoning you with them. In my opinion, a golf course is like a good book; there's an ebb and flow to it. The theme runs throughout the story, but it's presented, then fades away, then is presented again. If you're reading a drama and it continues to build constantly without a lessening of attention, the effect is lost. You build up and then soften, step back a ways, set the tone for the next stage of development. Mr. Ross did that so well.

"Its greatness eludes people at first unless they're well-versed in golf-course design. The little things, the angles, dips, contouring work around the greens, the bunkering. All that goes together to make the whole what it is. The whole is much greater than the sum of its parts. So many golf holes today are based upon individual, dramatic elements. The hole is an overwhelming ordeal, it's too dramatic.

"It feels so good out there playing. Every great player who's anybody has played there. You walk the fairways imagining the great players having the same shot you have. As a player you feel like you're in a contest with nature, you're not flung headlong into war. It's not so much made up with artificial fortifications. It's a game, not a war. Unfortunately, with a lot of new golf courses, the reverse is true. It's a question of, 'Who can survive?'

"Nobody can hit all those greens. As soon as you miss, there you are, faced with a delicate little chip or run-up shot off those mowed-down aprons. What shot do you play? People don't realize, the more options you give a good player, the harder it is to play a shot. The less options, the easier. The greens are crowned off on all sides, mowed very tight for 10 or 15 yards. They look so much easier than the

TEACHING SCHOOLS DRAW MIXED BAG OF GOLF ZEALOTS

To teach in the Pinehurst Golf Advantage Schools requires an intimate knowledge of the golf swing, some patience, a sense of humor and a little tact. But on occasion, a swift kick in the rear can help—or something similar.

Eric Alpenfels was trying his best one year to teach the wife of a prominent, successful and very demonstrative New York lawyer. But every time Alpenfels would advise the woman, her husband would overrule him with instruction of his own.

"We take them out on the course and on about the third hole I've had enough," says Alpenfels, the director of the schools. "I say, 'Listen, just because I watch *Matlock* every week doesn't mean I can practice law. So just shut up.' He looks at me and goes, 'Okay.' He didn't know what to say. For the rest of the week he kidded me about being that obnoxious."

Some 1,200 golfers attend schools throughout the year, taxing the stamina and resourcefulness of the teaching staff in a variety of ways.

They've had to babysit a 10-year-old who'd been deposited in an "advanced junior" school by parents traveling abroad. "His scuba-diving camp had been canceled, so they had to put him somewhere. All we had available was an advanced school. His mother said he was a five-handicap. He'd never touched a golf club in his life," Alpenfels says. "He was voted 'most improved' at the end of the school."

They've tried to teach the game to one man who, if he hit the ball out of the fairway, refused to go look for it. He'd just drop another and keep on going. They've taken early morning phone calls from a former student, a middle-aged woman from New York, who'd get up at 4:30 in the morning, go outside her apartment and hit balls into the Hudson River.

Once four Japanese golfers arrived in Pinehurst, and one of them announced, "I'm the interpreter."

"Fine. So we're standing around," says Alpenfels, "and we ask him, 'What's Johnny's handicap?'

"'Huh?'

"'What does Johnny think about this?'

"'Huh?'

"'How much golf has Johnny played?'

"'Oh no, he do fine.'

"This guy had convinced the others he'd be their interpreter, and he hardly knew a word of English."

So how did they learn any golf?

"Mime, mostly," Alpenfels says. "We'd just show them what to do and they'd do it.

"It turns out the supposed interpreter was a writer for a Japanese golf magazine. He sent me a copy of the article. It was in Japanese, of course. A few months later I'm giving a lesson to a man from D.C. who was a native of Japan. He translated the article for me."

What did it say?

"The guy liked the school."

PINEHURST MEMORABLE ROAD TRIP FOR WADKINS

Lanny Wadkins is lucky to have won 20 PGA Tour events and more than $5 million in prize money. To do so, he and his childhood buddies from Richmond, Va., had to survive a harrowing drive to Pinehurst each year in the car of Willow Oaks Country Club pro George Bird.

Wadkins is laughing one day at the memory.

"George and Leo Steinbrecher would take a group of about eight of us down every year for the Donald Ross Memorial," he says. "I remember this vividly. George said he'd give us a dollar for every car that passed him if we'd give him a dime for every one he passed. We lost money, I'll tell you that. It was a fun trip, a golf pro and a bunch of 13-year-old kids hauling it along those old two-lane roads. George had a big, old car, and we were bouncing the whole way. That car never saw a shock absorber. It was some trip. We stayed at the Holly Inn, and I'm not sure it's ever been the same since. Those are my earliest memories of Pinehurst."

One of Wadkins' few disappointments in golf is that he never won the North and South Amateur. He made it to the quarterfinals one year, to the semifinals another and lost 2-and-1 in the championship match in 1969 to Joe Inman, a Wake Forest University teammate. Vinny Giles beat both Lanny and brother Bobby Wadkins in the same day en route to finishing second to Eddie Pearce in 1971.

Golf Digest profiled Wadkins in its September, 1991, issue, and that 1969 match was mentioned. Inman told of Wadkins holing a bunker shot against him the summer before in the Carolinas-Virginia Team Matches. "The next year, we reach the final of the North and South Amateur, and it just so happened that we roomed together that week," Inman says. "The night before our match, a news station phoned Lanny and I heard him say, 'Joe's a good player, but there's nobody here I can't beat.' It got me all fired up. The next day I hit the flagstick twice in the first seven holes. On the 35th hole, Lanny's in the bunker and before he hit the shot, he looked up and gave me that same look he'd given me the year before. I couldn't help it, I said loudly, *'Don't you dare.'* Lanny lipped the cup with the shot. Scared the hell out of me. I barely hung on and won."

Wadkins dismisses the interview story.

"That sounds like a Joe Inman story to me," he says. "There are a whole lot of things that go with that story I won't tell you. But no, I never said that. If I had said it, I would tell you, but I did not.

"That was probably the most humiliating day of my life, because we'd driven there in my car, a '67 Mustang, I think, and we'd driven down and roomed for the week. So the day of the finals we had to get up, have breakfast and I drove to the golf course in my car. After it was over and I'd lost 2-and-1—notice I said 'I lost,' he didn't win—I then had to drive him back to Greensboro in my car listening to him tell me how wonderful he'd played. That's probably the most humiliating hour and 10 minutes I ever spent in my life."

Wadkins' emotions have never been a secret—and he obviously wasn't happy after missing a putt in his 1969 North and South loss to Joe Inman.

situation in a normal tour event, where you have two or three inches of rough all around. In reality, the good player is sitting 10 yards off the green and he says, 'Gee, do I chip with a sand wedge onto the green? Do I take a seven-iron, bump it onto the side of the crown? Or do I putt?' So he makes a decision, and as he's standing over the shot, he's thinking, 'Am I doing the right thing?' The element of doubt is the only way par will stand up to the best players. It's the same at Augusta. As soon as you play one you're not happy with, you second-guess yourself and you've got more doubt the next time you have one."

From Deane Beman, commissioner of the PGA Tour and a frequent visitor to Pinehurst during his amateur days at the University of Maryland:

"Pinehurst has had a very strong influence on the philosophy that we're now geared to on our TPC courses. Up until a year or so ago the architects who built our clubs were left to design them in their own style and image. The look had become very stereotyped, particularly around the greens with the heavy rough. We're making an effort to develop the interesting variety of pitch and chip shots that you find at Pinehurst. A couple of years ago we started a program at the TPC at Sawgrass to convert all the areas around the greens to that sort of bump-and-run instead of heavy, long grass. We're incorporating that into all of our new golf courses and converting some of our others. It's such an important part of the game that's been missing.

"I was disappointed when the old World Open didn't continue. I think Pinehurst is such an important place in golf history, and when the opportunity presented itself to return to Pinehurst, I felt it was something we should do. Understand that the tournament (the Tour Championship, formerly known as the Nabisco Golf Championships) has been very, very successful financially. The tour made the decision to go back to Pinehurst knowing that because of the difficulty of marketing and the number of people in the immediate area, it would cost us some money to play there. At other places we could make significantly more net income. But it's important enough to play there that the tour is subsidizing our going there. That's as strong an endorsement as we can give to a golf course."

And from Jay Sigel, one of the game's premier amateurs and a North and South regular who, much to his chagrin, has yet to win the tournament:

"The golf course has certainly changed over the years. They've had different grass on the greens. They let the waste areas fill in, then they cleared them out. I've played it both ways. At times there's been a lot of rough, at times no rough. Quite frankly, I think it will always be in the Top 10. I've seen everything there, and it doesn't matter to me how they do it, it's still great.

"The main thing is the greens have to putt smooth and they have to be firm. They don't have to be fast, but if they're firm and medium in speed, the size of the greens is reduced. The ball will roll off the slope if not hit perfectly, and that's the way it was designed to play.

"One thing that's special about Pinehurst is the caddies. There have been some outstanding caddies there. Fletcher Gaines stands out in my mind. I can't pick all the other names out. There was a great caddie named Carl McLaughlin. He was a tall, skinny guy. He was a high-quality individual who loved the game. I hope the caddie program stays strong. I truly believe Pinehurst deserves the caddie, the player deserves the caddie. Golf in general and No. 2 in particular shouldn't be played in a cart. You lose too much. There's too much to see. You can't see it driving a cart outside the fairway."

One facet of the evolution of No. 2 that has created the most controversy has been the surfaces of the greens. Until 1935, they were a sand and clay mix. Then they were planted with bermuda, which remained on the greens until 1973 and was overseeded with rye for the winter. Pinehurst's new owners, Diamondhead Corp., took the opportunity of a hard freeze one winter to replace the now-dead bermuda grass and root system with bent. (Diamondhead would later fall into financial arrears and Pinehurst would be acquired in 1984 by Club Corporation of America, its current owner). The new bent surfaces provided a better year-round putting surface, as the greens didn't need the two transition periods in fall and spring of bermuda to rye and then rye back to bermuda.

WILSON, CALLAWAY AMONG PRO HERITAGE

Pinehurst has had a variety of interesting characters and prominent golf figures employed as its golf professionals over the years.

One of the most revered was Willie Wilson, who was born in Melrose, Scotland, in 1877. On the advice of Harry Vardon, he came to the United States in 1902 and was employed as pro at York Golf and Tennis Club in Maine. He spent 43 winters in Pinehurst and once figured he'd given well over 100,000 lessons. His best-known pupil was Samuel Clemens. In Pinehurst, Wilson also handled the registration of guests and sometimes entertained them—to prove his ageless agility—by kicking at a sign suspended higher than his head.

The Callaway brothers were also integral parts of the golf scene. Donald Ross hired Harold, Clarence and Lionel in 1918. Harold spent several decades worth of winter seasons in Pinehurst, and one of his steady customers was Louis Fabian Bachrach, the photographer, whom Callaway knew primarily as a persistent slicer. Lionel Callaway would later develop the Callaway Handicap System that's used today as well as the Callaway Putting Guide—an apparatus with marks showing you how far to take the putter back for varying lengths of putts. He lived much of his life in Florida but returned to Pinehurst, where he lived until his death in 1988.

Another pro, George Carney, was once told by Philip D. Reed, board chairman for General Electric, that Reed would be willing to sit in a chair in Macy's window if he could break 70. As far as anyone ever knew, the window was never graced by Reed's presence.

THE STORY OF THE PUTTER BOY

There's probably not a more famous inanimate figure in golf than the Pinehurst "Putter Boy." He's been around since the very early days, in one form or another.

Frank Presbrey, Pinehurst's first advertising counselor, created a young boy that appeared in the resort's early advertising and calendars who was called, "The Golf Lad," "The Golf Boy," or "The Golf Calendar Lad." Later he was replaced on the calendars sent annually to hotel guests by photos of Donald Ross playing the Pinehurst golf courses.

In 1912, sculptress Lucy Richards used the lad as the model for her bronze statuette in sundial form. But since she wasn't a golfer, Ross demonstrated the proper grip and stance for her—but the image is not of Ross, who was a grown man at the time.

The shaft of the club created the shadow that would be used on the sundial to tell time, and in order to get the proper angle, the length of the club had to be inordinately long.

The statue was known as "The Sundial Boy" until the 1970s, when "The Putter Boy" name caught on. For many years the statue sat on a concrete base between the two large putting greens beside the clubhouse. It was moved in 1978 to the PGA/World Golf Hall of Fame. Just recently, "The Putter Boy" returned to prominence at Pinehurst Country Club and is now displayed near the new Donald Ross Memorial Garden.

JOHN HEMMER

Bent greens are less grainy and are smoother. But it's difficult to keep them as firm, and Ross designed the course to be played with firm greens.

But the PGA Tour began staging an annual event in Pinehurst in 1973, and for the next decade the World Open/Colgate-Hall of Fame Classic/Hall of Fame Classic was contested on No. 2. All but the first were held in August or September, two of the three hottest months of the year. The bent greens were kept moist to allow them to survive and became soft. Players hit their approach shots at the flagstick with abandon. The balls hit, stopped, and many were soon drained for birdies. "In the mid-1970s you could hit a three-wood to a green and it would would stay put," says Ken Crow.

So the greens were switched back to bermuda in 1979 to help preserve the course's original playing characteristics. But Pinehurst still had problems; the greens were better on its other five courses, and if the United States Golf Association would ever consider holding the U.S. Open on No. 2, it would never do so on bermuda greens. You simply can't get bermuda greens fast enough to the USGA's liking.

Mike Sanders was director of golf at Pinehurst from 1980 to 1986, before leaving to develop Pinehurst National Golf Club. He began researching the possibility of converting the greens back to bent before he left; that project was executed in 1987 under course superintendent Brad Kocher and new director of golf Don Padgett.

"Pinehurst had been talking to the USGA about bringing the U.S. Open here back when Lou Miller was the director of golf in late 1970s," Sanders says. "I continued to talk to them, but in the early '80s, Pinehurst was for sale and the banks were in control so, understandably, there was a reluctance to make any commitment until they saw what was going to happen to the resort.

"From the golf-course perspective, P.J. Boatwright was the key. I said, 'What do we have to do to get the U.S. Open?' He was very concerned with the bermuda greens and the transition period. If you had a problem with your transition period in spring and then the U.S. Open is coming the second week in June, you've got trouble.

"The bermuda greens created a problem from a resort standpoint as well. You don't have to go through an overseeding and transition period with bent. As far as this area goes, bent provides a better year-round surface. Guests come in and they have wonderful putting surfaces on five golf courses, and then

Course restoration specialist Ed Connor used computers in 1987 to file information about the green settings for Pinehurst No. 2 before the greens were torn up, rebuilt from ground up and planted with bentgrass. The green contours and swales could then be reproduced exactly as they had been. The arrows in the print-outs here of the 12th green indicate the direction the approach is coming from.

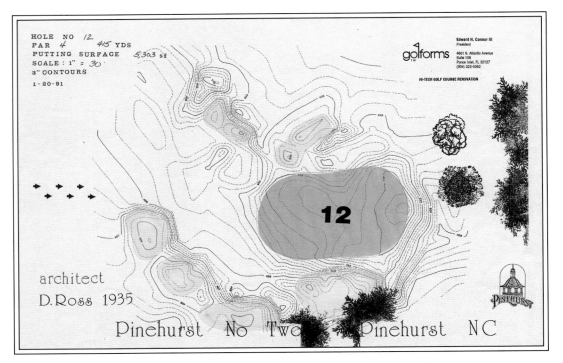

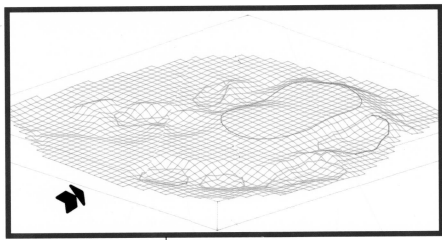

they play No. 2, a Top 10 course, and they pay a surcharge to play it, and they have bumpy greens during the transition period. They don't understand that."

But there was a key difference in the second conversion. With the input of Jack Nicklaus and his design staff and the use of a complex new computer program, the greens weren't just resurfaced. They were torn up and totally rebuilt. The substructures of all the greens were rebuilt to USGA specifications: four inches of gravel, topped by two inches of coarse sand, topped by 12 inches of a sand-peat moss mixture. The new foundations would allow the greens to drain better and remain firmer during the hot months when they received more water. Ed Connor of Golforms Inc., a golf-course renovation, architecture and construction firm, took what amounted to a three-dimensional,

computerized photograph of each green setting. That record allowed the new greens to be rebuilt with the same contours as before. The only change made was that the deep swale in the 18th green was lessened somewhat because mowers had been skinning off the grass making the curve.

(One sidelight of tearing up the greens was the discovery of a horse shoe that surely fell off the foot of a mule used in the original construction process.)

The result is a golf course that remains a national treasure and one on which the 30 top money winners on the 1991 PGA Tour would be tested Oct. 31-Nov. 1. The USGA is bringing its 1994 Senior Open to No. 2. Pinehurst officials—not to mention nearly the entire roster of the PGA Tour—would like to see a U.S. Open played here later in the decade. The results of the Tour Championship and the Senior Open will determine if No. 2 can stand up to today's players and equipment and if the Sandhills area has the infrastructure to support the demands of a U.S. Open.

"It will be interesting to see what happens," says Tom Fazio, who did some restoration work on No. 2 in 1978. "What would Donald Ross do if John Daly was going to play his golf course? Daly plays a totally different game than they played when Ross was alive. Ross worked on that golf course and adjusted and improved it continually. He died in 1948. Suppose he'd lived another 20 years. Would he have continued to do things to it? Probably so.

"It's the same thing at Augusta National. There's always some new adjustment. People complain about changes to old golf courses. You can't find one with more adjustments than Augusta. You can look back there and see what's been done every year. Because of our love for old golf courses, we have a tendency to say they've never been touched. But you can't *not* change a golf course. Golf courses are growing, living things. Nature itself adjusts a golf course.

"The tournament will be played at a time of year when the golf course can play hard and fast, if the weather cooperates. But I think No. 2 will stand the test of time. There's such character to it."

***

The practice green beside the first tee of No. 2 is cloaked in shadows early in the evening as Joel Hirsch tries varying his putting stance in hopes of turning his opening-round 77 into, say, a 75 the next day and improving his chances of qualifying among the top 64 entrants for match play. A thunderstorm threatens as dark clouds hover above.

"This is a little early for me in the season," *Hirsch says, stroking 18-footers.* "I'm not playing as well as I should be. It's really the beginning of the golf season. But this is a lot of fun. The people you get to meet are such a big part of it. Like the guys I played with today. Kelly has a wonderful game, but more importantly, he's a delightful young man. He's a gentleman. Julian's getting his career going, he'll be a fine amateur player. At my age, these young kids are so much fun to be around. It's quite enjoyable for me."

Unfortunately, the joy wouldn't last long for Hirsch. He would shoot a 78 on Tuesday and miss the qualifying cut. Taylor, who opened with a 75, followed with a 74; he lost to Doug Stone in his first-round match, 5-and-3. Mitchum's 68-73—141 won the qualifying medal; he would lose in the third round to Nicky Goetze, 5-and-4. David Eger was the eventual champion, winning the final over Tee Burton, 2-and-1.

"There's nothing like No. 2 to me," *Taylor says in the clubhouse locker room.* "You start on the first tee, you don't stop until you get to 18. You don't stop at the clubhouse at the turn. You just go play. The golf course is like the best things in life. When you see someone who's accomplished a lot or is very successful, they don't impress you by trying to show you how successful they are. They do it by action.

"You stand on the tee, and it doesn't look that difficult. There's no big, old pond to carry or railroad ties or big, giant tiers. You look at it and it appears simple. But the more you play it, the more you realize that if you don't drive to the proper approach angle to the green, you're not going to get it close. Like on 11. You stand on the tee and it looks like a football field out there. But if the pin's on the left, you've got to be on the right side of the fairway. If it's on the right, you've got to be center or left, or you're not going to have the angle to keep your shot on the green. It's a complete test. When you're done you know you've had to hit every shot."

But it's more than a great golf course. It's good times and good friends and relationships that will last forever.

"Joel Hirsch is just, to me, the epitome of amateur golf, along with guys like Bob Lewis and Jim Holtgrieve and Jay Sigel," *Taylor says.* "They just love the game. We're going to go out and play as hard as we can. Then we'll look over and watch Kelly hit it and say, 'That's great. I love to see it.' I wish him the best. I hope he makes it. And, I'll keep playing golf for the fun of it, with guys like Joel. I made a double bogey and Joel comes up and says, 'Come on, let's get it going.' It's just you, the golf course and the guys you're playing with. It's golf at its purest form."

And that's what Pinehurst is all about. ∎

THE GOLFER'S WISH

A golfing bug lay dying, his strength was failing fast,
The putt he'd sunk the day before was doomed to be his last,
His eyes were turning glassy, beyond the slightest doubt,
The soul which feared no bunker deep would soon go drifting out,
Then to his friends about him he turned and whispered low:
"I hope I'll find a Pinehurst in the land to which I go.

"I hope there'll be a Pinehurst in the realms beyond the stars,
Where all the golfers gather to brag about their pars.
I hope in some fair city where departed spirits dwell
And it may be up in Heaven or it may be down in Hell
That I'll find one haunt devoted to the glorious golfing kin
Where I can sit and tell them of the shots I've made to win.

"I want to sit among them, all those gabby golfing chaps
And talk to them of hazards, ditches, chocolate mounds and traps.
I'll play earth's courses over with those golfers gone before
If they only have a Pinehurst on that far-off golden shore.
Oh, I'll live my golf life all over, in the rough and through the fair,
And I'll be a happy angel, if they have a Pinehurst there.

"It is true that I've been nutty, it is true I've gone astray,
And I know that death can never wash my golfing sins away.
But the men I've met at Pinehurst have all talked the same as I,
So with golfers I'll be happy in the land beyond the sky
As a gabby golf nut angel I can face eternity
If they only have a Pinehurst and a hotel room for me."

© by Edgar A. Guest

PLAN of Nº 2 GOLF COURSE
PINEHURST COUNTRY CLUB ~ PINEHURST ~ N·C·

VILLAGE GREEN

No. 2: 1911

This is a landscape designer's plan of Pinehurst No. 2 from 1911. Thirteen of the holes remain largely in the same positions today. The two major differences are that the old course turned right at the second green, and three holes existed then to the left of the current 10th green (which in 1911 was the seventh hole). Eleven through 18 were exactly where they are today.

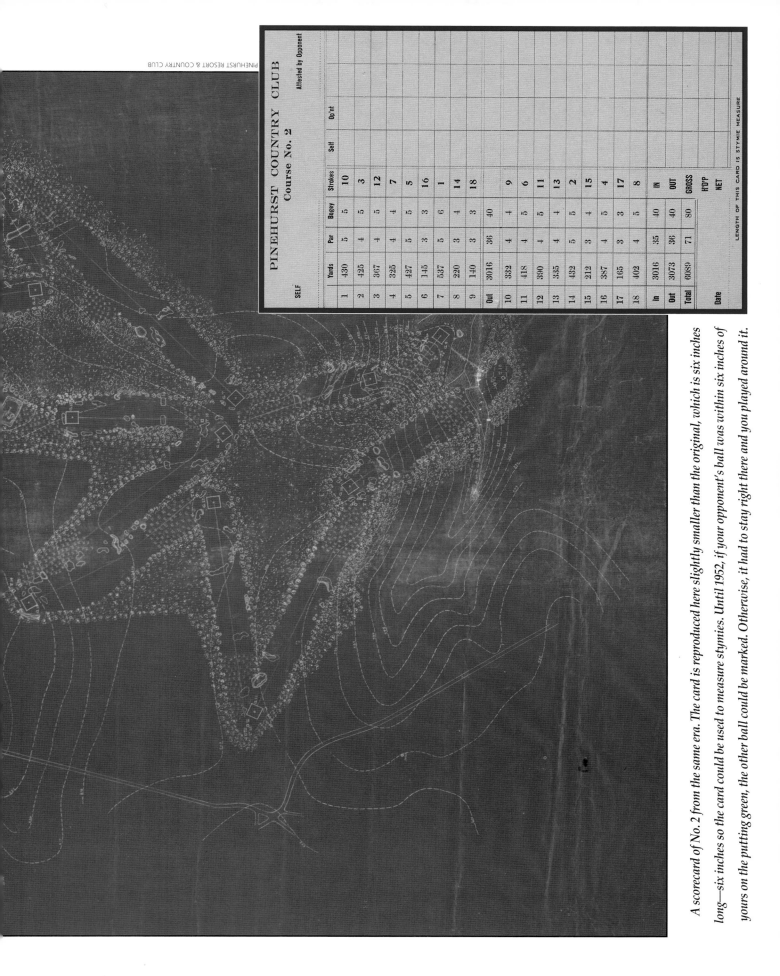

PINEHURST COUNTRY CLUB
Course No. 2

SELF

	Yards	Par	Bogey	Strokes	Self	Op'nt	Attested by Opponent
1	430	5	5	10			
2	425	4	5	3			
3	367	4	5	12			
4	325	4	4	7			
5	427	5	5	5			
6	145	3	3	16			
7	537	5	6	1			
8	220	3	4	14			
9	140	3	3	18			
Out	3016	36	40	Out			
10	332	4	4	9			
11	418	4	5	6			
12	390	4	5	11			
13	335	4	4	13			
14	432	5	5	2			
15	212	3	4	15			
16	387	4	5	4			
17	165	3	3	17			
18	402	4	5	8			
In	3016	35	40	IN			
Out	3073	36	40	OUT			
Total	6089	71	80	GROSS			
				HDP			
				NET			
Date							

LENGTH OF THIS CARD IS STYMIE MEASURE

A scorecard of No. 2 from the same era. The card is reproduced here slightly smaller than the original, which is six inches long—six inches so the card could be used to measure stymies. Until 1952, if your opponent's ball was within six inches of yours on the putting green, the other ball could be marked. Otherwise, it had to stay right there and you played around it.

PINEHURST NO. 2

DONALD J. ROSS, GOLF ARCHITECT

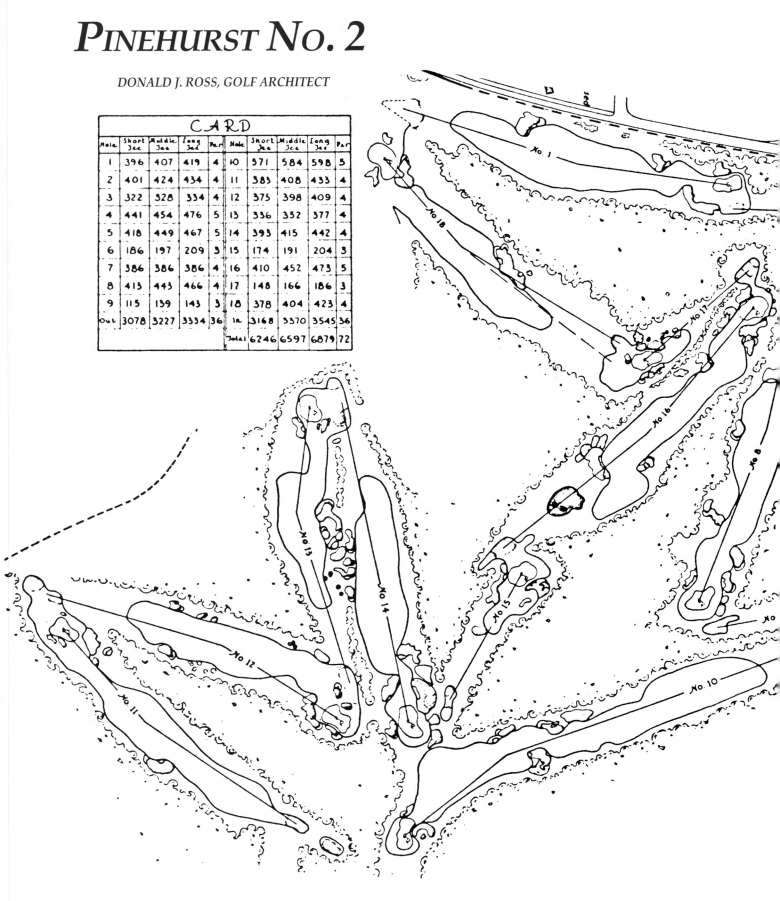

Hole	Short Tee	Middle Tee	Long Tee	Par	Hole	Short Tee	Middle Tee	Long Tee	Par
1	396	407	419	4	10	571	584	598	5
2	401	424	434	4	11	383	408	433	4
3	322	328	334	4	12	375	398	409	4
4	441	454	476	5	13	336	352	377	4
5	418	449	467	5	14	393	415	442	4
6	186	197	209	3	15	174	191	204	3
7	386	386	386	4	16	410	452	473	5
8	413	443	466	4	17	148	166	186	3
9	115	139	143	3	18	378	404	423	4
Out	3078	3227	3334	36	In	3168	3370	3545	36
					Total	6246	6597	6879	72

This 1936 map shows the No. 2 course as it was played in the 1936 PGA Championship. It includes Donald Ross's last major revision to the course: the addition of the fourth and fifth holes and deletion of two holes between the 10th and 11th.

MAP COURTESY W. PETE JONES

The new fifth hole (below) had been the ninth on an old

No. 5 course until Ross made major changes to No. 2 in 1935.

Ross apparently had an understanding with Bobby Jones on the

design of a new course in Augusta, Georgia. But when Jones saw

Cypress Point on the Monterey Peninsula in 1929, he developed a

kinship with that course's designer, Alister Mackenzie, and later tabbed Mackenzie for the co-design of Augusta National. Ross was a strict individualist, and Jones wanted an architect who would allow his participation. The changes to No. 2 were the efforts of a miffed architect to design the finest course in the South.

1

PAR 4

396	378	361

HANDICAP 11

The rightside bunker isn't as close to the green as it looks from the fairway.

onald Ross believed in opening his golf courses with fairly simple, straight-forward holes. He didn't want to give you something so difficult that you might start with a bad hole and have that lead to a bad round. But it needed to be strong enough to be a potential playoff hole. This hole fits that philosophy very well. It's not too long—a driver and a short iron, usually.

Right away you notice two characteristics of No. 2. All the greens are upside-down saucers, which effectively reduces them in size. A green might be 5,000 square feet, but when you take away the edges, the area you're hitting to is much smaller. And you've got a pretty generous driving area,

allowing you to aim for the side of the fairway that offers the best angle to the pin.

One tough pin is front-right because of a depth-perception problem that Ross presents frequently on No. 2. There's a bunker about 20 yards short of the green that looks from the fairway as if it's right beside the green. It's difficult to trust your eyes that it is indeed 135 or 140 yards to the pin with the bunker in front; the hole looks like it's closer. This happens a number of times—bunkers fool you into under-clubbing. Another excellent pin is back-left. You've got the full green in front of you but also you've got a lot of trouble to the left. It's almost impossible to pitch it close if you miss it left.

The first hole has gotten a lot of golfers off to good starts on big rounds: Ben Hogan birdied it in the first round of the 1940 North and South Open as he shot a 66, and Sam Snead scored a three en route to a 66 in the final round in winning in 1949. And Hale Irwin birdied it in shooting a 62 in winning the 1977 Hall of Fame Classic.

The second green sits below the fairway, guarded by a bunker front-right.

2

PAR 4

441	414	394

HANDICAP 3

Tom Watson scored a routine par on this hole to edge Johnny Miller in a playoff for the 1979 Colgate/Hall of Fame Classic title. The championship was Watson's second in a row after Miller, mired in a three-year slump, missed the green with his approach and couldn't get up and down.

The second hole plays from a slightly elevated tee to a blind landing area. The best driving position is left to left-center of the fairway. You're driving right at the bunkers on the left, which is a little unusual. You generally drive away from the bunkers, but here you're driving near them. The green is angled from left to right, and the view from the left side is wide open. This is a long hole; usually you're hitting a medium-to-long iron into the green.

One good pin that's kind of tricky is the front-left quarter of the green. It looks very simple, but you've got an upslope just short of the green, making it difficult to land the ball just short of the green and roll it up.

You've got to hit a perfect shot. But the back side of that left quarter slopes off and away from the green, so if you go over you don't just roll to the fringe, you could roll 15 or 20 yards away.

That's another key feature of the course: There's no buffer around the greens to catch a ball that rolls off. No. 2 is sort of like Augusta in that, "Where is the ball going to roll when it goes off the putting surface?" Since there's no rough, you can putt, chip or pitch the ball back to the green.

The other challenging pin position is back-right. There's a mound almost in the center of the green that you have to play over or around to get it close. This is one of the most difficult holes on the course.

3

PAR 4		
335	317	302
	HANDICAP 13	

Fly it at a backside flag on the third hole with caution: too much and you're dead.

Clayton Heafner trailed Sam Snead by three shots in the final round of the 1941 North and South Open when his approach shot flew the green, headed toward the hill behind the green and a sure double bogey. But the ball hit a tree, bounced on the green, and he made the putt for a three. But he still couldn't catch Snead, losing by three shots.

hree is one of the greatest short par-fours in all of golf. The key is position off the tee. You want to take a long iron and position it in the fairway, depending on where the pin is. If the pin's back-left, you want to be on the right side. If it's back-right, you want to be on the left. You're better off being 150 yards from the pin with a good angle than being 110 yards and having to hit over mounds and bunkers to the pin.

Any pin on the back can be scary. If the greens are firm and you fly it at the flag and take a little too much, you're dead. You'll roll over toward the fifth green if the pin's on the left, down onto the fourth fairway if the pin's on the right.

This green can be driven by long players. Davis Love III went for the green each match in 1984, when he won the North and South. Someone like Fred Couples could probably drive this green, too. But you bring out-of-bounds into the picture if you haul out the driver. There are homes along the left side, and if you get it started left you can be in someone's back yard.

One of the outstanding features of No. 2 is that there is no signature hole—all the holes fit together so well, and you're starting to see that. You've got a medium par-four to open with, then a long, difficult hole, now a short hole where position is more important than length. On No. 2, the whole is greater than the sum of its parts.

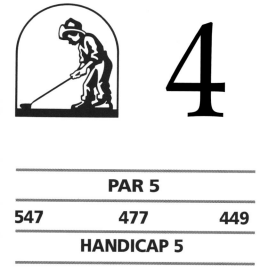

PAR 5

547	477	449

HANDICAP 5

Bunkers on each side of the fairway can penalize sloppy second shots.

Billy Joe Patton gained winning momentum here in 1962 against Hobart Manley in the North and South Amateur finals. After hooking his drive into the woods, Patton hit a five-iron through an opening in the trees, made four and watched as Manley three-putted after reaching the green with two drivers.

T he fourth and fifth holes were the last holes added to the golf course. They originally were the first and ninth holes of a nine-hole No. 5 course that was used primarily by employees. Both were par-fives when they were added to the course in 1935. The same year, Ross changed all the greens from the clay-sand mixture to grass. Those were the last major changes to No. 2, although Ross constantly fine-tuned the course until his death in 1948.

This hole was originally built with one tee, that being where the regular men's tee still sits. New tees have been added over the years on the other side of the sixth tee—one was built just prior to the 1951

Ryder Cup—that have stretched the hole from 477 yards to 547. But the new tee also straightens it out and actually makes the tee shot a little easier. There's a steep elevation change from tee to fairway.

Right-center off the tee opens the green up and keeps you away from the fairway bunker on the left. Long hitters can reach this green in two, but most players hit their second shots into a fairly level area 40 to 70 yards from the green. There are two bunkers, one on each side of the fairway, to keep you from getting careless with your second shot. Then you have a wedge into the green. This green is one of the easiest on the course. It's a great hole to make a birdie.

5

PAR 4		
461	427	417
HANDICAP 1		

It takes a solid drive and precise long iron to hit the fifth green in two.

Tom Kite called a stroke penalty on himself on this green in the 1978 Colgate/ Hall of Fame final round when his ball moved a fraction of an inch at address. That stroke cost him a potential playoff with Tom Watson as he finished with a 278 total, one behind Watson.

ive is probably the most difficult hole on the golf course. It's a very long hole with a sloped fairway and a very difficult green setting. This hole probably epitomizes Ross's design philosophy as well as any hole. He believed the true mark of a skilled golfer was his ability to hit a long iron. He made the remark before the 1936 PGA Championship was played here that the second shot on this hole was the hardest on the golf course. The way the green is angled and slopes to the left, it accepts a faded approach better, but you tend to draw the ball because the ball's above your feet.

The fairway accepts a faded tee shot best since it falls off from right to left. You can't see the landing area for your tee shot, so you've got to pick a target on the horizon—a pine tree, for example. You can play down the left side of the fairway to make it play a little shorter, but your angle into the green isn't very good from there. You're also flirting with mounds and deep rough over there. As far right as you can get opens up the green. The lie teases you into hitting a hook, and if you do that and the ball gets down in those bunkers or below them, you've got to be a magician to get it close. You can also guard against the hook and block it out to the right.

This is a typical Ross green. It's subtle without being severe. Back-left is a difficult position, as is front-right.

6

PAR 3

212	195	178

HANDICAP 15

A pin on the front of the sixth green is perfect to approach with a run-up shot.

Homero Blancas beat Deane Beman on the 24th hole in the quarterfinals of the 1962 U.S. Amateur. Blancas missed a short putt on 18 to win, then Beman missed several makeable birdies in the playoff. When they returned to the sixth hole, Blancas holed a 20-footer to end the match after Beman missed the green with his tee shot.

Six is a very tough par-three following a hard par-four. It's a stretch on the golf course where you take your pars and run. There are bunkers left and right. The green is open in front, allowing you to land the ball short and run it up, which is exactly what Ross had in mind when this hole (along with the parallel third) was added in 1923. There's a gentle downslope that will catch the ball and help roll it to the green. The sixth hole is generally played into the prevailing wind, making it play even longer.

Think about the clothes golfers wore in the 1920 and 1930s. They wore long-sleeve shirts with cuffs and jackets and ties, and most of the golf was played here in cold weather. All they could make was a swing with the arms and hands and wrists, turning it over and hooking it. That kind of swing was tailor-made for this hole. It was more of an on-the-ground game, not a fly-by-air game. If you take a long-iron or a fairway wood, aim at the right bunker and draw the ball, it will land on the downslope and bounce right up to the green.

Six holes into the course, the ebb and flow has already been established: three par-fours to open with, one medium length, one long, one short; a par-five that can serve up a birdie; then two back-breaking holes. This constant give-and-take makes Pinehurst No. 2 so fascinating and one of the America's Top 10 courses.

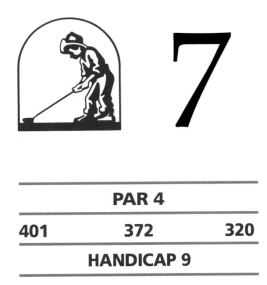

7

PAR 4
| 401 | 372 | 320 |

HANDICAP 9

A cluster of five bunkers guards the corner of the dogleg on the seventh hole.

Frank Stranahan gave Arnold Palmer a quick lesson in bunker play on this hole after closing him out 12-and-11 in the semifinals of the 1949 North and South Amateur. It was the second straight year Palmer lost to the eventual champion, as Harvie Ward ousted him 5-and-4 in 1948.

The greensite of the seventh hole has been intact on maps dating to 1911, but the configuration of the hole has changed. Prior to 1923, the third through sixth holes did not exist. Behind the second green was a tee to a short, par-four third hole that ran perpendicular to the second hole, the green sitting roughly where some new homes are today (to your left as you stand on the present seventh tee). Then the fourth hole was a straight hole to the present seventh greensite. In 1923, Ross added the third and sixth holes (which numbered three and four at the time; the current fourth and fifth holes were added in 1935), and made one dogleg hole of the old third and fourth holes.

The lure of going for the green and taking off the dogleg has always been a key feature of this hole. There once was a tree in the right corner of the bend, but it was destroyed one year by lightning, which opened up a nice avenue for long-hitters. Then the mounds and bunkers in the corner were moved from 235 to 275 yards from the tee during Tom Fazio's 1978 renovation to further deter bold tee shots. But it's still a hole on which long-hitters might be very bold on.

For most players, the line off the tee is to aim between the left and right bunkers. The center of the fairway is best. One difficult pin is in the front. If the greens are firm, it's hard to carry the ball to the flag and stop the ball by the hole.

8

The eighth hole was a weak par-five that's now a formidable par-four.

PAR 4

487	455	429

HANDICAP 7

Many top amateurs have won North and South titles en route to careers on the pro golf tour. Hal Sutton and Corey Pavin were so dominating in their final matches they closed their opponents out on eight—Sutton 12-and-10 over Kevin Walsh in 1980 and Pavin 11-and-10 over Steve Jones in 1981.

his hole has recently been redesignated a par-four, which is in keeping with the trend Ross started of wavering on how it should be played. A pre-1923 scorecard lists this hole (when it was the fifth) as a 467-yard, par-five hole from the "long tee," and a newspaper account shows it still played as a par-five as late as 1935, just before the current fourth and fifth holes were added. One year later, when four and five were opened and both designated par-fives, the eighth hole became a par-four. Then in 1949, the fifth hole was switched to a par-four and eight back to a par-five.

The hole has been, at best, a par-four-and-a-half for years, at only 487 yards, and was played as a four in all the PGA Tour events at Pinehurst from 1973 to 1982. It's a drive and long or medium iron for today's players. You've got another wide driving area; you want to avoid the bunkers on the right. The second shot is a little uphill, with a pretty severe slope off to the left of the green. That's designed to catch a bad shot from a good player. If you try to jump on a long-iron and turn it over too much, it will roll and roll to the left. There's a bunker short of the green on the right, eight to 10 yards from the green, that creates another depth-perception problem.

This is a strong par-four today, given the advances in equipment. Modern science simply overtook it as a par-five.

9

PAR 3

166	147	127

HANDICAP 17

A series of leftside bunkers make getting close to this pin difficult.

Mike Turnesa and Steve Doctor scored aces on No. 9 within one hour of each other in the 1950 North and South Open for the first hole-in-ones in the Open's history. Coupled with an ace by Harry Dee on the 17th, the slew of ones was dubbed "The Hole-In-One Orgy."

ine is the shortest par-three on the course, 166 yards to a green guarded front-left by a series of three bunkers. There's a small opening on the right side of the green where you can bounce the ball up. But since it's so short, Ross believed this was one hole you could be made to carry the ball the entire way. He didn't do that on the longer holes, but on a short one like this most of the entrance is guarded.

This hole runs in a reverse direction from the sixth, which points out another feature of most of Ross's better courses: the four par-threes run in four different directions, giving you a taste of every wind variable. If the wind is in its prevailing direction, from the west-to-southwest, it will be with you on this hole. It's against you on six, then from left-to-right on the 15th hole and right-to-left on the 17th.

This is a good birdie hole if you've got the right club for the distance and wind that day. But if the pin's on the left-front and you aim for it and are short, it's very difficult playing from those bunkers. There's also a steep penalty for having too much club. A severe slope behind the hole will catch the ball and run it into some thick foliage, which makes recovery next to impossible. Club selection can be difficult, too, because of the valley between the green and tee. It can make the hole appear farther away than it really is.

10

PAR 5		
578	491	475
HANDICAP 2		

Avoid at all costs this bunker 100 yards from the green on the 10th hole.

Sam Snead made a rare eagle on this hole in 1941, spawning a second-round 66 and his first of three North and South Open wins. Snead hit a driver and brassie to the front of the green, told his caddie to remove the pin and sank a 50-foot putt for the first eagle since Jimmy Thomson's in the 1936 PGA Championship.

Ten is an interesting hole in the history of No. 2, because at different points it was played as the seventh and later the eighth hole, and upon leaving the green you would play holes that went to the left, into the area where the No. 4 course sits today. If you look closely to the left of the green, you can see amid the pine trees an avenue of trees shorter than the others where old fairways existed.

This is the longest hole on the course. Some big-hitters can reach it in two, but generally speaking it's a great three-shot hole. The best drive is center to left-center if you play a draw. That opens up the fairway to the second shot, which must land right-center. There's a cross-bunker that angles into the fairway about 100 yards from the green. You want to avoid it at all costs. You figure with a par-five you've got a chance to make birdie, but a 100-yard bunker shot over a severe lip isn't going to get you close. So you've got to make a decision after your tee ball: Can I clear that bunker, and if I miss it a little, will I still clear it? If the answer is "No," it's better to lay up. That bunker narrows the fairway.

This is one hole you can't play with the knowledge of where the pin is, because you can't see the green from the tee or your second shot. The best thing is to play your second shot to the right side. That opens up the green the most.

11

PAR 4

453	410	363

HANDICAP 8

Bunkers guard this green left and right, making angle of attack crucial.

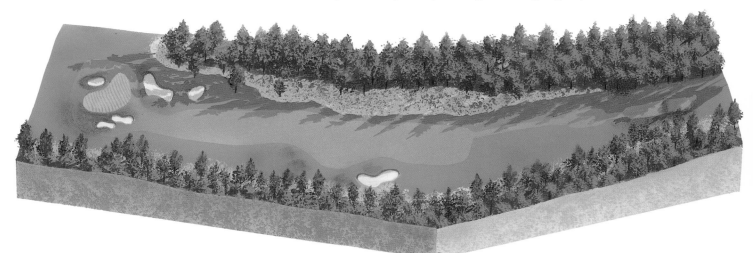

Ben Hogan made the most important shot in his most important tournament ever in the 1940 North and South. Winless in seven years of pro golf, Hogan exploded from the front-right bunker into the hole for a birdie en route to a first-round 66, setting the pace for his landmark first PGA Tour victory.

From here to 18 the layout of the course has remained the same at least since 1911 (see map on pages 188-189). But prior to 1935, you would leave what's now the 10th hole and forge into ground now occupied by course No. 4. At one point there were three holes, later two. Then you would rejoin the current layout on the 11th tee.

This hole exemplifies better than any the wide-open fairways Ross built that were, in fact, totally deceiving. They're not wide at all—if you want to get the ball close for birdie.

Eleven plays as a slight dogleg to the right, with natural area down the right side and woods beyond that. The fairway

measures 50 paces across in the landing area. But if the pin's on the right side of the green, just beyond the bunkers, you might have only seven or eight paces to clear the bunker and stop the ball close. Drive to the left of the fairway and the bunker's no longer a factor. It works the same when the pin's on the left. If you drive to the right of the fairway, you have no bunker to clear; from the left, however, you've got to fly another bunker and stop the ball on what should be a firm green. This is another hole that plays into the prevailing wind, making it even more difficult.

Twenty yards were added to the championship tee of this hole and 16 to the fifth hole during the summer of 1991.

12

PAR 4

415	351	335

HANDICAP 10

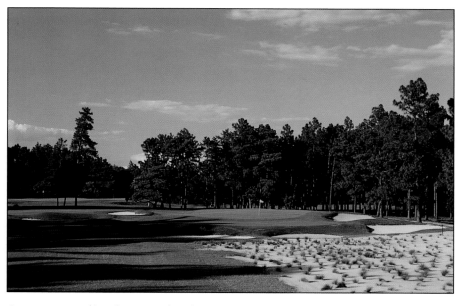

A waste area of hard-pan sand and wire grass stretches the right side of 12.

George T. Dunlap Jr. won more North and South Amateurs than anyone: seven between 1931 and 1942. He closed out John Ryerson 7-and-6 on the 12th hole in 1940 to collect his sixth championship.

welve is a medium-length par-four that, like so many holes, demands an accurate drive to one side or the other to ensure getting a good angle at the pin. Distance off the tee isn't as important as accuracy. The front-left of the green provides a particularly deceptive pin. It looks easy, but there's a swale running across the green from the left that will throw the ball off at an angle.

Notice how close the green is to the 13th tee. Classic golf courses were built compact, with little distance between greens and tees. There's a bunker bordering the left of this green that is, in fact, closer to the 13th tee than it is to the green it's guarding.

This hole has another stretch of hard-pan sand, pine needles and wire grass along its right side. Years ago, the fairway would give way to these areas on every hole. There was no "rough" in the modern sense. The wire grass is indigenous to the Sandhills area. This area is thought to have once been under the sea, and botanists speculate that when the sea receded, only the sturdiest, heartiest plants survived, and one was *Aristida stricta*. The plant is curious in that it can survive with little water and rarely bears seed. When Tom Fazio was hired to help restore No. 2 to its vintage state in 1978, he had hundreds of wire grass plants dug up from the wild and planted in the natural areas. That process has been repeated several times since then.

13

	PAR 4	
374	345	325
	HANDICAP 14	

The 13th hole is a short hole, but an elevated green makes club selection difficult.

It took Curtis Strange 36 holes to defeat George Burns 2-up for the 1975 North and South title. Strange had a much easier time winning the 1976 championship, closing out Fred Ridley on the 13th hole for a 6-and-5 triumph.

 This is another short par-four with a vintage Ross green placement. He designed courses by first selecting 18 natural green sites, then building holes around them. Notice on the 1911 landscape-designer plan on pages 188-189 how the green sits between topographical lines of 625 and 630 feet, some 15-20 feet higher than the landing area in the fairway.

This elevation—combined with the typical inverted-saucer green design—makes club selection crucial. If you're short by a hair, the ball won't fly to the green and instead will fall back off, into the level area of the fairway. The greens on No. 2 average 5,500 square feet compared, for example, to 7,000 at Pinewild. But when you discount all the edges and swales that account for 3,500 square feet per green, only 2,000 square feet have slopes less than three percent and thus are suitable for cupping (that compares to 3,800 at Pinewild).

Front-right is the toughest pin. Usually you're hitting a short iron, which gives you a better chance of stopping the ball close to that pin, but it's still a challenge. If you're short, the best recovery isn't necessarily the lofted wedge you might think. Leave that shot a little short and the ball will roll back to where you began. Some players prefer to bump the ball into the side of the hill, let it pop up and settle by the hole.

14

PAR 4

436	412	395

HANDICAP 4

There's a deep swale between the rightside bunker and the putting surface.

Hobart Manley began his immortal streak of five consecutive threes in the 1951 North and South final against Billy Joe Patton with a birdie here. Tom Watson also eagled the 14th in shooting a 62 in the fifth round of the 1973 World Open. He hit an eight-iron for his first eagle ever on a par-four.

Rarely did Ross conceal anything on his golf courses, and 14 is an excellent example of how you can see everything from the tee. The view from this tee is one of the prettiest on the course. Fairway bunkers right and left, mounds both sides. The pin position is clear, 436 yards away. It's simply a matter of hitting good shots. This was a par-five prior to 1923, then became a four.

There's another deceptive bunker around the green, this one cropping in from the right side about 20 yards short of the putting surface. If your drive is to the right side of the fairway, you can only see the top half of the flagstick, making distance judgment tricky. There are a number of swales and hollows around the green, putting the premium on chipping with the right club and the right angle of approach. There's a particularly deep hollow in back of that bunker on the right of the fairway.

This hole typifies another trend that runs throughout the course: hit your shot over the green and you've got an extremely difficult shot coming back. There's no rough to catch the ball, so it sometimes rolls 30 feet beyond the putting surface, leaving you a difficult shot back up the hill—with little room to stop the ball close to the hole. When the pin is in the back of the green, the best play is to take one club less, hit to the front or middle of the green and two-putt for par.

15

PAR 3

201	188	161

HANDICAP 16

It's hard to hold the 15th green because of the pronounced crowning effect.

Bill Campbell made the first hole-in-one in the 48-year history of the North and South Amateur in 1948 by hitting a four-iron into the hole. It was Campbell's first North and South, and he would go on to win the championship four times.

Fifteen is another long par-three that now has the wind blowing left-to-right if it's coming from its prevailing direction. Not surprisingly, most of the trouble is to the right of this hole. Two deep bunkers sit front-right, gathering any ball caught by the wind. The bunker on the left really doesn't come into play. Once again, Ross is calling for a long-iron shot which he was so fond of.

There's a deep swale right in front of the green that, again, can throw your depth perception off. Any pin toward the front of the green is tough to cover. You're hitting a long-iron, meaning the ball won't hit and light, and this green won't accept the run-up shot as easily as the sixth will.

The 15th green plays extremely small because of the roll-off around all the edges. If your shot is just a little short, long, left or right, it will trickle off the edge. The tee shot is one of the most exacting on the course.

Back-right is a particularly difficult pin position for players who like to draw the ball. To hit a right-to-left shot means they must start the ball at the rightside bunker, leaving them a difficult par if the ball doesn't turn over. Sam Snead used to shoot at that pin by hitting a fade to the center of the green and letting the ball's left-to-right spin carry it to the back-right corner.

PAR 5

531	470	415

HANDICAP 12

To reach 16 in two, you've got to fly the ball over three bunkers.

Johnny Miller hit what he calls his "best shot ever under pressure" here in a playoff in the 1974 World Open. Miller hit a three-wood second shot to eight feet and two-putted for birdie to win the title over Jack Nicklaus and Frank Beard (as well as Bob Murphy, who bogeyed 15, the first playoff hole).

ixteen features the course's one water hazard, and it's there by default. It was never built to be a hazard. There was a depression in the area to the front of the tee that simply would never drain very well, and it looked ugly. So Ross filled it in to make it look a little less scraggly. But it has nothing to do with playing the hole unless you're a short hitter playing the back tees into a strong wind.

Like the fourth, this hole had been gradually lengthened over the years with a new championship tee carved in the woods prior to the 1951 Ryder Cup.

The leftside bunkers make you play to the center or right-center of the fairway, although if you fade the ball you can aim straight for the green and let the ball work back into the middle of the fairway. The second shot here is one of the choicest decisions on the golf course. If you've hit a good drive, you can reach the green in two, but it's a full carry because the green sits on a rise and won't let you run the ball up very easily. There are two bunkers on the right-front of the green, which prevent you from hitting a draw, landing it short and letting it bounce up.

A lot of that decision is simply personal preference. If you're a good scrambler, you'll go for it and hope for the best. If not, you're better off laying up just over a fairway bunker that encroaches from the left and trying to hit a sand wedge close.

17

PAR 3		
190	162	149
	HANDICAP 18	

Right-front bunkers make this a difficult pin to get close to.

Harvie Ward made a remarkable bogey on the 17th in beating Frank Stranahan for the 1948 North and South title. Bunkered off the tee, Ward skinned his second over the green into the bunker back-left. But his third dropped inches from the cup, he tapped in for a bogey and kept his 1-up lead when Stranahan three-putted.

A anybody who says Donald Ross never put a bunker in front of a green or behind it never saw this hole in 1911 (see map on pages 188-189). He's got *seven* bunkers surrounding the green on this par-three, one directly in front and two behind the rear corners of the square, sand-and-clay based putting surface. He later revised that configuration, but there still are five bunkers around this green, and one stretching across two-thirds of the front of the green is pivotal in playing the hole. Rightside flags are difficult to approach on this hole for the right-to-left player, just as they are on 15.

Again, the flow of the holes on this course is so crucial: good birdie hole on 16, then you wrap up with an exacting par-three and an uphill par-four to a difficult green.

Club selection is important because if you're aiming at a flag over that bunker and come up short, you've got a difficult bunker shot. It's usually a five or six-iron for good players and is a medium-length par-three after two long ones and a short one. Here's another example of why this course should be played hard and fast. If the green is firm, it's tough to aim at a pin just over the bunkers and get it to stop. If the green is soft, you can take the bunkers out of play by aiming at the stick and knowing the ball will hold.

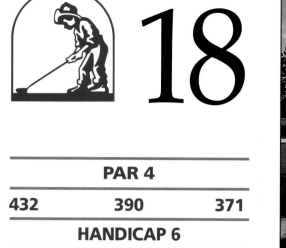

18

PAR 4		
432	390	371
HANDICAP 6		

The swale in the middle of the green guards all backside pin positions.

Few players drive into the rightside fairway bunker and survive—and that's what happened to Gene Andrews in the 1959 North and South Amateur final against Jack Nicklaus. It took Andrews four shots to reach the green, and Nicklaus made a six-foot putt for par and a 1-up victory.

Eighteen is one of the finest finishing holes in golf, particularly with the traditional back-left pin position. That's where the pin always is on Sundays of major tournaments or on North and South final Saturdays, and the best angle to approach that pin is the right side of the fairway. But to get to that side, you've got to flirt with a long, deep bunker that runs along the fairway. There's plenty of wire grass and some clumps of the gnarly love grass in that bunker that make playing from it even more difficult. Deposit a tee ball there and it's next to impossible to reach the green.

For the upteenth time, it seems (actually, the sixth), there's a bunker in front of the green that's really a good distance away, luring you into hitting too little club. The green features the renowned swale that seeps in from the right side, just shy of halfway back. Traditionalists say the swale isn't as severe today as it once was, but nonetheless it plays havoc with approach shots to rear flags. Land the ball into the downslope of the swale and it could go over the green; hit it five yards farther and into the upslope and it will kick back to the front. The proximity of the clubhouse to the green enlivens this hole, as bold approaches often carry too far, hit the downslopes around the greens and carom into the bushes, leaving a very tricky recovery from a drop area.

No. 1

Architect: Donald Ross. Originally opened as 18 holes in 1899; Ross revised in early 1900s.

The crowned green on the 18th hole of No. 1 is typical Donald Ross.

Pinehurst No. 1 is a great golf course for ladies, seniors, beginners, juniors and anyone who'd like to go back to the very start in Pinehurst.

The course measures only 5,780 yards from the men's tees (5,329 for the ladies), but plays longer than that since there are only two par-fives—and those are very short at 452 and 413 yards. The second hole, a par-four of 409 yards, and the 11th, a par-three of 216 yards, are among the strongest holes in Pinehurst.

If you've ever wondered why the first tee is located several hundred yards from the clubhouse, it's because the current first hole used to be the second hole. And the old first hole played along the fairway where the first hole of No. 5 is today.

Early maps of the first Pinehurst courses are difficult to decipher, but it's clear in studying a layout from the early 1900s that this course is routed in the same general vicinity as the first one. The pond in front of the 11th tee goes back to the beginning. Donald Ross reworked the course beginning in 1901 and built some new holes in 1913, when the first, second and 18th holes were torn up to build a practice range. It's also clear from a 1918 map that the current first, second, third, fourth, ninth, 10th, 11th, 14th, 15th, 17th and 18th exist today almost as they did then (but with different numbers). Ross added several new holes in 1939.

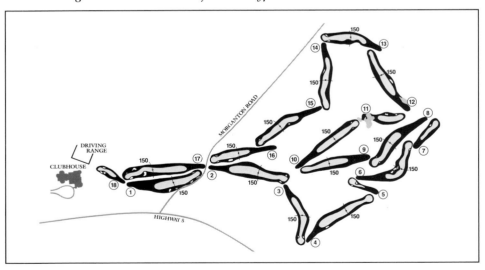

NO.	1	2	3	4	5	6	7	8	9	OUT	10	11	12	13	14	15	16	17	18	IN	TOT.
PAR	4	4	4	5	3	4	3	4	4	35	4	3	4	4	4	4	4	5	3	35	70
YDS.	366	409	336	452	148	348	156	335	339	2889	393	216	376	318	340	373	313	413	149	2891	5780
HCP.	5	1	13	9	15	3	17	11	7		8	6	4	14	12	2	18	10	16		

ALL YARDAGES FROM BACK TEES.

No. 3

Architect: Donald Ross. Originally opened as 18 holes in 1910.

The No. 3 course is the second of Pinehurst's short, older courses. It plays 5,593 yards from the men's tees (5,198 for the ladies) and opened in 1910 to rave reviews. A 1913 passage from the *Pinehurst Outlook* proclaims No. 3 "almost as popular as the No. 2 course, and in another year or so will, without question, be the finest golf course at Pinehurst. The general topography of the ground is decidedly of a more rolling character than the other two courses, and Donald Ross, who also laid this course out, has shown excellent judgment in placing the various holes."

Many of the holes exist as they did originally, though with different numbers. Some holes were lost to the new No. 5 course opened in 1961 and several new ones were built. The current first hole is the site of the old tennis courts, and the current second used to be the first—only it ran in the opposite direction.

The course actually was longer in its earlier days; a 1923 map lists its length as 6,209 yards. Water comes into play on only one hole. There's a pond on the par-three seventh hole that plays to 145 yards. That hole was the 14th hole in early days. "A carry of 120 yards is necessary to cross the pond, and on all sides are pits and traps and rough ground of all sorts," said the *Outlook*. Wild-hitters beware: woods and out-of-bounds frame the course.

The second hole of No. 3 was once the first hole—but it ran in the opposite direction.

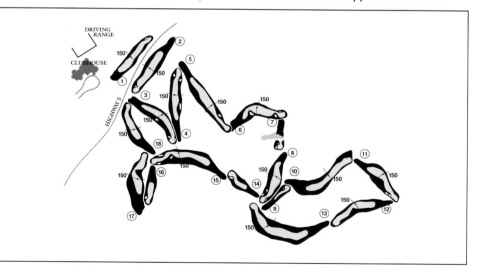

NO.	1	2	3	4	5	6	7	8	9	OUT	10	11	12	13	14	15	16	17	18	IN	TOT.
PAR	4	4	4	4	4	4	3	4	3	34	4	4	4	5	3	5	3	4	4	36	70
YDS.	287	341	332	386	398	348	145	282	150	2669	376	312	332	489	183	422	187	317	306	2924	5593
HCP.	17	5	9	1	7	3	15	11	13		2	14	8	4	6	12	10	18	16		

No. 4

Architect: Donald Ross. Originally opened as 18 holes in 1919.

*T*his course has been influenced by Donald Ross, Richard Tufts, Robert Trent Jones and Rees Jones. Perhaps more than any at Pinehurst, it links the old to the new. No. 4 is situated between the No. 2 and No. 1 courses as they fan out from the clubhouse.

From the back tees, it offers one of Pinehurst's sternest tests of golf. Robert Trent Jones rebuilt the course in 1973 to make it longer and more difficult and suitable for use (with No. 2) during the World Open. Son Rees rebuilt all the greens in 1983 and softened some of the harsher design features to make it a fairer test for average players.

The course has been reworked extensively since the first one that opened as an 18-hole course in 1919, for one reason to accommodate Donald Ross's revisions on No. 2. The area where the 12th and 13th greens of No. 4 sit today once was the site of, at different times, two and three holes of No. 2. In fact, the pond that you hit over on the par-three 13th once fronted the tee of the 10th hole of No. 2. Only the hole ran in a different direction, up toward your right as you stand on the 13th hole today and look at the green.

No. 4 can stretch to 6,890 yards from the blue tees and offers one of Pinehurst's best gambling holes, the par-five 12th. It's a dogleg left hole that wraps around a lake. Bold players can risk carrying more water and getting their second shots on the green.

The par-three 13th hole requires a full carry over a pond.

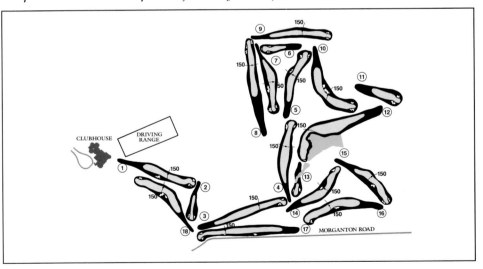

NO.	1	2	3	4	5	6	7	8	9	OUT	10	11	12	13	14	15	16	17	18	IN	TOT.
PAR	4	3	5	4	4	3	4	5	4	36	4	3	5	3	4	4	4	5	4	36	72
YDS.	431	181	486	441	371	192	382	519	399	3402	428	210	520	163	390	366	418	547	446	3488	6890
HCP.	5	17	9	1	13	15	11	7	3		6	10	4	18	14	16	12	2	8		

No. 5

Architect: Ellis Maples. Opened in 1961.

he next time you play No. 5, pay special attention to the par-four fourth hole, a short dogleg left that plays only 355 yards from the men's tees. Although the configuration of the hole has changed—it was once a straight-away hole—the green sits exactly today as it did in 1910, when Donald Ross completed the No. 3 course. This hole was originally the fourth on No. 3, then became the fourth on No. 5 in 1961.

No. 5 is another excellent test of golf, and it includes more water than any of the five courses that emanate from the main clubhouse. One of the water holes is the par-three 15th, the "Cathedral Hole" that features a green sitting in a cove of tall pines that resemble the pipes of an organ.

The first hole has an interesting history. It's a long, dogleg right par-four with the tee sitting beside the clubhouse and putting greens. Long ago, that site was the first hole of No. 1—a straight-away par-four of some 350 yards. Then there was a short par-three that angled off to the right, where the current green sits; that was the 10th hole of No. 4.

No. 5 has one of the most difficult holes in Pinehurst: the 453-yard, par-four ninth. Your drive must travel 250 yards uphill to a plateau to give you a sight of the green, which sits down to the right. The green itself also sits on a rise, making it difficult to bounce a long-iron or fairway wood onto it.

One of the prettiest holes in Pinehurst is the 15th, the "Cathedral Hole."

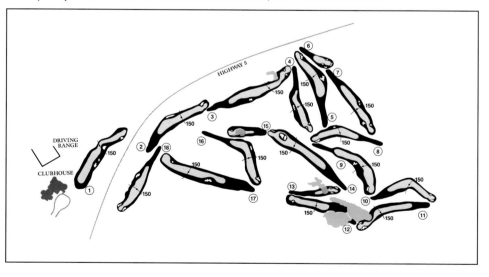

NO.	1	2	3	4	5	6	7	8	9	OUT	10	11	12	13	14	15	16	17	18	IN	TOT.
PAR	4	4	5	4	4	3	4	4	4	36	4	4	4	3	5	3	4	5	4	36	72
YDS.	395	403	452	393	421	165	401	377	453	3460	375	410	384	200	509	175	427	498	389	3367	6827
HCP.	3	9	7	13	5	17	11	15	1		12	2	16	14	4	18	6	8	10		

No. 6

Architects: Tom and George Fazio. Opened in 1979.

Course No. 6 is one of two at Pinehurst that have separate clubhouses and practice facilities. Both Nos. 6 and 7 are located on land that's much more rugged and dramatic than the topography where the first five courses were built.

No. 6 was built by Tom and George Fazio and opened in the spring of 1979. Played all the way back to its 7,098 maximum, some golfers feel this is the hardest golf course in Pinehurst. You can rack up some big numbers fast. The site is heavily wooded and there are several water hazards to negotiate. But if you're not too daring and hit the ball straight, No. 6 is a quite pleasant round of golf. Its 6,314 yardage from the men's tees is quite manageable.

The course underwent a facelift late in 1990 and early in 1991 as all the greens were rebuilt and some even recontoured, lessening the severity of some of the slopes.

No. 6 offers some of Pinehurst's most dramatic views as elevated tees give way to greens and landing areas far below. The 13th, for example, measures 210 yards from the back tees but plays much shorter because of the steep grade downhill. Sixteen is another downhill par-three that's surrounded on all sides by woods and, in front, a bunker. The par-five 10th is a bear. Water creeps in on both sides of the fairway. The green is elevated and deep and has more than its share of undulations.

The bunker fronting the green on the par-three 16th has had plenty of action since 1979.

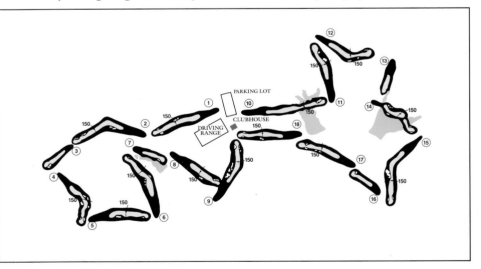

NO.	1	2	3	4	5	6	7	8	9	OUT	10	11	12	13	14	15	16	17	18	IN	TOT.
PAR	4	5	3	4	4	5	3	4	4	36	5	4	4	3	4	5	3	4	4	36	72
YDS.	430	523	198	413	406	520	212	370	437	3509	552	409	427	210	393	526	230	417	425	3569	7098
HCP.	7	3	17	9	11	1	15	13	5		2	12	8	18	14	4	16	10	6		

No. 7

Architect: Rees Jones. Opened in 1986.

No. 7 is Pinehurst's newest course, having opened in 1986. Like No. 6, the terrain is severely rolling. Down off the tee, back up to the green in many cases. Its four sets of tees range from 7,114 yards to 6,719 to 6,216 to 4,924.

The site includes more wetlands than other Pinehurst courses, and tougher environmental laws when No. 7 was built prohibited designer Rees Jones from touching them. The seventh hole, for example, requires your second shot to carry the "Devil's Gut"—an expanse of water and vegetation. It's a short hole, though, so usually you're hitting a lofted iron.

Two par-threes on the backside require nearly full carries over large expanses of sand. The 13th (161 yards from the white tees) is slightly uphill over a large berm, and the 15th (151 yards) requires a carry over "Rees's Fingers"—a large bunker with elongated strips of sand. The gold and blue tees on this hole are at a different angle from the forward tees. From the back, your shot must completely clear the sand. From the forward tees, you've got some fairway to work with.

The dramatic 18th is a par-five, downhill, to a green backed by a lake. The shallowness of the green makes it risky to try getting home in two. If you clear a bunker fronting the green, your ball might not stop before rolling over the green. A downhill third shot is tough to judge how hard to hit the ball.

The green on the 18th hole is surrounded by pot bunkers and backed by a lake.

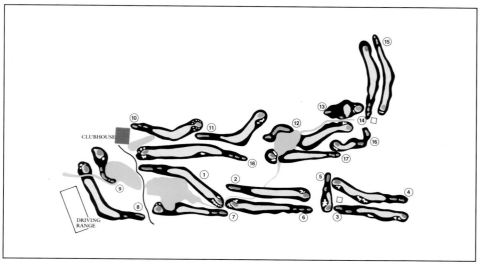

NO.	1	2	3	4	5	6	7	8	9	OUT	10	11	12	13	14	15	16	17	18	IN	TOT.
PAR	5	4	4	4	3	4	4	5	3	36	4	4	5	3	4	4	3	4	5	36	72
YDS.	514	452	405	423	201	447	388	530	204	3564	393	407	546	203	387	427	196	395	596	3550	7114
HCP.	7	1	11	9	17	3	13	5	15		14	8	4	16	12	6	18	10	2		

APPENDIX

Men's North and South Amateur Championship

Year	Champion	Score	Runner-up
1901	George C. Dutton		A.J. Wellington
1902	Charles B. Cory	3-and-1	E.A. Thomson
1903	T. Sterling Beckwith	1-up	John M. Ward
1904	Walter J. Travis	8-and-7	Charles B. Cory
1905	Dr. L. Lee Harban	1-up	Fred Herreshoff
1906	Warren K. Wood	2-up	C.L. Becker
1907	Allan Lard	12-and-11	Nathaniel F. Moore
1908	Allan Lard	5-and-4	John E. Porter
1909	James D. Standish Jr.	3-and-2	C.L. Becker
1910	Walter J. Travis	5-and-4	W.R. Tuckerman
1911	Charles Evans Jr.	6-and-4	Robert Hunter
1912	Walter J. Travis	6-and-5	Henry J. Topping
1913	Henry J. Topping	1-up, 37	Hamilton K. Kerr
1914	Reginald S. Worthington	6-and-5	Paul E. Gardner
1915	Fillmore K. Robeson	4-and-2	Henry J. Topping
1916	Philip V.G. Carter	5-and-3	Frank W. Dyer
1917	Norman H. Maxwell	2-and-1	William C. Fownes Jr.
1918	Irving S. Robeson	1-up	Robert A. Stranahan
1919	Edward C. Beall	4-and-3	Frank C. Newton
1920	Francis D. Ouimet	5-and-4	Samuel J. Graham
1921	B.P. Merriman	9-and-8	Gardiner W. White
1922	Henry J. Topping	3-and-2	Fillmore K. Robeson
1923	Frank C. Newton	6-and-5	Charles T. Lansing
1924	Fred W. Knight	1-up	B.P. Merriman
1925	Arthur W. Yates	10-and-8	William C. Fownes Jr.
1926	Page Hufty	2-and-1	L.E. Sherrill
1927	George Voight	4-and-2	Eugene V. Homans
1928	George Voight	1-up	John W. Dawson
1929	George Voight	9-and-8	William C. Fownes Jr.
1930	Eugene V. Homans	3-and-1	C. Ross Somerville
1931	George T. Dunlap Jr.	6-and-5	Samuel M. Parks Jr.
1932	M. Pierpont Warner	5-and-3	John B. Ryerson
1933	George T. Dunlap Jr.	6-and-5	Jack Toomer
1934	George T. Dunlap Jr.	4-and-3	Richard D. Chapman
1935	George T. Dunlap Jr.	1-up 38	Johnny Johnson
1936	George T. Dunlap Jr.	8-and-7	A.C. Giles
1937	Robert W. Dunkelberger	5-and-3	James T. Hunter
1938	Frank Strafaci	5-and-4	George T. Dunlap Jr.
1939	Frank Strafaci	1-up	Robert W. Dunkelberger
1940	George T. Dunlap Jr.	7-and-6	John B. Ryerson
1941	S.M. Alexander Jr.	3-and-2	Frank Strafaci
1942	George T. Dunlap Jr.	10-and-9	Powell Crichton
1943	Harry C. Offutt Jr.	2-and-1	Ronnie Williams
1944	Mal Galletta	8-and-6	George McAllister
1945	Ed Furgol	6-and-5	Frank R. Stranahan
1946	Frank R. Stranahan	6-and-5	H.S. Covington
1947	Charles B. Dudley	6-and-5	Felice Torza
1948	E. Harvie Ward Jr.	1-up	Frank R. Stranahan
1949	Frank R. Stranahan	2-and-1	E. Harvie Ward Jr.
1950	William C. Campbell	1-up 37	Wynsol K. Spencer
1951	Hobart Manley Jr.	1-up	Billy Joe Patton
1952	Frank R. Stranahan	8-and-7	Frank Strafaci
1953	William C. Campbell	2-and-1	Mal Galletta
1954	Billy Joe Patton	1-up 37	Alex Welsh
1955	Donald M. Bisplinghoff	5-and-4	William C. Campbell
1956	Hillman Robbins Jr.	1-up	William Hyndman III
1957	William C. Campbell	3-and-2	Hillman Robbins Jr.
1958	Richard D. Chapman	11-and-10	Herbert Durham
1959	Jack Nicklaus	1-up	Gene Andrews
1960	Charles B. Smith	5-and-3	Peter Green
1961	William Hyndman III	4-and-3	Richard D. Chapman
1962	Billy Joe Patton	7-and-6	Hobart L. Manley Jr.
1963	Billy Joe Patton	7-and-6	Bob Allen
1964	Dale Morey	3-and-2	Billy Joe Patton
1965	Tom Draper	1-up	Don Allen
1966	Ward Wettlaufer	4-and-2	Marion Heck
1967	William C. Campbell	10-and-9	William Hyndman III
1968	Jack Lewis	7-and-6	William Hyndman III
1969	Joe Inman	2-and-1	Lanny Wadkins
1970	Gary Cowan	5-and-4	Dale Morey
1971	Eddie Pearce	5-and-4	Vinny Giles
1972	Danny Edwards	3-and-1	Eddie Pearce
1973	Mike Ford	1-up, 38	Bill Harvey
1974	George Burns III	4-and-2	Danny Yates
1975	Curtis Strange	2-up	George Burns III
1976	Curtis Strange	6-and-5	Fred Ridley
1977	Gary Hallberg	5-and-3	Mike Donald
1978	Gary Hallberg	5-and-4	Hal Sutton
1979	John McGough	1-up	Scott Hoch
1980	Hal Sutton	12-and-10	Kevin Walsh
1981	Corey Pavin	11-and-10	Steve Jones
1982	Keith Clearwater	2-up	Jay Sigel
1983	Bryan Sullivan	8-and-7	Mike Taylor
1984	Davis Love III	4-and-3	John Inman
1985	Jack Nicklaus II	2-and-1	Tom McKnight
1986	Billy Andrade	3-and-2	Kurt Beck
1987	Robert Goettlicher	3-and-2	Billy Andrade
1988	Uly Grisette	2-up	Henry Cagigal
1989	Lee Porter	4-and-3	Eoghan O'Connell
1990	Tom Scherrer	1-up	Tee Davies
1991	David Eger	2-and-1	Tee Burton

World Open

Year	Champion	Score	Runner-up
1973	Miller Barber	68-74-73-74	Ben Crenshaw
		67-73-72-69—570	
1974	Johnny Miller *	73-63-73-72—281	Jack Nicklaus, Frank Beard, Bob Murphy
1975	Jack Nicklaus *	70-71-70-69—280	Billy Casper

Colgate/Hall of Fame Classic

Year	Champion	Score	Runner-up
1976	Raymond Floyd *	69-67-67-71—274	Jerry McGee
1977	Hale Irwin	65-62-69-68—264	Leonard Thompson
1978	Tom Watson	72-67-67-71—277	Hale Irwin, Tom Kite Howard Twitty

Hall of Fame Classic

Year	Champion	Score	Runner-up
1979	Tom Watson *	70-68-65-69—272	Johnny Miller
1980	Phil Hancock	71-67-67-70—275	Scott Simpson
1981	Morris Hatalsky	65-71-68-71—275	Jerry Pate D.A. Weibring
1982	Jay Haas *	70-70-70-66—276	John Adams

CHAMPIONS OF OTHER MAJOR EVENTS AT PINEHURST

1936 PGA Championship: Denny Shute
1951 Ryder Cup Matches: United States 9 1/2, Great Britian and Ireland 2 1/2
1962 U.S. Men's Amateur: Labron Harris Jr.
1971 PGA National Club Pro: Sam Snead
1972 PGA National Club Pro: Don Massengale
1973 PGA National Club Pro:
Rives McBee
1974 PGA National Club Pro:
Roger Watson
1988 PGA National Club Pro:
Robert Boyd
1965 Southern Amateur:
Billy Joe Patton
1977 Southern Amateur:
Vinny Giles
1966 Western Amateur:
Jim Weichers
1980 World Amateur Team
Championship: United States won men's and women's competitions.
1982 NCAA Championship: Houston team champion, Billy Ray Brown individual champion.
1983 PGA Senior Hall of Fame Classic: Rod Funseth
1989 U.S. Women's Amateur: Vicki Goetze

Low Competitive Rounds On No. 2		
Year	Player	Score
1973	Gibby Gilbert	62
1973	Tom Watson	62
1977	Hale Irwin	62
1974	Johnny Miller	63
1977	J.C. Snead	63
1978	Hale Irwin	63
1979	Dana Quigley	63
1979	Johnny Miller	63
1973	Ben Crenshaw	64
1977	Leonard Thompson	64

North and South Junior Boys		North and South Junior Girls	
1979	Mark Bucek	1979	Cathy Ayers
1980	Bruce Soulsby	1980	Debbie Thomas
1981	Woody Austin	1981	Kristal Parker
1982	Mike Taylor	1982	Robin Gamester
1983	Greg Parker	1983	Vanessa Castellucci
1984	Russell Mason	1984	Donna Andrews
1985	Kem Rodgers	1985	Karen Jefferson
1986	Francis Holroyd	1986	Shirley Trier
1987	Brian Craig	1987	Susan Slaughter
1988	Frederick Chew III	1988	Tonya Blosser
1989	Jack Patterson	1989	Barbara Paul
1990	Robert Dean	1990	Meredith Tucker
1991	Robert Dean	1991	Kim Marshall

North and South Open Championship

Year	Champion	Scores	Runner-up
1902	Alex Ross	75	Donald Ross
1903	Donald Ross	73-74—147	Jack Jolly
1904	Alex Ross	81-71—152 *	Jack Hobens
1905	Donald Ross	72-74—146	Alex Ross
1906	Donald Ross	72-74—146	Alex Ross
1907	Alex Ross	73-79—152 *	Donald Ross
1908	Alex Ross	72-71—143	Bernard Nichols
1909	Fred McLeod	77-71—148	Gil Nichols
1910	Alex Ross	73-68—141	Gil Nichols
1911	Gil Nichols	68-73—141	Donald Ross
1912	Tom McNamara	75-69—144	Charles "Chick" Evans **
1913	Tom McNamara	74-72—146	Mike Brady
1914	Gil Nichols	73-72—145	J.J. McDermott
1915	Alex Ross	71-75—146	Francis Ouimet **
1916	Jim Barnes	71-73—144	Clarence Hackney
1917	M.J. Brady	67-74—141	Fred McLeod
1918	Walter Hagen	76-72-73-72—293	Emmet French
1919	Jim Barnes	76-75-72-75—298	Mike Brady
1920	Fred McLeod	73-73-72-75—293	Clarence Hackney Walter Hagen
1921	Jock Hutchison	144-147—291	Fred McLeod George Fotheringham
1922	Pat O'Hara	73-75-72—220	Clarence Hackney
1923	Walter Hagen	70-68-76-75—289	Cyril Walker
1924	Walter Hagen	68-68-74-73—283	Cyril Walker
1925	Macdonald Smith	68-70-70-73—281	Walter Hagen
1926	Bobby Cruickshank	74-71-74-74—293	Arthur Yates ** Tom Harmon Jr. Macdonald Smith
1927	Bobby Cruickshank	68-75-73-69—285	Walter Hagen
1928	Billy Burke	73-69-74-75—291	Tommy Armour
1929	Horton Smith	74-71-67-76—287	Tommy Armour Roland Hancock
1930	Paul Runyan	72-77-72-70—291	Frank Walsh
1931	Wiffy Cox	69-74-74-71—288	Joe Turnesa
1932	Johnny Golden	74-69-72-71—286*	Craig Wood
1933	Joe Kirkwood	68-67-70-72—277	Harry Cooper
1934	Henry Picard	69-68-74-72—283	Horton Smith Harry Cooper George T. Dunlap Jr. **
1935	Paul Runyan	65-71-72-68—276	Felix Serafin
1936	Henry Picard	71-72-73-72—288*	Ray Mangrum
1937	Horton Smith	67-73-77-69—286	Paul Runyan
1938	Vic Ghezzi	68-73-68-70—279	Paul Runyan
1939	Byron Nelson	71-68-70-71—280	Horton Smith
1940	Ben Hogan	66-67-74-70—277	Sam Snead
1941	Sam Snead	69-66-73-69—277	Clayton Heafner
1942	Ben Hogan	67-68-67-69—271	Sam Snead
1943	Bobby Cruickshank	71-72-74-75—292	Joe Kirkwood
1944	Bob Hamilton	73-72-76-71—286	Bobby Cruickshank
1945	Cary Middlecoff	70-69-69-72—280	Denny Shute
1946	Ben Hogan	71-71-70-70—282	Sam Snead
1947	Jim Turnesa	71-66-74-73—284	George Schoux
1948	Toney Penna	72-73-70-70—285	Sam Snead, Julius Boros **
1949	Sam Snead	68-70-70-66—274	Johnny Bulla
1950	Sam Snead	68-71-66-70—275	Johnny Palmer
1951	Tommy Bolt	71-72-71-69—283	John Barnum

* Won playoff
** Amateur

Women's North and South Amateur Championship

1903	Myra D. Paterson	1926	Louise Fordyce	1949	Peggy Kirk	1970	Hollis Stacy
1904	Myra D. Paterson	1927	Glenna Collett	1950	Pat O'Sullivan	1971	Barbara McIntire
1905	Houghton Dutton	1928	Opal S. Hill	1951	Pat O'Sullivan	1972	Mrs. Michael Booth
1906	Myra D. Paterson	1929	Glenna Collett	1952	Barbara Romack	1973	Beth Barry
1907	Molly B. Adams	1930	Glenna Collett	1953	Pat O'Sullivan	1974	Mrs. J. Douglas Streit
1908	Julia R. Mix	1931	Maureen Orcutt	1954	Joyce Ziske	1975	Cynthia Hill
1909	Mary Fownes	1932	Maureen Orcutt	1955	Wiffi Smith	1976	Carol Semple
1910	Mrs. C.H. Vanderbeck	1933	Maureen Orcutt	1956	Marlene Stewart	1977	Marcia Dolan
1911	Louise Elkins	1934	Charlotte Clutting	1957	Barbara McIntire	1978	Cathy Sherk
1912	Mrs. J. Raymond Price	1935	Estelle Lawson	1958	Mrs. Philip M. Cudone	1979	Julie Gumlia
1913	Lillian B. Hyde	1936	Deborah Verry	1959	Ann Casey Johnstone	1980	Charlotte Montgomery
1914	Florence L. Harvey	1937	Estelle Lawson Page	1960	Barbara McIntire	1981	Patti Rizzo
1915	Mrs. Roland H. Barlow	1938	Jane Cothran	1961	Barbara McIntire	1982	Ann Sander
1916	Mrs. Roland H. Barlow	1939	Estelle Lawson Page	1962	Clifford Ann Creed	1983	Ann Sander
1917	Elaine Rosenthall	1940	Estelle Lawson Page	1962	Clifford Ann Creed	1984	Susan Pager
1918	Dorothy Campbell Hurd	1941	Estelle Lawson Page	1963	Nancy Roth	1985	Lee Ann Hammack
1919	Mrs. Roland H Barlow	1942	Louise Suggs	1964	Phyllis Preuss	1986	Leslie Shannon
1920	Dorothy Campbell Hurd	1943	Dorothy Kirby	1965	Barbara McIntire	1987	Carol Semple Thompson
1921	Dorothy Campbell Hurd	1944	Estelle Lawson Page	1966	Nancy Roth Syms	1988	Donna Andrews
1922	Glenna Collett	1945	Estelle Lawson Page	1967	Phyllis Preuss	1989	Page Marsh
1923	Glenna Collett	1946	Louise Suggs	1968	Alice Dye	1990	Brandie Burton
1924	Glenna Collett	1947	"Babe" Didrikson Zaharias	1969	Barbara McIntire	1991	Kelly Robbins
1925	Mrs. Melville Jones	1948	Louise Suggs				

Men's North and South Senior

1952	Judd L. Brumley	1972	William Hyndman III
1953	O.V. Russell	1973	Raymond Palmer
1954	Spencer S. Overton	1974	David Goldman
1955	B.F. Kraffert Jr.	1975	Harry Welch
1956	Tom Robbins	1976	Paul Severin
1957	J. Wood Platt	1977	George Pottle
1958	J. Wolcott Brown	1978	Edward Ervasti
1959	Walter F. Pease	1979	Dale Morey
1960	Tom Robbins	1980	Dale Morey
1961	Robert R. Bell	1981	Richard Remsen
1962	Col. William Lanman	1982	Brown McDonald
1963	James H. McAlvin	1983	Edward Ervasti
1964	James H. McAlvin	1984	Howard Derrick
1965	David Goldman	1985	Fred Zinn
1966	Curtis Person	1986	Joseph Faison
1967	Robert E. Cochran	1987	Gael Coakley
1968	Curtis Person	1988	Moot Thomas
1969	Curtis Person	1989	Denis Biron
1970	Robert E. Cochran	1990	Charles Smith
1971	David Goldman		

Women's North and South Senior

1958	Mrs. Harrison F. Flippin	1978	Mrs. I. Wayne Rutter
1959	Mrs. Charles E. Bartholomew	1979	Mrs. Ceil H. MacLaurin
1960	Miss Maureen Orcutt	1980	Mrs. Ceil H. MacLaurin
1961	Miss Maureen Orcutt	1981	Mrs. Betty Probasco
1962	Miss Maureen Orcutt	1982	Mrs. Jan Calin
1963	Miss Ada McKenzie	1983	Mrs. Barbara Young
1964	Mrs. John S. Haskell	1984	Mrs. Barbara Young
1965	Mrs. Reinert M. Torgerson	1985	Mrs. Barbara Young
1966	Mrs. John Pennington	1986	Mrs. Ceil H. MacLaurin
1967	Mrs. Frederick C. Paffard	1987	Mrs. Barbara Young
1968	Mrs. Douglass C. Coupe	1988	Mrs. Barbara Young
1969	Mrs. Philip J. Cudone	1989	Mrs. Betty Probasco
1970	Mrs. Philip J. Cudone	1990	Mrs. Betty Probasco
1971	Mrs. Harton S. Semple		
1972	Mrs. Philip J. Cudone		
1973	Mrs. Philip J. Cudone		
1974	Mrs. Philip J. Cudone		
1975	Mrs. Philip J. Cudone		
1976	Mrs. Ceil H. MacLaurin		
1977	Mrs. Ceil H. MacLaurin		

Donald Ross Memorial Junior Championship

1948	Charles B. Smith	1959	Bobby Littler	1970	David Thore	1981	Chris Kite
1949	Ken Worthington	1960	Don Hedrick	1971	David Thore	1982	Art Roberson
1950	Billy Ford	1961	David Bennett	1972	Chip Beck	1983	Danny Hockaday
1951	Joe Correll	1962	Russell Glover	1973	Chip Beck	1984	Matt Peterson
1952	Bobby Sisk	1963	Leonard Thompson	1974	Chris Tucker	1985	Kem Rodgers
1953	George Warren	1964	Leonard Thompson	1975	Charles Schaffernoth	1986	Doug Stone
1954	Ed Justa	1965	Mike Cheek	1976	Eric Moehling	1987	Robert Sevier Jr.
1955	Burnham Uhler	1966	Davis Williams	1977	Mike West	1988	Jason Widener
1956	Ed Justa	1967	Johnny Gregory	1978	Gray Linzel	1989	Trey Jervis
1957	George Smith Jr.	1968	Randy Hoft	1979	Chris Kite	1990	Brent Patrick
1958	Buddy Baker	1969	David Eger	1980	Seishi Tanaka	1991	Paul Carpenter

AFTERWORD

It is with great pride and pleasure that we at Pinehurst present this book celebrating the rich heritage of America's oldest and largest golf resort.

There is, quite simply, not another golf resort or country club in the nation that could bring together, between the hard covers of one volume, all of the legendary figures who've graced the premises of our village and club for almost 100 years.

Pinehurst was not the first place Americans played golf. But it was certainly a forerunner and catalyst to the game's development. Guests came from across the nation to Pinehurst, fell in love with the genius of Donald Ross and the game of golf. "Maniac Hill" served as a laboratory to early teaching pros and was one of the few practice ranges where golfers could compare ideas and philosophies on the golf swing. Richard Tufts would later contribute more to the development and simplification of The Rules of Golf than any individual.

Pinehurst, however, is not only famous for its golf, but also for its gun club and shooting school run for so many years by Annie Oakley and its championship tennis, lawn bowling and croquet facilities. Pinehurst's rich heritage provides the bellwether for the modern Pinehurst experience. Our job today is to provide a pleasant and comfortable experience for members and guests that combines modern comforts and southern hospitality with the charm of the past.

But we'll never rest on our laurels. In recent years, we have added Pinehurst No. 7, which has drawn great reviews, and a state-of-the-art conference facility while still maintaining the ambiance of the turn-of-the-century hotel. We've recently completed the remodeling of the pro shop and resort clubhouse. We've rebuilt our practice facilities and given course No. 6 a facelift. We are totally committed to Pinehurst and are very proud of our association with it.

These are exciting times in Pinehurst. We're delighted to have the 1991 Tour Championship at Pinehurst and eagerly look forward to hosting the 1994 USGA Men's Senior Open. We hope that those of you who know Pinehurst will enjoy this book and agree with us that it captures that singular experience and ambiance that is Pinehurst's alone. To newcomers, our wish is that this book helps acquaint you with our village and its history and that you, too, will fall in love with Pinehurst and will want to return again and again.

Robert Dedman
Chairman, Club Corporation
of America International

ACKNOWLEDGEMENTS

Pinehurst Stories, A Celebration of Great Golf and Good Times, is the combined effort of many individuals. I am deeply indepted to anyone who sat for an interview, provided a photograph, answered a question, told me a story. There are dozens and dozens of people to thank. The book would not have been possible without their time and help.

Pat Corso, President of Resorts of Pinehurst Inc., deserves the credit for initiating the project and providing the resources to make it as classy as the resort and club he operates. I thank him whole-heartedly for entrusting this project to me.

The many fine employees of the resort and country club who've assisted are far too numerous to name. But the administrative staff, including Beth Kocher and Melody Dossenbach; the golf staff, including Don Padgett, Ken Crow and Rich Wainwright; and the maintenance staff, headed by Brad Kocher, have been particularly helpful.

Zeke Cook and Sue Love of the Tufts Archives helped direct me through the vast array of documents and memorabilia donated by Pinehurst's founding family. Frank Pierce and his staff at Village Photography are responsible for the reproduction of many of the photographs contained herein. Thanks also to Cindy Fuquay of Raleigh for helping put the design package together and contributing her illustrations.

John Derr, Dick Taylor, Charles Price, Peter Tufts, Mike Sanders, Clyde Mangum, Marty McKenzie, Pete Jones and Michael Dann answered dozens of questions. The support, direction and background files of Ron Green of Charlotte were invaluable. And thanks to Bill Fields, Jim Wilson and Bart Willis for sniffing out typos and sentences that were duck-hooking into the woods.

The creative staff at Leslie Advertising not only designed the dust cover but went beyond with help and guidance on the selection of photographs.

Finally, thanks to David Kinney, publisher of Business North Carolina magazine in Charlotte, for helping give me the boost several years ago to plunge into making my business the printed word; and to Art Chansky of Four Corners Press in Chapel Hill, who taught me how to make a book.

LP

ABOUT THE AUTHOR

Lee Pace is a free-lance writer and publication editor living in Chapel Hill. A native of Hendersonville, N.C., he is a 1979 graduate of the University of North Carolina. After five years in newspapers and three in public relations and advertising, Pace began writing about Pinehurst and other golf subjects for various publications in 1987. He is golf editor of *Pinehurst Magazine* and is a frequent contributor to *Southern Links, Private Clubs, Golf Week, UNC Alumni Review, Business North Carolina* and the *ACC Football Yearbook*. His work on Pinehurst has also appeared in *Golf Digest, The Robb Report* and *Mid-Atlantic Country*.

CHRONOLOGY

**Some dates of interest
in the evolution of Pinehurst.**

1895   Holly Inn opens.

1896   Magnolia Inn opens.

1898   Nine holes of No. 1 Course open, length 2,561 yards.

1898   First clubhouse.

1899   18 holes of No. 1, length 5,176.

1900   Harry Vardon plays four exhibition rounds in Pinehurst. Donald Ross is hired as golf professional.

1901   Nine holes of No. 2, length 1,275 yards. Clubhouse enlarged. Carolina Hotel opens.

1903   Nine holes of No. 2 lengthened, 2,750 yards. Clubhouse enlarged.

1907   18 holes of No. 2 completed, length 5,860 yards; Donald Ross designer. Nine holes of No. 3 added, length 2,900 yards.

1910   18 holes of No. 3 open; Donald Ross designer.

1912   Six holes of No. 4 open for practice.

1913   Five new holes of No. 1 added by Donald Ross. New shop. Pine Crest Inn opens.

1914   Nine holes of No. 4 open.

1918   Walter Hagen wins first of three North and South Open titles with 293 total in the first year the event lasted 72 holes.

1919   18 holes of No. 4 completed; Donald Ross designer.

1921   Mid Pines golf course and hotel open.

1923   Present third and sixth holes of No. 2 replace old third and fourth. Manor Inn opens.

1927   Pine Needles golf course and hotel open.

1928   Nine holes of No. 5 open (present fourth and fifth of No. 2 were first and ninth holes of No. 5).

1933   Fairway sprinkler system installed on No. 2.

1934   Grass greens on first three holes of No. 2.

1935   Grass greens on all of No. 2. Course No. 5 abandoned. Present fourth and fifth holes of No. 2 replace old ninth and 10th.

1936   Grass greens on No. 3. Nine holes of No. 4 abandoned. Denny Shute wins PGA Championship on No. 2 with a 3-and-2 final victory over Jimmy Thomson.

1937   Grass greens on No. 1.

1938   Remaining nine holes of No. 4 abandoned.

1940   Present fifth, sixth and 11th holes of No. 1 replace old 10th and 11th. Ben Hogan wins North and South Open for first professional golf win.

1941   Sam Snead uses an eagle on the par-five 10th hole to help win the first of three North and South Open titles.

1948   Donald Ross Memorial Junior inaugurated following April passing of architect.

1950   Nine holes of No. 4 reopen.

1951   No. 2 lengthened from 6,952 yards to 7,007 for Ryder Cup Matches. North and South Open discontinued following victory by Tommy Bolt and replaced with Men's North and South Senior Amateur.

1953   Second nine holes of No. 4 reopen.

1958   Women's North and South Senior inaugurated.

1959   Jack Nicklaus wins the North and South Amateur, edging Gene Andrews 1-up.

1961   No. 5 course opens; Ellis Maples designer.

1962   No. 2 lengthed to 7,058 yards for U.S. Men's Amateur. Labron Harris Jr. defeats Downing Gray Jr. 1-up for championship.

1970   Pinehurst sold by Tufts family to Diamondhead Corp. (Dec. 31).

1973   Greens on No. 2 changed from bermuda to bent. Professional golf returns to Pinehurst for World Open, a 144-hole tournament won by Miller Barber by three strokes over Ben Crenshaw. No. 4 redesigned by Robert Trent Jones to be used with No. 2 for World Open.

1974   World Golf Hall of Fame opens. World Open reduced to 72 holes; Johnny Miller wins tournament in playoff with Jack Nicklaus, Frank Beard and Bob Murphy.

1977   World Open renamed Colgate/Hall of Fame Classic. Hale Irwin shoots 20-under-par 264 to win tournament.

1979   Greens on No. 2 changed from bent to bermuda. No. 6 course opens; Tom and George Fazio designers.

1980   Colgate drops sponsorship of PGA Tour event; it continues for three years as the Hall of Fame Classic.

1982   Hall of Fame Classic, beset by no title sponsor, no TV and dates opposite college football, discontinued, to be replaced the following year by the Hall of Fame Senior. Greens, tees and bunkers on No. 4 revised by Rees Jones.

1984   Pinehurst Hotel & Country Club acquired by Club Corporation of America.

1985   PGA of America purchases World Hall of Fame; name officially changes to PGA/World Golf Hall of Fame.

1986   No. 7 course opens; Rees Jones designer.

1987   Clubhouse for No. 7 opens.

1987   Greens on No. 2 rebuilt to USGA specifications.

1991   Greens rebuilt, some fairways recontoured on No. 6. Practice range rebuilt, resort clubhouse remodeled. PGA Tour returns to Pinehurst for the Tour Championship.

INDEX

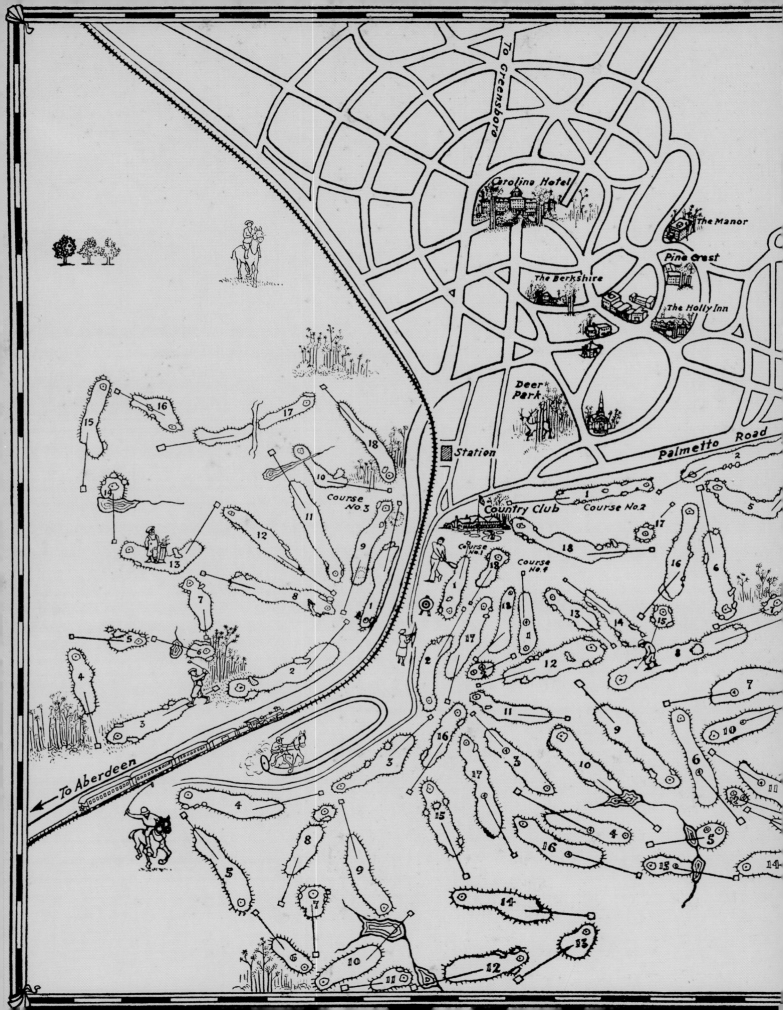